FORTRAN IV WITH WATFOR AND WATFIV

Prentice-Hall Series in Automatic Computation

George Forsythe, editor

PRENTICE-HALL INTERNATIONAL, INC., *London*

PRENTICE-HALL OF AUSTRALIA, PTY. LTD., *Sydney*

PRENTICE-HALL OF CANADA, LTD., *Toronto*

PRENTICE-HALL OF INDIA PRIVATE LIMITED, *New Delhi*

PRENTICE-HALL OF JAPAN, INC., *Tokyo*

PAUL CRESS
Canada Systems Group , Ottawa, Ontario

PAUL DIRKSEN
University of Waterloo, Waterloo, Ontario

J. WESLEY GRAHAM
University of Waterloo, Waterloo, Ontario

FORTRAN IV WITH WATFOR AND WATFIV

PRENTICE-HALL, INC.
Englewood Cliffs, New Jersey

A revision of
FORTRAN IV WITH WATFOR
by
Paul Cress, Paul Dirksen, and J. Wesley Graham

© 1970, 1968 by Prentice-Hall, Inc.
Englewood Cliffs, N.J.

13–329433–1

Current printing (last digit):

24   23   22   21   20

Library of Congress Catalog Card Number 74-129241

Printed in the United States of America

PREFACE TO THE REVISED EDITION

The WATFIV compiler was developed at the University of Waterloo to provide language and system capabilities additional to those of the WATFOR compiler. This **revised** edition describes the additional language capabilities, and points out some relatively minor incompatibilities between the two compilers. Both compilers are available and information about acquiring them can be obtained by writing to the Computing Centre, University of Waterloo, Waterloo, Ontario, Canada.

The name WATFOR was chosen to stand for WATerloo FORtran. When we began to write the new compiler, we needed a means of identifying it, and we chose the term WATFIV ("the one after WATFOR"), more or less as a convenience. As the compiler developed, we officially adopted the term; by a stroke of good fortune, it happens to be a short form for WATerloo Fortran IV.

This new compiler incorporates language features described in IBM's two SRL manuals, C28-6515 and C28-6817. In addition, we have incorporated character variables, as defined by the SHARE FORTRAN Committee (Proceedings of SHARE XXVIII, February, 1967). As with WATFOR, we have extended the language beyond these official specifications whenever we felt that the extension provided important new features without over-complicating the design of the compiler. Whenever one of these features is used, the compiler notifies the user by printing an extension message.

When this text is being used with the WATFOR compiler, the reader should ignore Chapters 21 and 22, as well as Appendices C and D. If the WATFIV compiler is being used, the reader should consult Appendix D, which lists the important differences between WATFOR and WATFIV; these differences affect the material in Chapters 1 to 20. Also, the reader can use the material in Chapters 21 and 22.

We have listed the error messages for WATFOR in Appendix B, and those for WATFIV in Appendix C. We have purposely used a "sideways format" for the WATFIV messages to make them obvious, and thus avoid confusion for the reader.

We trust that these new additions to the text will add to its usefulness.

Waterloo, Ontario, Canada.   P. H. Cress
September, 1970.   P. H. Dirksen
     J. W. Graham

PREFACE

The WATFOR compiler was developed at the University of Waterloo to satisfy important requirements in both education and research. It is important to have a fast compiler to handle the fast-growing volume of undergraduate student problems in an economical way. Of equal importance is the need to provide diagnostics which are as complete as possible, in order to give a good measure of independence to the student as he debugs his programs.

In the area of research, much computer time is consumed in the development of programs, before they can become useful in production. WATFOR expedites this process by employing rapid compilation which results in fast turn-around; furthermore, the error diagnostics help catch many obscure programming blunders.

This book was written to describe the FORTRAN IV language, with particular emphasis on its implementation with the WATFOR compiler. WATFOR provides a large number of extensions and modifications to the FORTRAN IV language, and we trust that this presentation of WATFOR, coming from its home territory, will be useful.

The material has been collected from notes and problems that have been in use at the University of Waterloo during the past eight years.

We have attempted to present the material in a
manner which has received majority acceptance
from students over the years.

The reader will note that the book
begins with the immediate introduction of a program.
We have found that it is important to begin work
with the computer as soon as possible - preferably
immediately after the first lecture. The interest
of the student is then usually so strong that he
is motivated to proceed with his work in Computer
Science as quickly as possible.

We have chosen to use a rather informal
style. Each new concept is introduced by
considering an example and then discussing it.
Usually the concepts are not tied together formally
until a number of examples have been considered.
This use of examples is consistent with our belief
that "an example is worth a thousand words" and
this belief has been justified many times by the
responses of our own students.

The book is concerned exclusively with
a description of the FORTRAN IV language. It does
not have an introduction to the digital computer,
a discussion of input-output devices, or a dissertation
upon number systems. It is assumed that the reader
either has already learned such material, or else
is learning it concurrently by using one of the
many other available reference books. We assume
that teachers are well-versed in this other
material, and are fully capable of presenting it
to their students.

There has been no use of flow charts, since most of the examples are logically very simple. Once again we assume that teachers will introduce flow charts as part of their teaching techniques.

We are indebted to the efforts of R. G. Stanton of York University and R. J. Collens of the University of Waterloo, who assisted in editing the text. We are also grateful to J. A. Brzozowski for his suggestions during the early stages of preparing the manuscript. Miss Susan Tyrer has provided an important contribution by checking out all examples on the computer. Finally, we would like to thank Miss Laurel Thorpe for her careful typing of successive forms of the manuscript.

Waterloo, Ontario, Canada.   P. H. Cress
May, 1968.   P. H. Dirksen
    J. W. Graham

TABLE OF CONTENTS

CHAPTER 1

INTRODUCTION TO FORTRAN

This chapter will serve as a general introduction to the FORTRAN language. No attempt will be made to be rigorous, since rigor at this stage tends to introduce details which are unnecessarily confusing to the beginner. The object of this chapter is to introduce the novice to many of the basic ideas in the FORTRAN language and to put him in a position to solve problems as quickly as possible. The remainder of the book expands upon this introduction and considers the various aspects of the language in more detail. The experienced FORTRAN user will probably prefer to skip this chapter.

1.1 BASIC PRINCIPLES

FORTRAN is a language which is useful for expressing many common problems in a form suitable for computer processing. It seems reasonable, therefore, to begin a discussion of FORTRAN by considering a number of problems and examining their formulation using the language.

Example 1.1 illustrates how one could calculate the square of 4 and print the result. This, of course, is too trivial a problem to be considered for solution using a computer, but nevertheless it serves to illustrate a number of important points. More challenging problems will follow!

```
C EXAMPLE 1.1
C THIS PROGRAM CALCULATES THE SQUARE OF 4
      X=4.
      Y=X*X
      PRINT,X,Y
      STOP
      END
```

This example consists of seven *statements*, the first two of which are *comments* describing the problem. Comment statements are recognizable by the letter C to the left and will appear in most examples for identification purposes; they serve no other useful purpose. The third statement assigns the value 4 to the *real variable* X. The fourth statement assigns to Y the value of X multiplied by itself. Note that multiplication is denoted by the symbol *. The fifth statement prints the values of X and Y side by side. The sixth statement brings the process to a halt. The END statement has a special purpose which will be explained in Section 1.2.

It is important to note that the statements are interpreted sequentially, beginning with X=4. and proceeding until the process is halted. The seven statements, taken collectively, are referred to as a *program*.

The problem can be further extended by requesting that the squares of 5, 6, 7, 8, etc. be

calculated and printed. The solution is illustrated
in Example 1.2.

```
C EXAMPLE 1.2
C CALCULATE SQUARES OF 4,5,6,7,ETC.
      X=4.
    8 Y=X*X
      PRINT,X,Y
      X=X+1.
      GO TO 8
      END
```

Note that, after the result is printed,
the value of X is increased by 1, and *control* is
transferred back to the statement which has *state-*
ment number 8. The statement number is merely a
means of identifying any statement, and does not
necessarily reflect the position of the statement
in the program. Once control is transferred, Y is
recomputed, this time using the current value of X,
which is 5. Control resumes sequentially; the results
are printed and X is incremented. Then control is
transferred once again. It is obvious that the
process will continue in a *loop* endlessly, but will
calculate squares of integers beginning at 4 as
required. A means of halting the process will be
considered in Example 1.3.

The statement X=X+1. is worthy of comment.
This is obviously not an equation, which underlines
the fact that "=" is not used in its usual arithmetic
sense. In FORTRAN, "=" means "is assigned the
value". As a result, the statement is properly
interpreted to mean "X is assigned the value X+1".

In Example 1.3 below, a condition has been

3

placed upon the transfer of control to the statement numbered 8. After X is incremented, control proceeds to the IF statement, which allows a transfer if and only if X is less than or equal to 9. If X has been incremented to 10, control is not transferred to the statement numbered 8, but proceeds to the next sequential statement which is STOP. Note that "less than or equal to" is written as .LE. in FORTRAN.

```
C EXAMPLE 1.3
C CALCULATE SQUARES OF 4,5,6,...,9
      X=4.
    8 Y=X*X
      PRINT,X,Y
      X=X+1.
      IF(X.LE.9.)GO TO 8
      STOP
      END
```

The word IF is followed by an expression in parentheses which, when evaluated, gives the answer "true" or "false". This is referred to as a *logical-valued expression*, or, more briefly, a *logical expression*. If the logical expression is true, the statement that follows it (in the same line) is carried out; if it is false, the next sequential statement is taken.

All constants used to date contain the decimal point, even though they are integers. In a later chapter we will find that this is not always necessary, but for the time being the programmer should use the decimal point in all constants. Note that the statement number is not a constant which enters into calculations, and it *never* contains a decimal point.

1.2   PREPARATION FOR THE COMPUTER

Once a program has been written, it is necessary to ,put it into machine-readable form so that it can be processed by a computer.   The most common way of doing this is to punch the program into cards using a special machine called a **key-punch**.   Normally we punch one statement per card; the statement number (if any) appears in columns 1 to 5 inclusive, and the rest of the statement begins in column 7 or beyond.   No statement should use columns 73 to 80 of the card.   Comment statements are an exception, as they are identified by a "C" in column 1 followed by whatever message is required. As in other statements, columns 73 to 80 should not be used.

When punching cards the user will notice that only upper case is available for the letters. He is allowed to leave blank columns whenever he feels it will make the program more readable.   For example, GO TO could be written and key-punched as GOTO, and either form is acceptable to the computer. The rule is to insert blanks at will; the computer will ignore them.

Figure 1.1 shows an interpreted card deck containing the program for Example 1.3.

Note that two special cards are required, one at each end of the deck.   These cards ($JOB and $ENTRY) are called *control cards*, and are not part

of the FORTRAN language. They are necessary to
instruct the *supervisor* or *monitor* and may vary
from computer to computer. The reader should consult
his installation's operating manual for the precise
format of these special control cards.

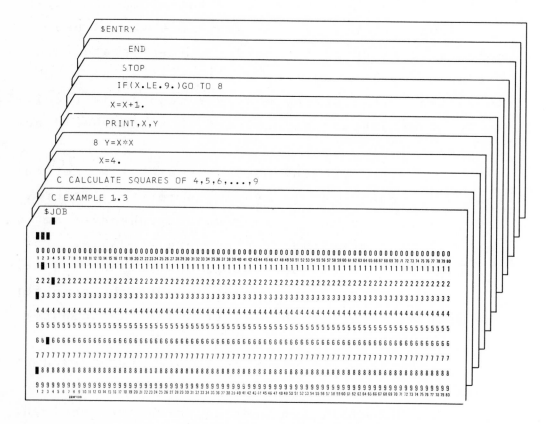

Figure 1.1

The reader will notice that the special
FORTRAN statement END has been used as the last
statement of every program. In fact, every FORTRAN
program *must* have the END statement as its last
statement. When the card deck is read into the
computer, this is a signal that the program has
been completely read in. Execution can then begin
with the first *executable statement* in the program.
Execution is terminated when the STOP statement is
encountered. It is important to understand this
difference between the STOP and END statements;
END signals the physical end of the card deck which
contains the program, whereas STOP terminates the
processing. The END statement is always the last
statement, but the STOP statement can appear anywhere in a program. It is also important to note
that END is a *non-executable statement*, as are
comment statements.

We will now consider the means by which
answers are communicated to us by the computer.
When the program deck, as illustrated in Figure 1.1,
is submitted to the computer, the results appear on
the printer as illustrated in Figure 1.2.

```
0.4000000E 01    0.1600000E 02
0.5000000E 01    0.2500000E 02
0.6000000E 01    0.3600000E 02
0.7000000E 01    0.4900000E 02
0.8000000E 01    0.6400000E 02
0.9000000E 01    0.8100000E 02
```

Figure 1.2

Note that all values are printed in the format

$$0.xxxxxxxE \; yy$$

which is a computer notation meaning .xxxxxxx times 10 to the power yy. Thus the constants 6.125 and 132. would print out as 0.6125000E 01 and 0.1320000E 03 respectively. The reader may consider this somewhat messy; in later chapters we will discuss methods for improving the appearance of computer output.

The reader is now in a position to attempt the first set of exercises which are merely extensions of the ideas in Example 1.3.

1.3   EXERCISES

1.1   Calculate a table of squares for the integers ranging from -10 to 10 inclusive.

1.2   Compute a table of squares for the even integers from 2 to 40 inclusive.

1.3   Compute a table of cubes for the odd integers ranging from 1 to 23 inclusive. Note that the statement

$$Y=X*X*X$$

can be used.

1.4   Tabulate the function

$$y = x^3+x+2$$

for x = -1, 0, 1, 2, ..., 8.
Notice that lower case letters are not

available on the key-punch so upper case
must be used.

1.4 COMPILERS

Programs written in FORTRAN cannot be
processed directly on any computer. They must be
translated into the language of the computer by
a *compiler*. A compiler is a special program read
into the computer when the monitor encounters the
$JOB control card. This special program is capable
of translating FORTRAN statements into what is
referred to as *machine language*. The compiler
which is the subject of this book is called WATFOR.

WATFOR not only compiles the FORTRAN
program, but detects errors in *syntax* while doing
so. For example, the statement

$$I+J = K*K$$

is meaningless in FORTRAN. The WATFOR compiler
would detect this and inform the programmer by
printing an error message. A list of all WATFOR
error messages is given in Appendix B.

1.5 TIMING

It is important to note that every
program processed on a computer using WATFOR goes
through two distinct phases, one following the
other in time. First the program is *compiled*, and
then it is *executed*. We refer to these two phases
as *compile time* and *execution time*.

WATFOR detects errors, not only at compile
time, but at execution time as well. For example,
the consecutive statements

X=0.
Y=3./X

would be compiled, but of course Y cannot be computed,
since division by zero is undefined. This would be
detected by WATFOR at execution time, and an
appropriate error message would be printed.

1.6   MORE EXAMPLES

Example 1.4 evaluates the function

$$b = \frac{a^2+3a-2.3}{a+4.1}$$

for a = 1.25, 1.50, 1.75, ..., 3.00. (Note that the
dot in 2.3 is, as always in this book, a decimal point.)

```
C EXAMPLE 1.4
C EVALUATE FUNCTION
      A=1.25
    5 B=(A*A+3.*A-2.3)/(A+4.1)
      PRINT,A,B
      A=A+.25
      IF(A.LE.3.)GO TO 5
      STOP
      END
```

Here we have introduced two new real
variables, A and B. This begs the question: "What
real variable names can be used in FORTRAN?".
Before answering this question, we must define the
term *FORTRAN symbolic name*. A FORTRAN symbolic
name is any sequence of up to six characters chosen

10

from the letters, the digits, and the character $; it
must not begin with a digit. Thus CAT, $12, MABLE,
and J12 are examples of symbolic names, whereas
CHARLIE and 2P are not.

A FORTRAN real variable can be any
FORTRAN symbolic name not beginning with any of
the letters I to N inclusive. Thus MABLE and J12
are not real variables. In a later chapter we
will see how to use symbolic names beginning with
the letters I to N inclusive.

Every statement in which a variable is
assigned a value is referred to as an *assignment
statement*. Assignment statements which are used
in this example are

    (i)   A=1.25
   (ii)   B=(A*A+3.*A-2.3)/(A+4.1)
  (iii)   A=A+.25

Note that a single variable always appears to the
left of the equals sign and an *expression* to the
right of it. An expression can be a simple constant
as in (i), or can be quite involved as in (ii). In
(ii), we see that / is used for division, and that
parentheses are used as in algebra to group sub-
expressions which are to be considered as single
units. In (iii), we see that the variable to the
left of the equals sign can also appear in the
expression to the right of it.

The statement PRINT,A,B is referred to
as an *input-output statement*, or, more briefly, an
I/O statement. Using this statement, we can print
the *values* of any of the variables which have been

11

assigned by the program. It is important to
recognize that the values represented by the
variables are printed, not the variables them-
selves.

The IF and STOP statements are known as
control statements because they control the
sequence in which the statements are executed.

Example 1.5 illustrates a FORTRAN program
for computing the cubes, squares, square roots and
cube roots of all the integers from 1 to 10 inclusive.

```
C EXAMPLE 1.5
C CALCULATE CUBES, SQUARES, AND ROOTS
      X=1.
    7 A=X**3.
      B=X**2.
      C=SQRT(X)
      D=X**(1./3.)
      PRINT,X,A,B,C,D
      X=X+1.
      IF(X.LE.10.)GO TO 7
      STOP
      END
```

Here the exponentiation operator **
is illustrated. The expression X**3. means X^3,
and the expression X**(1./3.) means $X^{1/3}$.

The FORTRAN *function* SQRT is introduced
for computation of the square root. The letters
SQRT are always followed by an expression contained
in parentheses. The computer first evaluates the
expression, then its square root. If the value
for the expression is negative, the WATFOR compiler
will produce an execution-time error diagnostic.

A few of the many other functions available
are SIN, COS, ABS, ALOG, and EXP; these are used to
calculate sine, cosine, absolute value, natural
logarithm, and exponential respectively. Each of
these evaluates the appropriate function of the
parenthesized expression immediately following it.
In the case of SIN and COS, the real expression
represents radians, rather than degrees.

These functions are referred to as *built-in*
functions, since they are a part of the language.
In later chapters we will see how the user can define
his own functions.

Example 1.6 calculates the sum of squares
of the first 50 integers and prints the results.

```
C EXAMPLE 1.6
C CALCULATE SUM OF SQUARES
      SUM=0.
      X=1.
   32 SUM=SUM+X**2.
      X=X+1.
      IF(X.LE.50.)GO TO 32
      PRINT,SUM
      STOP
      END
```

This example illustrates the use of
initialization. The statements

```
      SUM=0.
      X=1.
```

are executed only *once* and are said to *initialize*
the values of X and SUM prior to entering the loop.
SUM is used to accumulate the total, while X is
incremented by 1 each time through the loop. When

13

X reaches 51, the process drops out of the loop
and proceeds to print the computed sum of squares.

Examples 1.7 and 1.8 point out common
errors committed by FORTRAN programmers.

```
C EXAMPLE 1.7
      X=3.
      Y=X**2+A
      PRINT,X,Y
      STOP
      END
```

When the computer attempts to calculate
the expression X**2+A, it cannot do so, since A has
not been previously assigned a value. The variable
A is referred to as an *undefined variable*, and
WATFOR would cause an error message to be printed.

```
C EXAMPLE 1.8
      X=3.
      Y**2.=X
      PRINT,X,Y
      STOP
```

The statement Y**2.=X is invalid, since a
variable must be used to the left of the equals sign in
an assignment statement; here the expression Y**2.
appears to the left.

1.7   EXERCISES

In Example 1.3, we introduced .LE. which
means "less than or equal to". In the course of
solving these and other problems, the reader may
find it useful to know the complete list of such

operators. It is as follows:

.EQ. equal to

.NE. not equal to

.LT. less than

.LE. less than or equal to

.GT. greater than

.GE. greater than or equal to

These are discussed in detail in Chapter 12.

1.5 Write a FORTRAN program to tabulate the function

$$z = \frac{w^2 + w + 3}{w - 2}$$

for w = 3, 3.5, 4, 4.5, ..., 9.5, 10.

1.6 Modify the previous problem so that the denominator is w − 5 rather than w − 2. Note that you must arrange to skip over the value w = 5.

1.7 Tabulate the function

$$s = a^2 + \sin b$$

for a = 1, 2, 3, 4, 5, 6;
and b = 0, .125, .25, .375, .5.

1.8 Compute the sum of squares of the even integers between 10 and 40 inclusive.

1.9 Compute the average of the integers between 15 and 49 inclusive.

1.10 Write a program to tabulate the function

$$y = \frac{x^3 + 7x - 5}{x^3 - 3x^2 - 4x + 12}$$

for x = -4, -3, -2, ..., 7, 8, 9.

Note that, prior to each division, one must test to see whether the denominator is zero.

1.11 Consider the n terms of the geometric progression

$$a, \ ar, \ ar^2, \ ..., \ ar^{n-1}.$$

Compute these terms for values 3, 4, 8, of a, r, and n.

1.12 Using the built-in functions SIN and COS, tabulate the function

$$y = \sin^2 x + \cos^2 x$$

for x = 0., .1, .2, ..., 1.0.

Recall that the value of x represents radians.

CHAPTER 2

REAL ARITHMETIC

A number of examples of FORTRAN programs using real arithmetic were discussed in Chapter 1. The purpose of this chapter is to formalize and extend some of the ideas already introduced.

2.1 REAL CONSTANTS

Probably the best way to describe FORTRAN *real constants* is to give a number of examples, followed by a discussion of each. The following is a selection which consists of most of the possible variations of real constants.

a)	(i)	12.34	(v)	1234.567
	(ii)	-12.34	(vi)	.0001234
	(iii)	+12.34	(vii)	670000.0
	(iv)	0.	(viii)	1234567.

b)	(i)	12.34E3	(vi)	12.34E+03
	(ii)	+12.34E3	(vii)	12.34E0
	(iii)	-12.34E3	(viii)	12.34E50
	(iv)	12.34E-3	(ix)	1234567.E6
	(v)	12.34E+3	(x)	0.E0

Every real constant contains a decimal point explicitly as part of it. This is the case even if the constant happens to be an integer as in a) (viii). Each constant can have a + or - sign to the left, and if no sign is present, the constant is assumed to be positive. No constant can contain more than seven digits, including non-significant zeros. The greatest precision possible is seven significant decimal digits as indicated in Examples a) (v), a) (viii), b) (ix).

Group b) has real constants which use the exponent notation. The constant 12.34E3 means 12.34×10^3. In all cases, the signed integer following the E indicates the power of ten which is used to multiply the number which precedes it. This notation is generally used to handle very large or very small real constants. Thus the number -0.123×10^{-60} would be written as -0.123E-60 in FORTRAN. As is the case for group a), the greatest precision possible is seven significant decimal digits. The largest real constant which can be used is .7237005E+76 and the smallest in magnitude (except for zero) is .5397605E-78. These unusual-appearing limits are a function of the IBM 360 hardware. Under normal circumstances, the programmer need only be aware of their approximate magnitudes, namely, 10^{76} and 10^{-78}. More detail on 360 hardware will follow in a subsequent chapter.

The following are examples of errors frequently made when using real constants.

12.34E6.	No decimal allowed after the E.
123,456.7	No comma allowed.
−123456	No decimal point.
+123.456E90	Too large.
123.456789	Too many digits.
123.450000	Too many digits (zeros count).

2.2 REAL VARIABLES

Variables capable of being assigned values which are real constants are said to be *real variables*. A real variable can be any valid FORTRAN symbolic name which is declared in a REAL *declaration statement*. For example, the statement

REAL X, T, MABLE, NUMBER

declares each of X, T, MABLE, and NUMBER to be real variables. This is a non-executable statement and is placed prior to the first executable statement in a program. The reason we have such a statement is because there are other types of variables and constants in FORTRAN. These will be outlined in subsequent chapters.

The reader may be wondering how we managed to get by without the REAL statement in Chapter 1. The answer is that, in the absence of any other declaration, symbolic names are real variables provided they do not begin with the letters I to N inclusive. This is often referred to as the *default declaration* or *implicit declaration*.

2.3 REAL-VALUED EXPRESSIONS

Any expression which, when evaluated, produces a real result is said to be a *real-valued expression*, or, more briefly, a *real expression*. Some examples are:

(i)	(X+3.64)/2.3
(ii)	(X+Y)*(2.1-A)
(iii)	6.892
(iv)	A
(v)	-A
(vi)	A*B**2
(vii)	A/B*C
(viii)	-8.2**2
(ix)	A**B**C
(x)	3.2E50*7.9E40
(xi)	3.2E-50*7.9E-40

The conventions for evaluating expressions are similar to those encountered in algebra. In Example (i), the sum X+3.64 is evaluated first because it is contained in parentheses; then the division by 2.3 is performed.

In Example (ii), both quantities in parentheses are evaluated separately, and then multiplied. Note that the * must be used; the expression (X+Y)(2.1-A), while legal in algebra, is not valid in FORTRAN.

Examples (iii) and (iv) indicate that a real constant or a real variable is a trivial example of a real expression.

Example (v) illustrates the use of the

20

unary minus. Example (viii) also contains a unary
minus.

In Example (vi), B**2 is evaluated, and
the result is subsequently multiplied by A. This
is because of the priority of operators. The
operators in order of decreasing priority are

$$**$$

$$* \text{ and } /$$

$$+ \text{ and } - \text{ (including unary + and -)}$$

Example (vii) seems to be ambiguous, as it
is not obvious whether $\frac{ac}{b}$ or $\frac{a}{bc}$ would be calculated.
The rule is that the expression is evaluated from
left to right, unless the priority of operators
dictates otherwise. Thus A/B is calculated and the
result is subsequently multiplied by C.

In Example (viii), the result is $-(8.2)^2$.
A unary minus in an expression is always treated
as if there were a zero preceding it. Thus, -8.2**2
produces the same result as 0.-8.2**2.

Example (ix) illustrates the only exception
to the rules as stated to this point. When successive
exponentiations are involved, the computation proceeds
from right to left. Thus A**B**C would be equivalent
to A**(B**C).

Examples (x) and (xi) show situations
which give rise to computed results which are out
of the range of magnitude for real constants. In
the first case, the result is too large and an error
message would be printed indicating an *overflow*
condition. In the second case, the result is too
small and an error message would indicate an

underflow condition.

It is not possible to have two consecutive operators in FORTRAN. Thus the expression X*-8.2 is illegal and must be written as X*(-8.2). However, recall that **, denoting exponentiation, is a single operator.

2.4 REAL ASSIGNMENT STATEMENTS

The general form of a *real assignment statement* is

real variable = real expression

Examples are:

```
Y=(A*B-3.2)/7.6E-8
SUM=SUM+3.0
```

The computer first evaluates the real expression, then assigns the result to the real variable on the left of the equals sign.

2.5 SOME EXAMPLES

The following examples will serve to illustrate further some of the rules and, in some cases, will point out interesting difficulties encountered when using real arithmetic.

Example 2.1 indicates how we could compute an approximation to π using thirty-one terms of the series

$$\frac{\pi^3}{32} = \frac{1}{1^3} - \frac{1}{3^3} + \frac{1}{5^3} - \frac{1}{7^3} + \cdots$$

```
C EXAMPLE 2.1
      SUM=0.
      X=1.
      S=1.
    6 SUM=SUM+(1./X**3)*S
      S=-S
      X=X+2.
      IF(X.LE.61.)GO TO 6
      PI=(SUM*32.)**(1./3.)
      PRINT,PI
      STOP
      END
```

The variable S alternates between +1 and
-1 in order to add or subtract the new term each
time through the loop. There is no particular
reason why the example is set up to go through the
loop thirty-one times. As an exercise, the reader
may wish to compute and print the approximation
each time through the loop to observe how the
accuracy increases as each term is added.

```
C EXAMPLE 2.2
      X=3.1
      Y=3.1E20
      Z=Y-Y+X
      T=Y+X-Y
      PRINT,Z,T
      STOP
      END
```

In Example 2.2, we would expect Z and T to
be assigned identical values. In actual fact, Z
becomes 3.1 and T becomes zero! This happens because
computation of expressions proceeds from left to
right, and real constants retain only seven digits

of precision. When computing Z, the quantity Y-Y
is evaluated first, yielding zero; then X is added
to produce the result 3.1. When computing T, the
quantity Y+X is evaluated first. Since the computer
retains only seven significant digits, the result
is 3.1E20 because X is insignificant relative to
Y. Then Y is subtracted, producing the zero result
for T. This points out that operations which are
associative in ordinary algebra are not necessarily
associative in FORTRAN.

```
C EXAMPLE 2.3
      X=.2
      Y=X+X+X+X+X
      PRINT,Y
      STOP
      END
```

In Example 2.3, we would expect the result
for Y to be 1.0. However, when run on the computer,
the output is 0.9999999E 00, which is slightly in
error. This happens because the IBM 360 records
its real constants using hexadecimal, rather than
decimal, arithmetic. It is impossible to convert
.2 to a hexadecimal equivalent using a finite number
of hexadecimal digits. The computer truncates the
hexadecimal number, and thus ends up with only an
approximation to .2. When this is added to itself
four times, as in the example, the error is increased
by a factor of 5, with the result that Y is not
exactly as expected.

As a further explanation of this problem,
suppose the IBM 360 recorded its real constants using

decimal rather than hexadecimal arithmetic. Then
one-third would be approximated by the decimal
fraction .3333333. If this were added together
three times the result would be .9999999 rather
than 1.

This example illustrates a point which
needs to be kept in mind when one is doing
computations in real arithmetic. The actual numbers
used are frequently only good approximations, and
hence may contain errors. These errors can increase
during the course of a computation. Thus it is
likely that the final result is not accurate to
seven significant digits. Unfortunately, there
is no general rule for predicting the accuracy of
the results.

2.6 REAL BUILT-IN FUNCTIONS

In Chapter 1 we introduced the real
function SQRT, and mentioned some others such as
SIN, COS, EXP, etc. A complete list of available
functions and their characteristics can be found
in Appendix A. However, a number of observations
are useful.

Every FORTRAN function has a name such
as SIN, COS, or SQRT, and this is always a FORTRAN
symbolic name. The fact that SIN begins with an
S is consistent with the fact that its value is a
real constant. The function name is always
accompanied on the right by an *argument list*
enclosed in parentheses. Often this list has only
one argument. For example, X is the argument in

reas A and B are the arguments in
These arguments can be any expressions,
ey are of the proper type. For example,
ᴏᵢɴ(X**2+2.3*X-8.4) is legal provided that the
argument within the parentheses, when evaluated,
produces a real constant. On the other hand,
SIN(3) is illegal since the constant 3 is not a
valid real constant (3. would be valid).

All functions are treated as if they
were variables and can be used as components of
expressions. The following are all legal real
expressions.

```
(X+COS(X**2))/(A+2.0)
SIN(A)*SIN(B)+2*(A+B)
SIN(A+COS(X))
SQRT(SQRT(X))
```

The last example shows how a function
can have, in its argument list, an expression which
contains the function itself.

```
C EXAMPLE 2.4
      SUM=0.
      SUMOLD=0.
      X=1.
      S=1.
    6 SUM=SUM+(1./X**3)*S
      IF(ABS(SUM-SUMOLD).LT..00001)GO TO 7
      SUMOLD=SUM
      S=-S
      X=X+2.
      GO TO 6
    7 PI=(SUM*32.)**(1./3.)
      PRINT,PI
      STOP
      END
```

Example 2.4 shows how the ABS function can be used to terminate the loop when approximating π (see Example 2.1). Here, the statement

IF(ABS(SUM-SUMOLD).LT..00001)GO TO 7

will cause a transfer out of the loop when the absolute value of the difference between two consecutive values of SUM is less than .00001.

```
C  EXAMPLE 2.5
C  CALCULATE TABLES
      X=1.
    9 A=SIN(X)
      B=COS(X)
      C=SQRT(X)
      D=EXP(X)
      PRINT,X,A,B,C,D
      X=X+.1
      IF(X.LT.2.)GO TO 9
      STOP
      END
```

Example 2.5 computes tables of sine, cosine, square root, and exponential for X ranging from 1 to 2 at increments of .1. Note that the argument is considered to be in radians when SIN and COS are used. Note also that .LT. (meaning "less than") rather than .LE. is used in the IF statement. It would appear, therefore, that the computation would not be done when X is two. In fact, this computation does get done since the accumulated error in the evaluation of X causes X to be slightly less than 2 rather than exactly equal to it.

```
C EXAMPLE 2.6
      X=0.
    5 Y=EXP(X)+SIN(X+.1)+X*ABS(X)
      PRINT,X,Y
      X=X+.5
      IF(X.LE.5.)GO TO 5
      STOP
      END
```

Example 2.6 shows how we could tabulate the function

$$y = e^x + \sin(x+.1) + x|x|$$

for x = 0, .5, 1.0, 1.5, ..., 5.0.

In this case .LE. is used in the IF statement because .5 can be accurately converted to hexadecimal notation. Thus, X can be accurately computed at each stage. The reader can broaden his understanding of such matters by studying the properties of hexadecimal arithmetic and observing computer output in specific instances.

2.7 EXERCISES

2.1 Given that A=2, B=3, C=4, and D=2 evaluate the following FORTRAN expressions by hand and also by using the computer, to compare the results.

(a) A*B/C**D   (d) A**B**D

(b) A*(B/C)**D-7.   (e) -B**A-C**D

(c) C/A/B*D

2.2 (a) Write a program which tabulates the
function x^{-3} for x = 1, 3, 5, 7,
..., 51.

(b) Make the necessary changes to the
program in (a) to tabulate the
function

$$(-1)^{\frac{x-1}{2}} x^{-3}$$

over the same range.

2.3 Define S_n as the sum of the first n terms
of the series

$$\frac{1}{1^3} - \frac{1}{3^3} + \frac{1}{5^3} - \frac{1}{7^3} + \ldots$$

Note that the nth term can be written as
$t_n = (-1)^{n-1}(2n-1)^{-3}$.
Write a program which tabulates
S_n and t_n for n = 1, 2, 3, ..., 50.

2.4 The program written for Exercise 2.3
calculates S_{50} by adding the terms in the
order t_1, t_2, t_3, ..., t_{50}. Modify the
program so the addition is done in the
reverse order. Are the computed answers
for S_{50} identical? Which result would
you expect to be more accurate? Why?

2.5 (a) Compute a table of the sine, cosine,
and tangent for the angles from 0° to
45° at intervals of 1°. Verify your
results by consulting published
tables.

(b) Modify the program in (a) to compute the tables at intervals of 5 minutes. To conserve computer time, do the tabulation up to 5 degrees only.

2.6 Tabulate the function

$$f(x) = e^{\sin x} + |x|$$

for x = -5, -4, -3, ..., 5.

2.7 Write a program to evaluate the expression

$$y = \frac{\pi}{2} \sin^2 (3\theta + \frac{\pi}{4})$$

for $\theta = 0, \frac{\pi}{8}, \frac{2\pi}{8}, \frac{3\pi}{8}, \frac{4\pi}{8}, \ldots, \pi$

where π = 3.141593

2.8 The roots of

$$ax^2 + bx + c = 0$$

can be calculated using the formula

$$x = \frac{-b \pm \sqrt{b^2 - 4ac}}{2a} ,$$

provided a $\neq$ 0 and b^2 - 4ac is not negative. Write a program which computes the roots and prints them, together with one of the following codes, according to circumstances.

code 0   not a quadratic or a linear equation, no roots

code 1   not a quadratic, one root only

code 2   equal roots

code 3   distinct real roots

code 4   complex roots

30

CHAPTER 3

INTEGER ARITHMETIC

The FORTRAN language has a completely separate set of facilities for handling computations with *integers*. These facilities may seem redundant since real arithmetic (Chapter 2) encompasses operations upon integers, which are a subset of the real numbers. However, the separate facilities provide certain advantages to the programmer. Proper use of the integer features can enable the programmer to obtain more accurate results for certain types of problems; often he will use less computer time in the process.

3.1   INTEGER CONSTANTS

Examples of valid FORTRAN *integer constants* are:

(i)	+1234	(iv)	0
(ii)	−1234	(v)	987654321
(iii)	1234	(vi)	+0003

The common characteristic of all integer constants is the absence of a decimal point; it is always assumed to be immediately to the right of the farthest-right digit. Examples (i) and (ii) illustrate the use of the sign. If the sign is absent, the constant is assumed to be positive.

Integer constants can be any integer n in the range

$$-2147483648 \leq n \leq 2147483647$$

These unusual-looking limits are a function of the IBM 360 hardware. Under normal circumstances the programmer need only be aware of their approximate magnitude, namely, 10^9. In other words, integer constants are capable of having any nine-digit integer as their value.

The following are examples of invalid integer constants.

(i)   1,234   Comma not allowed.
(ii)   13E12   Exponent not allowed.
(iii) 18.0   Contains a decimal point.
(iv)   111222333444   Too large.

3.2   INTEGER VARIABLES

Variables capable of being assigned values which are integer constants are said to be *integer variables*. An integer variable can be any valid FORTRAN symbolic name which is declared in an INTEGER type statement. For example, the statement

INTEGER A,B,SUM,TOTAL

declares each of A, B, SUM and TOTAL to be integer variables. This statement is non-executable and is placed prior to the first executable statement in a program.

In the absence of any other declaration, symbolic names which begin with the letters I to

N inclusive are declared as integer variables by
default.

3.3 INTEGER-VALUED EXPRESSIONS

Any expression which yields an integer
constant when evaluated is said to be an *integer-
valued expression*, or, more briefly, an *integer
expression*. Some examples are:

```
  (i)    (I+3)*20
 (ii)    (I+J)/(3-K)+I**4
(iii)    6
 (iv)    MABLE
  (v)    -MABLE+3
 (vi)    14/3
(vii)    1234*1234*1234*1234
```

Examples (i) and (ii) illustrate that all
the arithmetic operators used in real expressions
can also be used in integer expressions. The operators
follow the same rules of priority, and parentheses
can be used. Examples (iii) and (iv) show the
simplest possible integer expressions, and Example (v)
uses the operator unary minus.

Example (vi) is worthy of discussion.
Since 14/3 is an integer expression, it yields the
integer result 4; the remainder is ignored. Similarly
(-14)/3 yields -4 and 2/3 yields zero.

Example (vii) is a legal integer expression
which would produce unexpected results. Since $(1234)^4$
is too large to be an integer constant, the computer
would produce a result which is incorrect. No
warning message is given, and it is the programmer's

responsibility to ensure that this type of thing does not occur. The unexpected results are related to the way in which integer constants and integer arithmetic are handled by the computer hardware.

3.4 INTEGER ASSIGNMENT STATEMENTS

The general form of an *integer assignment statement* is

integer variable = integer expression

Examples are

```
I=(J+3)/K
J=J+1
```

The computer first evaluates the integer expression, then assigns the result to the integer variable to the left of the equals sign.

3.5 SOME EXAMPLES

Example 3.1 computes a table of the squares and cubes of the integers from -2 to 5 inclusive.

```
C EXAMPLE 3.1
      INTEGER SQUARE,CUBE
      I=-2
    6 SQUARE=I**2
      CUBE=I**3
      PRINT,I,SQUARE,CUBE
      I=I+1
      IF(I.LE.5)GO TO 6
      STOP
      END
```

When the reader runs this example on the
computer, one of the first things he will notice
is that the computer output of integer constants is
more readable than is the case for real constants.
The E notation is not used and decimal points are
not printed. Output for Example 3.1 is shown in
Figure 3.1.

-2	4	-8
-1	1	-1
0	0	0
1	1	1
2	4	8
3	9	27
4	16	64
5	25	125

Figure 3.1

Example 3.2 computes all of the prime
factors of each of the integers from 2 to 30
inclusive.

The essence of the method is to find a
prime factor of J by successively dividing by 2,
3, 4, etc., until a remainder of zero is encountered.
This test is made in the statement

```
IF(J/TEST*TEST.NE.J)GO TO 3
```

Because of the nature of integer arithmetic, the
expression J/TEST*TEST will not be equal to J unless

the division is exact. Once a prime factor is
found, it is factored out of J and the process is
repeated to find the next prime factor. This
procedure is terminated when the factoring process
has reduced J to unity.

```
C EXAMPLE 3.2
      INTEGER TEST
      I=2
  6 J=I
      PRINT,J
      TEST=2
  5 IF(J/TEST*TEST.NE.J)GO TO 3
      PRINT,TEST
      J=J/TEST
      IF(J.EQ.1)GO TO 4
      GO TO 5
  3 TEST=TEST+1
      GO TO 5
  4 I=I+1
      IF(I.LE.30)GO TO 6
      STOP
      END
```

Note the operators .NE. (not equal) and
.EQ. (equal) have been introduced in this example.

3.6   INTEGER BUILT-IN FUNCTIONS

Only a few built-in functions are available
for use in integer arithmetic. There are no integer
functions for sine, cosine, square root, exponential,
logarithm, etc., because these functions would not be
of much use in a world restricted to integers. One
useful function which is available is IABS. It
computes the absolute value of an integer expression.
Others can be found in the table in Appendix A. Note

that all integer functions begin with one of the
letters I to N inclusive.

3.7 EXERCISES

3.1 Given that I=2, J=3, K=4, and L=2, evaluate
the following FORTRAN expressions by hand,
and also by using the computer; compare
your results.

(a) I*L/K**J   (d) K**J/I/J/L

(b) I**K/L*J   (e) K**J**I

(c) J/I*I

3.2 Write a program to determine which of the
positive integers from 1 to 25 inclusive
are perfect squares. For each of these
integers, the output is to be 1 if the
integer is a perfect square; otherwise,
the output is to be 0.

3.3 Tabulate the function

$$k = 2^n$$

for n = 1, 2, 3, ..., 50.
Notice that, after n=30, unexpected results
are printed for the required function.

3.4 Write a computer program to compute n!
(factorial n) for n = 0, 1, 2, ..., 10.
Note that n! can be defined as follows

$$0! = 1$$
$$n! = n\ (n-1)!$$

3.5 (a) Write a program to produce all the
right-angled triangles which have 3
sides of integral lengths (each hypo-

tenuse is to have length less than 100.)

(b) Modify the program in (a) to produce all right-angled triangles which have sides of integral lengths, and which have perimeters of less than 100.

3.6 (a) Write a program that converts a quantity expressed in millimeters to a corresponding quantity expressed in metres, centimetres, and, millimetres. For example, 3821 millimetres equals 3 metres, 82 centimetres and 1 millimetre.

(b) Repeat (a), converting seconds into days, hours, minutes, and seconds.

(c) Write a program to convert a positive decimal integer to a sequence of zeros and ones which represent the binary equivalent.

3.7 A positive integer is said to be prime if it has no integral factors other than one and itself (1 is not considered prime).

(a) Write a program which tests a given positive integer greater than two to determine whether or not it is prime. The program should divide by all possible integer divisors between one and the number itself. If any division is exact, the integer being tested is not a prime. The program should print the integer, together with an indication of 1 if it is prime, and 0 if it is not prime.

38

(b) Note that it is not necessary to divide by all integers between one and the number itself. For example, only odd integers are necessary if the trial divisor two has already been used. Also, it is only necessary to test divisors whose squares are less than or equal to the integer being tested. Write a new program incorporating these improvements.

(c) Modify the program in part (b) so that it can be used to compute all prime numbers greater than two and less than 200.

3.8 Find all twin primes in the set of prime numbers less than 200. Twin primes are consecutive odd numbers such as 11 and 13.

3.9 From the set of prime numbers less than 200, find all pairs of primes such that the larger is just one more than twice the smaller, i.e., pairs of primes of the form j, $2j+1$ (e.g., 2 and 5; 3 and 7; 5 and 11.)

3.10 Write a program which takes a positive four-digit integer, reverses the order of the digits, and prints the resulting integer. For example, 1289 would become 9821.

3.11 It is generally not possible to multiply a six-digit integer p by another six-digit integer q and obtain accurate results.

This is because the result pq has twelve digits; this exceeds the precision of an integer constant. However, an accurate result can be obtained by segmenting the problem

First express p and q as

$$p = a \times 10^3 + b$$

$$q = c \times 10^3 + d$$

where a, b, c, and d each have 3 digits. Then use the formula

$$pq = (a \times 10^3 + b)(c \times 10^3 + d)$$

The computation can proceed using a, b, c and d, and recording the result in two integers, one containing the first six digits, and the other containing the last six digits.

(a) Write a program to perform this extended-precision integer arithmetic, and try it for several values of p and q. It should work for negative as well as positive values of p and q.

(b) Modify the program in (a) so it works properly if p and q have up to 9 decimal digits. Can you explain why it is difficult to go beyond 9 decimal digits?

CHAPTER 4

MIXED-MODE ARITHMETIC

In each of Chapters 2 and 3, a particular mode of operation has been discussed. In the former, computation with real variables and constants was considered; in the latter, computation involved integer variables and integer constants. The FORTRAN language allows complete freedom to mix both types of computations in arithmetic expressions and assignment statements. Such expressions are referred to as *mixed-mode expressions*. In actual fact, the computer stores and handles the two types of constants quite differently. Thus, although mixed-mode is legal, it is important to study the details of how the computations are done so that the programmer can achieve predictable results.

4.1 EVALUATION OF EXPRESSIONS

The following are examples of mixed-mode expressions:

(i)	A+I
(ii)	SIN(A+I)
(iii)	I-1.3+J
(iv)	2/3*6.2
(v)	3+SIN(X)
(vi)	123456789+B
(vii)	X**5

In Example (i) the computer will convert the integer constant, which is the current value of I, to a real constant. Then the result will be added to the real constant which is the current value of A. The final result is a real constant. Since the result of the expression is a real constant, the expression is, by definition, a real-valued expression. Thus it is possible to use it as the argument of a built-in function such as SIN, as illustrated in Example (ii).

The general rule is that when a binary operation takes place between two expressions, one of which is real-valued and the other integer-valued, the integer value is automatically converted to a real value before the operation takes place; the final result is a real constant. There is one exception to this rule; it will be illustrated in Example (vii).

The usual rules of priority are observed, as is the convention that evaluation of expressions proceeds from left to right. Thus the expression in (iv) gives rise to the result zero, represented as a real constant. This is because 2/3 is evaluated first; thus the integer constant 0 is produced. Then this integer constant is converted to a real constant because it must enter into multiplication with the real constant 6.2. The final result is zero, represented as a real constant.

In Example (v) the sine would be evaluated first. Then the integer constant 3 would be converted to the real constant 3.0; the addition is then performed.

Example (vi) illustrates how accuracy
may be lost. The integer constant 123456789 must
be converted to a real constant before computation
can proceed. But this cannot be done accurately,
since real constants can represent a precision
of at most seven digits. Thus the conversion
produces the real constant 1234567.E2, which is
subsequently added to the current value of B.

Example (vii), although a mixed-mode
expression, is handled differently. The integer-
valued exponent is used to instruct the computer
to multiply the current value of X by itself 5
times. The rule is that, whenever an integer-valued
expression appears as an exponent, it is never
converted; its integer value is merely used to
indicate the number of multiplications that must
be done.

The expression X**5.0 is not a mixed-
mode expression but it seems natural to discuss
it at this point. Whenever the exponent is a
real-valued expression, and X is different from
0, the exponentiation is evaluated using logarithms.
Thus the expression X**5.0 could not be evaluated
if X happened to have a negative value. This
suggests the rule that integer-valued expressions
should be used in exponents whenever possible.
However, if the calculation $X^{1/5}$ must be done, the
exponent is, of necessity, a real-valued expression,
namely (1./5.). Under these conditions, if X has
a negative value an error message will be printed.

As has been pointed out in the chapter

on real arithmetic, expressions such as SIN(3) or
SQRT(4) are illegal. This is because the arguments
of such built-in functions must be real-valued
expressions. It is interesting to note that while
SQRT(4) is illegal, SQRT(4+0.) would be legal, since
4+0. is a mixed-mode expression producing a real-
valued result.

4.2 MIXED-MODE ASSIGNMENT STATEMENTS

Two general types of mixed-mode assignment
statements will be discussed.

    (i)   real variable = integer expression
    (ii) integer variable = real expression

In case (i), the integer constant which
is the computed value of the integer expression
is converted to a real constant, and is assigned
to the real variable. Note that this could result
in reduced accuracy, since integer constants can
have greater precision than real constants.

In case (ii), the real constant which is
the computed value of the real expression must be
converted to an integer constant prior to assignment
to the integer variable. This is done by truncating
any fraction which is a part of the real constant.
For example, 123.76 becomes 123, -86.98 becomes -86
and .0042 becomes zero. Large real constants such
as 12.3E20 cannot be accurately converted to integer
constants. In cases like this, inaccurate assignment
will occur, and it is the programmer's responsibility
to see that this situation does not arise.

4.3   MIXED-MODE BUILT-IN FUNCTIONS

The FORTRAN language provides built-in
functions which facilitate the conversion of real-
valued expressions to integer-valued expressions
and vice-versa.   They are IFIX and FLOAT respectively.
For example:

IFIX(X+2.4)

would evaluate the real expression X+2.4 and convert
the result to an integer constant using the same
rule as outlined for mixed-mode assignment statements.
On the other hand,

FLOAT(I+2)

would evaluate the integer expression I+2 and convert
the result to a real constant, subject to the same
restrictions already discussed for mixed-mode
assignment statements.   This suggests another
method of computing the illegal expression SIN(3);
it can be written as SIN(FLOAT(3)), which is legal.

4.4   EXTENDED ASSIGNMENT STATEMENT

The WATFOR compiler allows *extended
assignment statements* as a useful extension to
the FORTRAN language.   Examples are:

    (i)   X=Y=2.4
    (ii)   X=Y=Z=A=B=-3.56+SIN(T)
    (iii) I=J=9
    (iv)   I=X=J=123456789

In case (i), the real variables X and Y
are both assigned the value 2.4; in case (ii),

45

all five of X, Y, Z, A and B are assigned the real
value of the computed expression $-3.56+SIN(T)$.
In Case (iii), we see that assignments can be made
to integer variables as well.

When using mixed-mode assignments,
as in case (iv), it is important to know the exact
way in which the extended assignment statement is
implemented in WATFOR. The general form is

$$v_1 = v_2 = v_3 = \ldots = v_n = \text{expression}$$

This is equivalent to

$$v_n = \text{expression}$$
$$v_{n-1} = v_n$$
$$.$$
$$.$$
$$.$$
$$v_2 = v_3$$
$$v_1 = v_2$$

Example (iv) is therefore equivalent to
the three statements

```
J=123456789
X=J
I=X
```

When X is assigned in the second statement, accuracy is lost. This means that, when I
is assigned in the third statement, it ends up with
a value different from that of J. This could have
been avoided by arranging the original statement
as follows:

$$X = I = J = 123456789$$

Note that, in each example of the extended assignment statement, the only expression involved is to the right of the farthest-right equals sign. The item to the left of *every* equals sign must be a variable which is to be assigned. It follows, therefore, that the statement

$$X = X + Y = Z = T * 2.0$$

is invalid.

4.5 EXERCISES

4.1 Given that I=2, J=3, A=4.2, B=2.0, evaluate the following FORTRAN expressions by hand. For verification, also evaluate the expressions using the computer.

(a)   J/I*A   (c)   J**I+A**B

(b)   A*J/I   (d)   J**I+A**I

4.2 Tabulate the function

$$y = x^5$$

for x = 1, 2, 3, ..., 25, using the two expressions X**5. and X**5; compare your results.

4.3 Find

$$\sum_{n=0}^{10} \frac{x^n}{n!}$$

for x = .1, .2, .3, ..., 1.0.

4.4 A program is required to convert inches to metres, centimetres, and millimetres (recall that 2.54001 cm. = 1 inch).

(a) Write the program without using any built-in functions.

(b) Write the program using the built-in function IFIX.

CHAPTER 5

SIMPLE INPUT AND OUTPUT

By now the reader has learned some of
the basic concepts of the FORTRAN language.
However, one idea has not been described in detail.
Most examples presented have used some form of the
PRINT statement to *output* values. This has been
the only way available for the computer to
communicate results to the user. This chapter
will present some of the details and rules for
printing values.

As well, the programmer often wishes to
introduce new data to the program at execution
time. This is accomplished by the READ statement
which is also described in this chapter.

This style of *input* and *output* is called
format-free, and is valuable and useful to the
reader who is learning to program. In later
chapters, other methods of performing I/O will
be described.

5.1 OUTPUT DURING EXECUTION

We have seen the PRINT statement used in
many examples, but let us review it by considering
Example 5.1.

```
C EXAMPLE 5.1
      A=B=C=20.
      D=E=F=-25.
      I=J=739
      K=L=-52
      PRINT,I,A,K,D
      STOP
      END
```

The line printed would be

739   0.2000000E 02   -52   -0.2500000E 02

The 'PRINT,' is followed by a list of variables separated by commas. At execution time, the values of these variables are printed across the page with spaces inserted for clarity. Each value is printed to full precision. If the statement

PRINT,I,A,K,D,J,B,L,E,C,F

is executed, the number of values to be printed cannot fit on one line. In this case, the values are printed across the page for the full width of the page; then a new line is started.

The number of values per line depends on the type of variable and the particular printer used. On most standard printers, the first eight values of Example 5.1 would appear on the first output line, followed by the last two values on the second output line.

Example 5.2 shows that constants as well as variables may appear in the PRINT list.

```
C EXAMPLE 5.2
      X=3.0
      PRINT,2,X,500032
      STOP
      END
```

The resulting line would be

```
2    0.3000000E 01        500032
```

This feature is useful when *debugging*
programs. If the programmer is having difficulty
in determining why his program will not work,
statements of the form PRINT,1 and PRINT,2 ,
etc., can be inserted at appropriate places in
the program. The output will then help him trace
the order in which the statements are executed.

Finally, Example 5.3 demonstrates that
expressions may appear in the PRINT list.

```
C EXAMPLE 5.3
      I=25
      J=3
      Z=92.
      X=25.
      PRINT,X,X*Z/I,I+I/J,ABS(SIN(X))
      STOP
      END
```

In this case, the expressions are evaluated and the
resulting values are printed. Notice that any
arithmetic expression may be used, including those
using built-in functions. The type of value
printed is determined by the type of expression.

One rule must be kept in mind. No
expression in the PRINT statement may start with a

left parenthesis. Thus the statement PRINT,(A+B)/C is invalid, while the statement PRINT,+(A+B)/C is valid.

5.2   INPUT DURING EXECUTION

It is often necessary to perform computations upon data which are *read* into the computer at execution time. Values are normally punched on data cards, which are read by the program as it is being executed by the computer. Example 5.4 is a simple program to introduce the READ statement.

```
C EXAMPLE 5.4
      READ,N
      M=N+2
      PRINT,M
      STOP
      END
```

In the example, notice that the variable N is not assigned a value in an assignment statement, but is used in an arithmetic expression. The statement READ,N causes a value, obtained from a data card, to be assigned to the variable N at execution time. Thus the READ statement is another way of assigning values to variables.

A suitable data card for this example might have the integer constant 25 punched in the first two columns of the card. In this case, the value printed for M would be 27.

Many problems will require more than one data card, and it is important to note the position

of the data cards relative to the FORTRAN program.
They always follow the $ENTRY control card, as
illustrated in Figure 5.1.

$JOB

——————

——————   FORTRAN PROGRAM

——————

$ENTRY

——————   DATA CARDS

——————

Figure 5.1

Example 5.5 illustrates how a program can
be written to find the average of 50 real numbers
punched on 50 separate data cards.


```
C EXAMPLE 5.5
C CALCULATE AVERAGE OF 50 NUMBERS
      I=1
      SUM=0.0
   14 READ,X
      SUM=SUM+X
      I=I+1
      IF(I.LE.50)GO TO 14
      AVG=SUM/50.
      PRINT,AVG
      STOP
      END
```


Each time the READ statement is executed,
another card is read from the set of data cards.
Since the READ statement will be executed 50 times,
there must be 50 data cards present. What happens

53

if there are more than or fewer than 50 data cards?
If there are more, only the first 50 will be used,
and the rest will be ignored. If there are fewer,
an error message is issued when the data are depleted;
it indicates that insufficient data cards are present.

We will now describe the rules for
punching constants onto data cards. Any valid form
of real constant may be read in for the corresponding
real variable in the READ list. On the other hand,
if integer variables are to be assigned values by
use of the READ statement, then integer constants
must be punched on the corresponding data cards.

Example 5.6 shows that a number of variables,
separated by commas, may follow the READ,. This
example causes four values for X, Y, Z, and N to
be read, and calculates $X^N + Y^N + Z^N$. If the
value read for X is zero, the program is terminated.

```
C EXAMPLE 5.6
  1 READ,X,Y,Z,N
    IF(X.EQ.0.)GO TO 2
    W=X**N+Y**N+Z**N
    PRINT,X,Y,Z,N,W
    GO TO 1
  2 STOP
    END
```

The data for this program can be punched
in a number of ways. The first and most logical
way is to place the four required constants on one
card. The constants are separated by one or more
blanks or by a comma. We give three examples of
data cards punched in this manner. In each case,

the data need not start in column 1 of the data
card.

```
3.0 6.2 9.E-2 5
9.2,6.4,9.E+2,3
67.        39.            40.6,1
```

Alternatively, we can punch the four
required values on four consecutive cards. There
are many other possibilities, any of which must
satisfy the following two rules.

(i)   Each time a READ statement is encountered
      in the course of execution of the program,
      a *new* card is read.

(ii) If necessary, additional data cards will
      be read until the list of variables has
      been *satisfied*, that is to say, values
      have been assigned to all the variables
      in the READ list.

Thus, if there are not sufficient constants on the
first data card, further data cards will be read
until the list is fully satisfied. Blank cards are
ignored, since they contain no constants and may be
placed anywhere in the data deck. If the READ list
is satisfied and there are still more constants on
the current data card, these are ignored.

This brings up an important point.
Example 5.6 uses the value 0.0 for X as a termination
criterion. If the last data card contained only the
value 0.0, the program would terminate with an error
message. Rule (ii) above tells us the reason for this.

The variables Y, Z, and N could not be assigned, since the data deck is depleted. Therefore, the last card should contain 0.0, followed by any two real constants and any integer constant.

To emphasize rule (i), consider the following statements:

```
READ,A          READ,A,B
READ,B
```

The statements on the left, when executed in succession, require that two data cards be supplied, as each of the statements initiates the reading of a new card; the statement on the right requires only one data card but could have two.

Finally, READ statements such as the following, which contain constants or expressions, are considered invalid.

```
READ,1,3.9
READ,X+Y,SIN(Z)
```

5.3 EXERCISES

5.1 (a) Example 5.5 is designed to find the average of 50 real values. Modify the program in such a way that it determines the average of an arbitrary number of values. Assume that the values are positive and not zero. A common trick is to place a special data card as the last card in the deck. This card might contain the value zero for this problem. However, if zero is one of the possible data values,

another value would have to be chosen
as a termination criterion.

(b) Another method of reading an arbitrary
number of data values is to have a
special value read as the first item
of the data. This special value is
the number of items of data that follow
in the data deck. For example, if 50
real numbers were to be read, the
special initial card could contain
the integer value 50. Modify the
program in part (a) so that it
incorporates this technique.

5.2 It is required to compute the average of
five real numbers read in from data cards.
The following program will do the job.

```
READ,A,B,C,D,E
PRINT,+(A+B+C+D+E)/5.0
STOP
END
```

All of the data could be punched in one
card. Alternatively, five cards, each
with one number punched on it, will do.
How many other ways are there to punch
the data?

5.3 A data deck has n values for x. Write a
program which reads the values and computes

$$\sqrt{\frac{1}{n-1}\left(\Sigma x^2 - \frac{(\Sigma x)^2}{n}\right)}$$

where

$$\Sigma x = \text{sum of the values of } x$$

$$\Sigma x^2 = \text{sum of the squares of the values of } x.$$

5.4   A data deck contains 100 integer values.
Write a program which reads these data
and determines the following.

(a)   The total of all negative integral
values.

(b)   The total number of integers which
are negative.

(c)   The total of all positive integral
values.

(d)   The total number of all even integers.

(e)   The total number of all odd integers.

(f)   The total number of all odd negative
integers.

5.5   Repeat Exercise 2.8 using the READ statement
to input arbitrary values of A, B, C;
determine the required roots.

CHAPTER 6

CONTROL STATEMENTS

As the reader has seen by now, FORTRAN statements are executed sequentially, starting with the first executable statement of a program. He has also seen that it is possible to alter this normal sequential flow by using IF-statements or GO TO statements. These statements are examples of control statements; their purpose is to allow the programmer to make decisions during the course of execution of his program and to exercise control over the order in which the statements of his program will be executed.

All but one of the control statements of FORTRAN will be introduced in this chapter. However, some of them will be more fully illustrated in subsequent chapters; in particular, Chapter 7 is devoted to the special control statement DO.

6.1 UNCONDITIONAL GO TO

The use of the GO TO statement has been illustrated in previous examples, and its meaning should be fairly obvious. However, let us review a few points about this control statement by considering the examples which follow.

```
C EXAMPLE 6.1 - UNCONDITIONAL GO TO
      INTEGER SUM,I
      SUM=0
      I=1
  129 SUM=SUM+I
      PRINT,SUM
      I=I+1
      GO TO 129
      END
```

Example 6.1 is a trivial program using
the unconditional GO TO; each time the GO TO statement is reached, control transfers to the statement
numbered 129. Of course, control proceeds
sequentially from there until the GO TO is
encountered again.

Presumably this program calculates the
sum of all the positive integers without ever
terminating. Obviously we must have a way of
stopping the program, and this is the purpose of
conditional control statements. Before discussing
these, however, consider Example 6.2, which shows
some common errors that can be made with a statement as simple as the GO TO statement.

```
C EXAMPLE 6.2 - IMPROPER USE OF GO TO
    2 INTEGER X,SUM
      SUM=0
      READ,X
      SUM=SUM+X
      GO TO 2
      PRINT,SUM
      STOP
      END
```

Here, the GO TO attempts to transfer control to a non-executable statement; transfer must always be made to executable statements. Notice also that it is impossible to get to the unnumbered PRINT statement since it immediately follows the GO TO; thus, to ensure that the PRINT statement may be executed, the statement following the GO TO should be assigned a number, and some means of transferring control to this statement should be provided. See Example 6.3 which illustrates this.

6.2   IF STATEMENTS

There are two kinds of IF statements in FORTRAN - logical IF and arithmetic IF. Both are examples of conditional control statements, since they allow the programmer the facility of making tests at execution time and possibly altering control within the program, depending on the results of the tests.

The reader has seen examples of logical IF statements in previous chapters; Example 6.3 uses one to illustrate an improvement to Example 6.2. The improved program will terminate when a zero value is read in for X.

The IF statement causes a test to be performed on the value of X; if X is equal to zero, control will transfer to the statement numbered 117; otherwise, control passes on to the next sequential statement.

```
C EXAMPLE 6.3 - SUMMING NUMBERS
      INTEGER X,SUM
      SUM=0
    2 READ,X
      IF(X.EQ.0)GO TO 117
      SUM=SUM+X
      GO TO 2
  117 PRINT,SUM
      STOP
      END
```

Suppose it is desired to read in values
for X, positive or negative, but to sum only the
positive values. Again, the program prints the
value of the sum, and terminates when a zero value
is read. Example 6.4 shows how this might be
accomplished using two logical IF statements.

```
C EXAMPLE 6.4 - SUMMING POSITIVE NUMBERS
      INTEGER X,SUM
      SUM=0
   58 READ,X
      IF(X.EQ.0)GO TO 23
      IF(X.GT.0)SUM=SUM+X
      GO TO 58
   23 PRINT,SUM
      STOP
      END
```

Note that the expression between the
parentheses of the logical IF has either of two
values - true or false. Thus, it is either
true or false that X has a value greater than
zero; there is no other possibility. Such an
expression is an example of a logical-valued
expression. Much more will be said about such

62

expressions in a subsequent chapter; it will suffice to describe the general form of the logical IF statement here. The general form is:

IF(a)s

Here, 'a' stands for any logical-valued expression and 's' stands for any executable FORTRAN statement with two exceptions: s cannot be a DO statement (see Chapter 7) nor another logical IF statement. Thus, in the statement

IF(X.GT.0)SUM=SUM+X

X.GT.0 corresponds to 'a', while SUM=SUM+X corresponds to 's'.

If the logical value of expression 'a' is false, control passes to the next executable statement in the program following the logical IF; if 'a' is true, the statement 's' which forms part of the logical IF is executed, and then control passes on to the next executable statement following the logical IF (except, of course, in case 's' is another control statement, as in Example 6.3).

In essence, the logical IF statement allows us a two-way choice - do something or do not do something - based on a test performed at execution time. The arithmetic IF statement is somewhat different, in that it allows a possibility of a three-way choice. Example 6.5 is a modification of Example 6.4, but uses an arithmetic IF statement to do the same problem.

```
C EXAMPLE 6.5 - USE OF ARITHMETIC IF
      INTEGER X,SUM
      SUM=0
   62 READ,X
      IF(X)62,5,133
  133 SUM=SUM+X
      GO TO 62
    5 PRINT,SUM
      STOP
      END
```

The arithmetic IF statement in the program, namely,

$$IF(X)62,5,133$$

works in the following fashion; a test is performed
on X and, if X is negative, control transfers to
the statement numbered 62; if X is zero, control
transfers to the statement numbered 5; if X is
positive, control transfers to the statement
numbered 133.

Actually, what appears between the
parentheses of the arithmetic IF statement may be
any real- or integer-valued expression. Consider
the next example, which is a program to tabulate
the function

$$y = \frac{x^2 - 3x + 2}{x - 3}$$

for x = 0, 1, 2, 3, 4, ..., 10,

but skips the value where the denominator
vanishes.

```
C EXAMPLE 6.6 - USE OF ARITHMETIC IF
      X=0.
    7 IF(X-3.)12,2,12
   12 Y=(X*X-3.*X+2.)/(X-3.)
      PRINT,X,Y
    2 X=X+1.
      IF(X-10.)7,7,85
   85 STOP
      END
```

Notice that, even when we are interested
in only a two-way choice for the result of the
test on the value of the expression, three statement numbers of executable statements must be
provided following the closing parenthesis of the
IF; they always correspond to a negative result, a
zero result, or a positive result, from left to right.
Control will transfer from the arithmetic IF to a
statement which is numbered by one of the three
statement numbers. For this reason, the next
executable statement following an arithmetic IF
should be numbered, since otherwise there is no
way that control can ever pass to that statement.
Example 6.7 illustrates this possibility; the
statement PRINT,X can never be executed.

```
C EXAMPLE 6.7 - FAULTY STATEMENT NUMBERING
    3 READ,X
      IF((X-5.)*(X+3.))1,2,3
      PRINT,X
    1 Y=X*X-14.3*X
      PRINT,Y
      GO TO 3
    2 STOP
      END
```

The question might be asked: When does one use a logical IF, and when does one use an arithmetic IF? Usually this will be answered by experience. The logical IF statement is often easier to understand, is more descriptive because of its structure, and is very natural to write when coding a program; but the arithmetic IF is sometimes convenient because it allows the three-way choice. Historically, earlier versions of the FORTRAN language did not have logical IF statements.

6.3 COMPUTED GO TO

The computed GO TO statement is a conditional control statement that allows a many-way choice for transfer of control. This feature is often convenient when different calculations must be performed on some values depending on a code or a 'key' that can be associated with the values.

To illustrate this, suppose the height of each student in a school is punched on a separate data card along with a code specifying the sex of the student: 1 for male, 2 for female. A card with a code of 3 is used to indicate the end of the data. Example 6.8 is a program to calculate the average height of males and females in the school.

The computed GO TO

GO TO(14,29,17),SEX

transfers control to one of the statements numbered

14, 29, or 17, depending on the value read for the code variable SEX. If the value of SEX is 1, control transfers to statement 14 to perform the calculations for a male student; if the value of SEX is 2, control transfers to statement 29 to process the data for a female. The last data card has a value of 3 for SEX, and control transfers to statement 17 to print the averages. (Note that the last card must contain a dummy value for HEIGHT to satisfy the read list.)

```
C EXAMPLE 6.8 - AVERAGE HEIGHT
      INTEGER SEX,FEMALE,MALE
      REAL HMALE,HFEMAL
      HMALE=HFEMAL=FEMALE=MALE=0
    3 READ,HEIGHT,SEX
      GO TO(14,29,17),SEX
   14 HMALE=HMALE+HEIGHT
      MALE=MALE+1
      GO TO 3
   29 HFEMAL=HFEMAL+HEIGHT
      FEMALE=FEMALE+1
      GO TO 3
   17 PRINT,HMALE/MALE,HFEMAL/FEMALE
      STOP
      END
```

This example has shown a three-way choice for transfer of control, since only three statement numbers were included. Computed GO TO statements may have any number of choices as the following sample statements show.

```
GO TO(16,3,3,8,14,16),JACK
GO TO(1,2,3,4,5,5,4,3,2,1),K
GO TO(99,28),LPT
```

If the first statement were executed, control

would pass to statement number 16, if the value of JACK, called the index, had the value one; similarly, if JACK had the value 2, control would pass to statement 3; if JACK had the value 4, control would pass to statement 8; and so forth.

There are only a few simple rules to remember about the use of the computed GO TO, and these are:

(i)   The index must be a simple integer variable

        e.g., GO TO(12,2,63),2*I+1

        is invalid.

(ii)   If the value of the index exceeds the number of statement numbers in the GO TO, control passes to the next executable statement following the GO TO. For example, control would pass to statement 5 if the following were executed:

```
    I=99
    GO TO(3,17,4),I
  5 SUM=SUM+1
```

(iii) All the statement numbers in the list must be numbers of executable statements.

A common error when using computed GO TO's is to forget the comma following the parenthesized list of statement numbers.

Another use of computed GO TO's is that of a *switch*, as illustrated in Example 6.9.

```
C EXAMPLE 6.9 - COMPUTED GO TO AS A SWITCH
      INTEGER SWITCH
      SWITCH=1
   16 READ,X
      GO TO(3,5),SWITCH
    3 SWITCH=2
      SUM=-X
      GO TO 16
    5 SUM=SUM+X
      IF(X.NE.0.)GO TO 16
      PRINT,SUM
      STOP
      END
```

Note that the statement numbered 3 and the two statements following it are executed only once.

6.4 ASSIGN AND ASSIGNED GO TO STATEMENTS

The assigned GO TO statement is very much like the computed GO TO statement in that it allows a many-way choice for transfer of control. However, the choice of statement to which control is transferred depends on the previous execution of a special statement called the ASSIGN statement. To see what these statements look like and how they work together, suppose the following statements were executed sequentially in a program:

```
      ASSIGN 15 TO IX3
      GO TO IX3,(3,7,15,8)
```

As a result of executing the GO TO, control will be transferred to the statement numbered 15, since the previous execution of the ASSIGN statement associated that statement number with the variable IX3 mentioned

in the GO TO. The numbers appearing in the GO TO
statement are a list of statement numbers which
are potential targets for transfer of control
from the GO TO.

Example 6.10 shows that different
statement numbers may be associated with a
variable, thus allowing a many-way branch.

```
C EXAMPLE 6.10
      ASSIGN 3 TO JUMP
    5 GO TO JUMP,(7,3,6)
    6 PRINT,999999
    7 STOP
    3 PRINT,888888
      ASSIGN 6 TO JUMP
      GO TO 5
      END
```

The output for this program consists of the
following two lines:

```
888888
999999
```

The assigned GO TO can be used in much
the same way as the computed GO TO, that is, as a
switch which can transfer control to one of many
points in a program, depending on the most recent
assignment of a statement number to the integer
variable associated with the GO TO. It has the
advantage that, when reading over a program, the
effect of the assigned GO TO is easier to follow,
particularly where the equivalent computed GO TO
has a very long list of statement numbers. Also,
the assigned GO TO usually takes less time to
execute on a computer than the equivalent computed

GO TO. However, the computed GO TO is quite useful when transfer of control can be made to depend on some code or key.

The rules for the ASSIGN statement and the assigned GO TO statement are quite simple, namely,

(i)   The variable used in these statements must be an integer variable.

(ii) This integer variable should not be used for any other purpose in a program since this could lead to troubles at execution time. For example, the following two statements appearing in a program would be considered invalid.

```
ASSIGN 5 TO JUMP
JUMP=JUMP+3
```

(iii) The statement to which an assigned GO TO transfers control *must* be one of the statements numbered in the list of the GO TO. Thus, although any executable statement's number may be mentioned in an ASSIGN statement, when an assigned GO TO is executed, a previously-executed ASSIGN statement must have assigned one of the numbers in the list to the variable of the GO TO. Failure to do this results in an error.

Finally, one must not forget that the forms of the computed and assigned GO TO are slightly different:

```
Computed GO TO    GO TO(26,3,35,8),K
Assigned GO TO    GO TO JUMP,(4,7,57,22)
```

71

6.5   STOP STATEMENT

A STOP statement has appeared in almost every sample program shown so far. It is really a control statement, and is mentioned here for completeness since its meaning by now should be clear.

By way of explanation, it should be stated that the STOP statement does not actually stop the operation of the computer; its effect is to terminate execution of the program, thus freeing the computer to start working on some other person's program. It might be added that, in earlier versions of FORTRAN used on smaller computers, the STOP statement did bring the computer to a halt, thus requiring some sort of operator action before the computer could be started up on another program.

There is an additional form of the STOP statement which consists of the word STOP followed by a constant of up to five digits, e.g., STOP 673 It has the same effect as the simple STOP, but in addition the constant is displayed on the computer operator's console (usually a typewriter connected to the computer). This gives a record of the STOP statement which terminated execution of the program. Since it is usually the case, in present-day large computer installations, that the programmer does not have access to the operator's console output, this form of the STOP statement is of limited usefulness and, in some installations, it is not allowed. In this case, WATFOR treats such a STOP statement like a simple STOP.

Note that a program may have any number of STOP statements; the first one encountered at execution time terminates program execution. Note also that the first executable statement following a STOP statement should have a statement number; otherwise, there is no possibility of its being executed.

6.6   PAUSE STATEMENT

The PAUSE statement is another control statement which, when encountered, involves the computer operator and thus, because of its limited usefulness and potential nuisance value, is not permitted at some installations.

There are three forms:

(i)   simple PAUSE, e.g., PAUSE

(ii)   PAUSE with a constant, e.g., PAUSE 125

(iii)   PAUSE with a message, e.g.,
          PAUSE 'MOUNT TAPE 25'

When a PAUSE statement is executed, a message is displayed on the operator console and further execution of the program is temporarily suspended until the operator responds, usually by typing something on the console. Control then proceeds to the next statement following the PAUSE statement. The message the operator receives is the constant in the statement (00000 for simple PAUSE) or the actual letters between the quote marks.

Thus the PAUSE statement would be used

only if the program had encountered some special
problem which involved operator assistance, e.g.,
mounting a special data tape at a certain point
in the program's execution.

6.7 CALL AND RETURN STATEMENTS

The CALL and RETURN statements are
mentioned here only for completeness. They are
control statements used with subprograms
and will be discussed in a subsequent chapter.

6.8 CONTINUE STATEMENT

This control statement consists of the
word CONTINUE only. It is a do-nothing statement
in the sense that, when executed, control passes
through it to the next executable statement.
One might well question the usefulness
of such a statement in FORTRAN. If it does not
do anything, why bother to have it? The principal
use of CONTINUE statements is with DO-loops, which
are discussed in the next chapter.

6.9 EXERCISES

6.1 (a) A certain course is divided into
          four sections. A separate data card
          is punched for each student in the
          course; it contains a student number
          and a section code. The section code
          is punched as 1 for section 1, 2 for
          section 2, etc. A card with a code

of 5 is used to indicate the end of
the data. Write a program to calculate
the number of students in each section.
Use the computed GO TO feature.

(b)   The school administration wishes to
know how many males and females are
in each section. In order to ascertain
this, a second code specifying the
sex of the student is punched in each
data card; the code is punched as 1
for male and 2 for female. Add this
facility to your program; this time
the program should print the number
of males and females in each section.
Again use computed GO TO's.

6.2   Tabulate the function

$$y = f(x) + g(x)$$

for x = 1, 2, 3, ..., 10,
where $f(x) = x^2 - 16$

and $g(x) = \begin{cases} 1 \text{ if } f(x) < 0 \\ x^2 + 16 \text{ if } f(x) = 0 \\ 0 \text{ if } f(x) > 0 \end{cases}$

Use an arithmetic IF statement.

6.3   (a)   A teacher has completed the marking
of a set of examinations for a class,
and would like to calculate the
average mark for the class. Each
student's number and mark are punched
on a data card. Write a program to
find the average.

(b) The teacher would like the following
information for the class:
  (i) Maximum mark
  (ii) Minimum mark
  (iii) Number of students in each of
      the following categories:
      A: over 75%
      B: 66% to 75% inclusive
      C: 60% to 65% inclusive
      D: 50% to 59% inclusive
      E: under 50%
  Include these features in your
  program of part (a).

6.4 In addition to the information requested
in 6.3 (b), the teacher would like to know
the average mark in each of the five
categories. Re-write the program to include
this facility. Use the ASSIGN and the
assigned GO TO statements.

6.5 Write a program which uses IF statements
to determine the largest of three positive
integer values read from a data card.
Modify the program to handle
  (i) four positive integer values
  (ii) five positive integer values.

6.6 Write a FORTRAN program which reads three
numbers and prints one of the following
codes:
      0 if the numbers do not represent
        the sides of a triangle

1   if they represent the sides of a
    triangle which is neither isosceles
    nor equilateral
2   if they represent the sides of an
    isosceles triangle
3   if they represent the sides of an
    equilateral triangle

Write the program so that it will process
an arbitrary number of sets of three
numbers, and will terminate upon reading
a set of three numbers, all of which are
0.

CHAPTER 7

THE DO STATEMENT

The DO statement is one of the most
powerful statements in the FORTRAN language.
It was put into the language by the original
designers because they realized that many of
the calculations performed by programs are
essentially repetitive. Thus, for example, we
would normally not take the trouble to program
a computer to find the square root of 2, but might
consider doing so if we required a table of square
roots of all the integers from 2 to, say, 10000.
The DO statement is a control statement which
facilitates the programming of repetitive computations.

7.1   INTRODUCTORY EXAMPLES

Let us see how a DO statement works
by comparing two sample programs which perform
a repetitive calculation. Example 7.1 prints
a table of the integers 1 to 100 and their
squares; Example 7.2 achieves the same result
but uses a DO statement.

```
C EXAMPLE 7.1 - SQUARES OF INTEGERS
      I=1
   65 ISQ=I*I
      PRINT,I,ISQ
      I=I+1
      IF(I.LE.100)GO TO 65
      STOP
      END


C EXAMPLE 7.2 - SAME PROBLEM USING DO
      DO 13 I=1,100
      ISQ=I*I
   13 PRINT,I,ISQ
      STOP
      END
```

The action of the DO statement

$$DO \ 13 \ I=1,100$$

might be paraphrased as: "Perform repetitively
all the statements following the DO, up to and
including the statement numbered 13, for I starting
at 1 and increasing by 1 for each repetition as
long as I is less than or equal to 100. Then
continue on in the program." It can be seen that
the DO statement has control over some of the
statements that follow it in the program. Thus,
in Example 7.2, the two statements

```
      ISQ=I*I
      PRINT,I,ISQ
```

would be executed one hundred times with I ranging
in value from 1 to 100.

As can be seen, although Examples 7.1
and 7.2 achieve the same result, the latter example

is a somewhat shorter program than the former.
This is one of the advantages of using a DO statement. Another advantage is that a loop in a
program is more easily recognized if it is headed
by a DO statement. Some FORTRAN compilers use
this fact to produce a faster-executing machine-
language program than might be possible if loops
were not controlled by DO statements.

      Before proceeding to other examples, let
us introduce some jargon that is usually associated
with the DO statement by referring to Example 7.2.
The statement numbered 13, i.e., PRINT,I,ISQ, is
called the *object* of the DO statement. The object
is always the statement whose number is referenced
in the DO. The set of statements following the DO,
up to and including the object, is called the *range*
of the DO. Thus the range of the DO statement in
Example 7.2 is the two statements

$$ISQ=I*I$$
$$PRINT,I,ISQ$$

      The values of I, 1, 100 used in the DO
statement are called the *DO-parameters*, with the
variable I also called the *index* of the DO.

      A loop in a program controlled by a DO
statement is commonly called a *DO-loop*.

      Example 7.3 is a program which sums the
first 250 integers using a DO statement. The range
of the DO is executed 250 times, each time with
the index INT increased by 1.

```
C EXAMPLE 7.3 - SUM OF INTEGERS WITH DO-LOOP
      INTEGER TOTAL
      TOTAL=0
      DO 63 INT=1,250
   63 TOTAL=TOTAL+INT
      PRINT,TOTAL
      STOP
      END
```

In this example, the range of the DO consists of the single statement which is the object of the DO.

Example 7.4 illustrates that the index of the DO need not be employed in any statements within the range, since its primary purpose is to count the number of times the loop is repeated.

```
C EXAMPLE 7.4 - TABULATION USING A DO
      X=0.
      DO 4 J=1,25
      Y=(X*X-3.*X+2.)/(X+5.)
      PRINT,X,Y
    4 X=X+1.
      STOP
      END
```

Example 7.5 shows that the value by which the index is incremented after each passage through the range may be specified to be different from 1, and the initial value may be greater than 1. The example sums all the odd integers from 27 to 99. The final constant 2 in the DO statement specifies the increment to be applied.

```
C EXAMPLE 7.5 - SUM OF ODD INTEGERS
      INTEGER SUM,COUNT
      SUM=0
      DO 43 COUNT=27,99,2
   43 SUM=SUM+COUNT
      PRINT,SUM
      STOP
      END
```

Example 7.6 shows that the DO-parameters may be integer variables as well as integer constants. The program prints a table of the first M integers and their squares, where the value of M is read from a data card.

```
C EXAMPLE 7.6 - SQUARES OF INTEGERS
      READ,M
      DO 93 J=1,M
   93 PRINT,J,J*J
      STOP
      END
```

To review the function of the DO statement, Example 7.7 shows how the same result could be obtained using a logical IF.

```
C EXAMPLE 7.7 - SAME AS EXAMPLE 7.6
      READ,M
      J=1
   93 PRINT,J,J*J
      J=J+1
      IF(J.LE.M)GO TO 93
      STOP
      END
```

7.2   GENERAL FORM OF DO STATEMENT

The general form of the DO statement is specified as follows:

$$DO \ n \ i = m_1, m_2, m_3$$

Here n stands for the statement number that identifies the object of the DO.   The DO-parameters are i, m_1, m_2, and m_3, with i also being called the index.   The value m_1 is called the *initial value*, m_2 is called the *test value*, and m_3 is called the *increment*.

The DO statement exercises control over the statements in its range by first setting the index to the initial value m_1 when the DO statement itself is executed; then the statements of the range are executed in turn.   After the object has been executed, the increment m_3 is added to the index i and, if the resulting value is less than or equal to the test value m_2, control is automatically transferred back to the first statement in the range for repetition of all statements in the range.   This looping action continues each time the object statement is executed, as long as the incremented value of i is less than or equal to the test value m_2.   When the test value is exceeded, control passes to the next executable statement following the object; the DO-loop is then said to be *satisfied*.

It is unfortunate that the DO statement is encumbered with a relatively large number of rules.   These do not detract from its power, and are very easily learned and mastered.   At any rate,

the WATFOR compiler will give an error message if
these rules are violated; this fact makes it easy
to correct the program.

Rule 1: The DO index must be an integer variable
and the other DO-parameters must be unsigned
integer constants greater than zero or integer
variables whose values are greater than zero.
Furthermore, if the increment value is not
explicitly stated, it is assumed to be 1
Thus DO 3 I=1,10 is the same as DO 3 I=1,10,1
The following are valid DO statements:

```
DO 14 JACK=KEN,LEN,MEL
DO 38 IGNATZ=3,MX3,2
DO 12345 I=J,510,L
DO 627 KB3=K,J,62
```

The following are not valid DO statements
because they violate Rule 1.

```
DO 6 K=-5,+15,+3
DO 53 X=.1,2.8,.2
DO 143 K=J,2*M+3,L+5
DO 652 A=0,10
DO 19 J=14
```

Rule 2: Because the testing of the incremented
value of the index is done following execution
of the object of the DO, the range of the DO
is always performed at least once, even if the
initial value is greater than the test value
when the DO-loop is entered.

Thus the range of the following DO statement will be performed once:

```
DO 175 I=17,3
```

Rule 3:   The DO-parameters may not be modified by
statements within the range of the DO.   (It
is perfectly legal to modify them outside the
range.)   For example, the following DO-loop
violates this rule:

```
      DO 12 I=J,K,L
      L=3
      READ,I
   12 J=I+2
```

Rule 4:   The object of the DO must be an executable
statement, but not STOP, PAUSE, RETURN, another
DO, an arithmetic IF, any GO TO, or a logical
IF containing any of the previously named.
Here is where the CONTINUE statement comes in
handy.   Examples will be given in the next
section.

Rule 5:   It is possible to exit from a DO-loop before
it is satisfied.   For example, an IF statement
within the range could transfer control out of
the loop.   It is not valid, however, to attempt
to branch into the range of a DO from outside
the range.   In short, the only way to get into
the range of a DO is to enter through the
controlling DO statement itself.   An example
which violates this rule follows:

```
      GO TO 12
      DO 3 J=1,25
   12 ISQ=I*J
    3 PRINT,I,ISQ
```

Rule 6:   If control passes from the DO-loop because
it is satisfied, the value of the index is to be
considered indefinite,   that is, it may have the

last value it had while in the loop, or that value plus the increment, or some value completely different. Because this is a compiler implementation feature, it is not safe to use the index in this situation, if the program is expected to produce the same results with different compilers.

If control passes from the loop by means of an IF or GO TO, for example, the value of the index is usable outside the loop, and is the value the index had when control passed from the loop.

A few words should be said about what happens if the index never actually equals the test value, as would be the case for a statement such as DO 17 I=1,6,2. The range would be performed for I equal to 1, 3, and 5, since a further increment of 2 to I would increase it beyond 6. This is easily determined from the definition of the DO statement. The following examples are given as further illustrations of this rule.

(i)	DO 2 I=1,9,3	3 times
(ii)	DO 65 JACK=2,9,5	2 times
(iii)	DO 9 J12K=2,9,11	1 time
(iv)	DO 721 KB3=3,25,3	8 times
(v)	DO 16 L=11,1000,37	27 times

The last result was determined by the following formula which can be used to calculate the number of times the loop is executed.

$$\text{number of times} = \begin{cases} \left[\dfrac{m_2 - m_1}{m_3} \right] + 1 & \text{if } m_2 > m_1 \\ 1 & \text{if } m_2 \le m_1 \end{cases}$$

86

The square brackets mean 'the greatest integer
value less than or equal to', and m_1, m_2, and m_3
are the DO-parameters. The reader can verify that
this result holds for cases (i) to (iv).

7.3   USE OF CONTINUE

Let us consider a few more examples
which illustrate points arising from Rules 1 to
6. Example 7.8 shows where the use of a CONTINUE
statement is absolutely necessary. The problem
is this: A collection of data cards has been
punched, each containing two real numbers. A
program is to be created which reads the data
cards in turn, and prints out each pair of values
in the order: larger, smaller. It does this until
the data cards are exhausted or a data card is
found with the two values equal. The first data
card will contain an integer value which is the
count of the number of data cards with pairs.
Before terminating, the program is to print out
the number of data cards read, exclusive of the
first data card.

There are several points to note about
this example. Probably the most important is the
use of the CONTINUE statement as object of the DO.
This is necessary here since, following any
executions of statement 1, the object of the DO
must be reached in order to increment and test the
index for further repetitions of the loop. Statement 3 cannot be the object, since we want to
execute it only if X is greater than Y. Thus the

use of the dummy CONTINUE statement solves the
problem.

```
C EXAMPLE 7.8 - PRINTS LARGEST,SMALLEST
C N IS THE NUMBER OF DATA CARDS
      READ,N
      DO 4 I=1,N
      READ,X,Y
      IF(X-Y)1,2,3
    1 PRINT,Y,X
      GO TO 4
    3 PRINT,X,Y
    4 CONTINUE
      I=N
    2 PRINT,I
      STOP
      END
```

Also note that the program illustrates
that it is perfectly legal to transfer out of the
range of a DO, or to transfer within the range
provided the statement transferring control is
also within the same range. The program also
shows how to get around the difficulty imposed by
Rule 6. The extra statement I=N following the
CONTINUE is there to ensure that the value of I
is defined properly for the PRINT statement in
case control reaches the PRINT statement by
satisfying the DO-loop.

The next three examples are variations
of the same program. They all solve the following
problem: Read a data card containing an integer
value n. Then read n more data cards each containing
a positive real value. Find the largest real value,
and print it before terminating. (Here n might be
the number of students in a class, and the real

88

values might be the marks in a particular course. The
program would find the highest mark.) Basically,
the program works like this: Initialize a variable
BIG to zero. Then read n followed by the n values
in turn, each time checking whether the value just
read is larger than the current value of the
variable BIG, and replacing BIG with it if so. (This
will certainly be true the first time, since BIG is
zero and all the values are positive.) Finally,
after all the cards have been checked using the
DO-loop, the last value of BIG is printed out.

Example 7.9 is likely the simplest way
of doing the problem.

```
C EXAMPLE 7.9 - FINDING LARGEST NUMBER
      BIG=0.
      READ,N
      DO 2 I=1,N
      READ,X
    2 IF(X.GT.BIG)BIG=X
      PRINT,BIG
      STOP
      END
```

This example shows that a logical IF
statement is valid as object of a DO. In this
case, the index is tested after full completion
of execution of the logical IF; this will include
the statement BIG=X whenever the logical expression
X.GT.BIG is found to be true.

Example 7.10 differs from 7.9 only in
that a CONTINUE is used as object of the DO,
although it is superfluous. Some programmers
prefer always to place a CONTINUE as object since

89

this does no harm and avoids any problems that
might arise.

```
C EXAMPLE 7.10 - SAME AS 7.9
      BIG=0.
      READ,N
      DO 2 I=1,N
      READ,X
      IF(X.GT.BIG)BIG=X
    2 CONTINUE
      PRINT,BIG
      STOP
      END
```

Example 7.11 is another variation which
requires a CONTINUE for the object because this
time the IF tests for values of X less than BIG.

```
C EXAMPLE 7.11 - SAME RESULT AS 7.9, 7.10
      BIG=0.
      READ,N
      DO 2 I=1,N
      READ,X
      IF(X.LT.BIG)GO TO 2
      BIG=X
    2 CONTINUE
      PRINT,BIG
      STOP
      END
```

7.4   NESTED DO-LOOPS

The final topic to discuss is what happens
when a DO statement appears within the range of
another DO. This is as simple as the previous
topics, and only one rule need be added to
handle it.

<u>Rule 7</u>: All statements in the range of the inner
        DO must also be in the range of the outer DO.

        DO statements satisfying this rule are
said to be *nested*.

        Example 7.12 illustrates improperly
nested DO-loops.

```
C EXAMPLE 7.12 - IMPROPER NESTING
      DO 1 I=1,5
      DO 2 J=1,5
    1 L=I+5
    2 PRINT,L
      STOP
      END
```

        In essence, Rule 7 states that the object
of the inner DO of the nest must appear physically
no later in the program than the object of the
outer DO. It does not exclude the fact that nested
DO-loops may end on the same statement. In fact,
Example 7.13 illustrates that this is sometimes a
convenient situation. The program evaluates $x^2 + y^2$
for values of y equal to -2, -1, 0, 1, 2, for each
value of x equal to 0, 2, 4, ..., 10, i.e., at
the points of a grid in an x-y coordinate plane.

```
C EXAMPLE 7.13 - EVALUATION OF X**2+Y**2
      DO 17 I=1,11,2
      X=I-1
      DO 17 J=1,5
      Y=J-3
   17 PRINT,X,Y,X**2+Y**2
      STOP
      END
```

The first or outer DO statement causes
all statements up to and including 17 to be
executed for I ranging from 1 to 11 in steps of 2.
Since the second or inner DO statement is in this
range, all the statements past it up to and
including 17 are to be executed additionally under
control of the inner DO for J ranging from 1 to
5.   Thus the statements

```
Y=J-3
PRINT,X,Y,X**2+Y**2
```

are executed 30 times,whereas the statements

```
X=I-1
DO 17 J=1,5
```

are executed 6 times.   This, of course, produces
the desired result.

A slight modification in the problem
will show that nested DO's sometimes may not
share the same object statement.   This time we
evaluate

$$\frac{x^2 + y^2}{x - 4}$$

but we do not permit x to be equal to 4.   Example
7.14 shows that a CONTINUE statement must be
used to ensure that the nested DO's have separate
object statements.

```
C EXAMPLE 7.14 - EVALUATE (X**2+Y**2)/(X-4)
      DO 17 I=1,11,2
      X=I-1
      IF((X-4.).EQ.0.)GO TO 17
      DO 23 J=1,5
      Y=J-3
   23 PRINT,X,Y,+(X**2+Y**2)/(X-4.)
   17 CONTINUE
      STOP
      END
```

Note that Example 7.15 appears to be another solution to the problem. However, it violates Rule 5, since the IF statement in the outer DO attempts to branch into the range of the inner DO.

```
C EXAMPLE 7.15 - ILLEGAL BRANCH ATTEMPT
      DO 17 I=1,11,2
      X=I-1
      IF((X-4.).EQ.0.) GO TO 17
      DO 17 J=1,5
      Y=J-3
      PRINT,X,Y,+(X**2+Y**2)/(X-4.)
   17 CONTINUE
      STOP
      END
```

Figure 7.1 indicates DO formations which violate Rule 7.

Figure 7.2 shows properly nested DO's, and also indicates legal (solid arrow) and illegal (broken arrow) transfers of control.

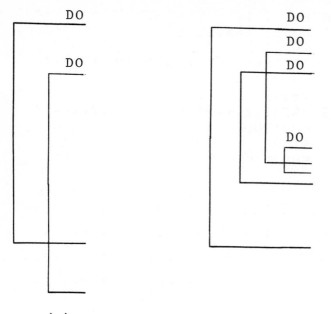

Figure 7.1   Improper Nesting

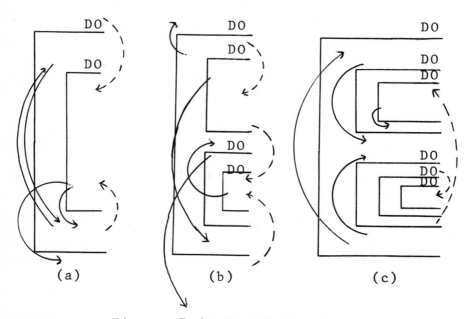

Figure 7.2   Valid Nesting

Figure 7.2 (c) shows DO loops nested to
a depth of four. Usually there is a limit to the
nesting depth imposed by the compiler, but this
is reasonably high, say 20; consequently, most
programs can be accommodated.

The DO statement finds its major use
with subscripted variables; these are the topic
of the next chapter.

7.5   EXERCISES

7.1   Repeat Examples 1.3, 1.4, 1.6, 2.1, 2.5,
3.1, 5.5, using DO statements to control
any loops.

7.2   Repeat Exercises 2.3, 2.4, 3.4, 4.3,
using DO statements to control any loops.

7.3   Tabulate the following functions using
DO statements to control any loops.

(a) $k = i^2 + i + 1$
for i = 0, 1, 2, ..., 10

(b) $y = (x^2 + 10)/(x + 3)$
for x = 5, 6, 7, ..., 15

(c) $f(x) = (x^3 + 3x + 16)/(x^2 - 4)$
for x = -5, -4, -3, ..., 10

(d) $f(x,y) = (x^2 - y^2)/(x^2 + y^2)$
for x = 0, 1, 2, ..., 5;
and y = 3, 5, 7, ..., 15 for each
value of x

(e) $f(x,y) = (x^2 + 3x + y^2)/(xy - 5y - 3x + 15)$
for x = 2, 3, 4, ..., 7;

and y = 0, 1, 2, ..., 5, for each
value of x

7.4 Compute the number of points with integer-
valued co-ordinates that are contained
within the ellipse

$$\frac{x^2}{16} + \frac{y^2}{25} = 1$$

7.5 A rectangular area is defined by the
relationships

$$N1 \leq x \leq N2$$
$$N3 \leq y \leq N4$$

where N1, N2, N3, and N4 are integers
greater than zero. In this area, there
are (N2-N1+1)(N4-N3+1) points which have
integer-valued co-ordinates. These points
are called the set A. Suppose the
following data were read by a program.
  (i)   N1, N2, N3, N4
 (ii)   the co-ordinates of a point, P, taken
        at random.
Write a program which uses DO-loops to
compute the distance from the point
P to each point in set A. The printed
output should have a separate line for
each of the distances. Each line should
contain the co-ordinates of the point in
A, together with the computed distance.

CHAPTER 8

SUBSCRIPTED VARIABLES

Subscripted variables are an extremely useful feature of the FORTRAN language since they allow flexible and general programs to be written. Indeed, they are so useful and important that it is rare to find a FORTRAN program of any size which does not use at least one of them. This is partly because they facilitate programming the repetitive calculations that are so common in computation and, in this respect, are often used with DO-loops. Also, they allow the programmer to refer to whole collections of values using one name much in the same way a mathematician refers to a set, e.g., the set of marks for a class or the set of prime numbers less than 100.

The notation used with subscripted variables is similar to the mathematical notation for vectors and matrices and facilitates the programming of problems that use these concepts.

8.1 NOTATION AND USE

Consider the problem of calculating the average mark in a certain course for a class of five students. Each student's mark is to be printed along with the class average. Example 8.1 is a simple program to solve this particular problem. Note that a different real variable

97

name is given to the mark of each student, and each
mark is punched on a separate data card.

```
C EXAMPLE 8.1 - AVERAGE MARK
      READ,A
      READ,B
      READ,C
      READ,D
      READ,E
      TOTAL=A+B+C+D+E
      AVRGE=TOTAL/5.
      PRINT,A,AVRGE
      PRINT,B,AVRGE
      PRINT,C,AVRGE
      PRINT,D,AVRGE
      PRINT,E,AVRGE
      STOP
      END
```

This approach to the problem is
obviously inflexible in that a great deal of
modification would have to be made to the program
if there were a different number of students in
the class, say 12 or 30. Indeed, it would be
impossible to use the approach if the number of
students was not known beforehand, but was to be
read in as data to the program.

Let us approach this problem again, and
introduce the idea of a *subscripted variable*.
Suppose we consider all the students' marks as a
set named, say, m. Then we could refer to a
particular student's mark by writing the name of
the set, m, with a subscript which identifies the
student. Thus m_1 refers to the mark of student
number one, m_2 to the mark of student number two, and
so on. (Of course, we would have to agree upon some

method for numbering the students.) In general, we
would call the ith student's mark m_i, where i would
have some value between 1 and the number of students
in the class, inclusive. Thus the use of a subscript with the set name allows us to refer to a
particular element of the set. This notation has
been found to be useful in mathematics and engineering,
and is carried over into FORTRAN in the following
way: the subscript is written inside parentheses
following the set name.

eg. M(1), M(2), M(16), M(I)

The variable M is referred to as a subscripted
variable.

Since a particular element of the set
has a value, this element can be used in a program
in exactly the same way that other variables have
been used in the programs seen so far.

Example 8.2 uses a subscripted variable
to find the average mark for a class of 30 students.

```
C EXAMPLE 8.2 - CLASS AVERAGE
      DIMENSION MARK(30)
      INTEGER SUM
      SUM=0
      I=1
   22 READ,MARK(I)
      SUM=SUM+MARK(I)
      I=I+1
      IF(I.LE.30)GO TO 22
      AVE=SUM/30.
      I=1
   53 PRINT,MARK(I),AVE
      I=I+1
      IF(I.LE.30)GO TO 53
      STOP
      END
```

Aside from the DIMENSION statement,
which will be explained later, the program looks
much like many of the examples seen before. There
is a loop, controlled by a logical IF statement,
which causes successive data cards to be read,
each containing a mark. The first time through
the loop, I has the value 1, and is used as a subscript for variable MARK in the READ statement.
Thus the value of MARK(1) is read in and accumulated
into SUM. Since I is incremented within the loop,
successive repetitions of the loop read in values
for MARK(2), MARK(3), MARK(4), ..., MARK(30).
Thus it is an easy matter to read in any number
of marks, and the program could be modified quite
simply to do this, if the class contained, for
example, 25 students. In fact, this will be done
in the next section.

8.2 ONE-DIMENSIONAL ARRAYS

What is the purpose of the DIMENSION
statement? It is another example of a declaration
statement and, as such, has no effect at execution
time. It is used strictly at compile time to
provide the compiler with certain information about
the variable named in it.

With reference to Example 8.2, the
information it provides is this:

    (i) It identifies MARK as the name of a set
         of values; a particular member of the
         set will be referenced in the program
         by the use of the name MARK followed by

a subscript enclosed in parentheses.

(ii)   It informs the compiler that there are
        30 elements in the set, and that enough
        memory must be allocated to store values
        corresponding to these elements.

(iii)   It contains a tacit promise that the
        value of any subscript used with MARK
        will never be less than 1 or greater
        than 30.   Thus it would be impossible
        to refer to MARK(-5) or MARK(79).

The value 30 used in the DIMENSION
statement is called the *dimension* of MARK.   Any
variables that are to be used with subscripts must
have their dimensions declared before they are
used in the program.   Subscripted variables are
also referred to as *dimensioned variables* or *arrays*.

The names for arrays follow the usual
rules of FORTRAN.   Thus, each element of MARK is
an integer value, and will be treated as such by
the compiler.   It is possible to have arrays of
other than integer type, as subsequent examples
will show.

Example 8.3 is a modification of 8.2,
and illustrates the flexibility of programs which
use subscripted variables.   This new version declares
MARK to have 30 elements, but does not assume that 30
student marks will be read.   Instead, the first data
card contains an integer constant which specifies
the actual number of student marks which follow it
on cards.   Thus the program is general, in the sense
that it can be used with a class of any size up to

a maximum of 30. The program simply reads in the
particular class size at execution time; no
modifications are required to the program itself.

```
C EXAMPLE 8.3 - GENERAL PROGRAM FOR AVERAGE
        DIMENSION MARK(30)
        INTEGER TOTAL
        TOTAL=0
        READ,N
        DO 26 I=1,N
        READ,MARK(I)
    26  TOTAL=TOTAL+MARK(I)
        AVRGE=TOTAL/N
        DO 4 I=1,N
     4  PRINT,MARK(I),AVRGE
        STOP
        END
```

Note that Example 8.3 uses DO statements
to control the looping. Note also that the program
does not necessarily use all 30 locations reserved
for MARK; in fact only the first N are used.

The answers printed for Example 8.2 may
differ slightly from those for Example 8.3; the
former program uses mixed-mode arithmetic to
calculate the average, whereas the latter uses
integer arithmetic for this calculation. In both
cases, the average is a real number.

It should be apparent by now that a
subscripted variable may be used in the same ways
that a simple variable may be used, that is, in
READ statements, assignment statements, IF statements, etc. Example 8.4 shows the use of a subscripted variable on the left side of an assignment
statement and in a PRINT statement. The program

prints the first ten Fibonacci numbers which are
defined by the following rules:

$$f_1 = 1$$

$$f_2 = 1$$

$$f_{i+2} = f_{i+1} + f_i \qquad i \geq 1$$

Thus, each Fibonacci number after the second is
obtained by adding together the previous two. Thus,

$$f_3 = f_2 + f_1 = 2$$

$$f_4 = f_3 + f_2 = 3$$

$$f_5 = 5, \quad f_6 = 8, \quad \text{etc.}$$

Note that all Fibonacci numbers have integer values.

```
C EXAMPLE 8.4 - FIBONACCI NUMBERS
      INTEGER F(10)
      F(1)=1
      F(2)=1
      DO 1 I=1,8
    1 F(I+2)=F(I+1)+F(I)
      DO 43 J=1,10
   43 PRINT,F(J)
      STOP
      END
```

The program illustrates other features
about subscripted variables. Since we want the
array F to represent integer values, we declare
its name in an INTEGER statement. It is also possible to declare the dimensions of arrays in type-
declaration statements, and hence the single statement

INTEGER F(10)

103

serves both purposes. It would be perfectly legal
to use a DIMENSION statement to declare the dimension
of F, for example,

```
    DIMENSION F(10)    or    INTEGER F
    INTEGER F                DIMENSION F(10)
```

However, using one statement saves extra key-punching,
and localizes all the information about F. The
dimension must be declared only once; for example,
the following pair of statements is invalid.

```
            DIMENSION F(10)
            INTEGER F(10)
```

The assignment statement

$$F(I+2)=F(I+1)+F(I)$$

shows that subscripts may be expressions and not
just simple values as in previous examples. The
statement is the object of the DO, and hence is
repeated eight times. The first time, I has value
1 and the statement is essentially equivalent to
$F(3)=F(2)+F(1)$. Next time through the loop, I has
value 2, and the calculation performed is
$F(4)=F(3)+F(2)$. Thus, going eight times through the
loop computes the third to tenth Fibonacci numbers –
the desired result.

A subscript may in fact be *any* integer-valued
or real-valued expression; if real, the value is
converted to an integer by truncating any fractional
part. For example, X(17.38) is taken as X(17) if X
is an array. Although this feature is occasionally
convenient, the programmer is cautioned against
using real-valued subscripts because the necessary

104

conversion is costly in computing time.

Example 8.5 contains one modification to
the previous example.

```
C EXAMPLE 8.5 - USE OF IMPLIED DO
      INTEGER F(10)
      F(1)=1
      F(2)=1
      DO 1 I=1,8
    1 F(I+2)=F(I+1)+F(I)
      PRINT,(F(I),I=1,10)
      STOP
      END
```

The PRINT statement contains a new
feature not seen in previous examples, although
the I=1,10 part may look familiar. The construction

$$(F(I),I=1,10)$$

is called an *implied DO* because it is a means of
causing a looping action within the PRINT statement.
The statement

$$PRINT,(F(I),I=1,10)$$

means, effectively: "Print values of F(I) for I
ranging from 1 to 10".   The ten values so printed
would be strung out across the printer line as
follows:

1   1   2   3   5   8   13   21   34   55

The same effect could be achieved by the equivalent,
though more cumbersome, statement

PRINT,F(1),F(2),F(3),F(4),F(5),F(6),F(7),F(8),F(9),F(10)

The parameters of the implied DO have the

same significance as those of a DO statement; accordingly, an increment may be specified. Thus, to print out the third, fifth, seventh, and ninth Fibonacci numbers, we could use the statement

    PRINT,(F(I),I=3,10,2)

The same effect could be obtained from

    PRINT,(F(2*I+1),I=1,4)

but the former method is superior since its execution involves fewer computations and hence is faster.

It is important to note that the outer parentheses and the comma preceding the DO index are always necessary when constructing an implied DO. The only executable statements in which the implied DO is allowed are the input and output statements.

One simplification that could be made to the program is shown by Example 8.6.

```
C EXAMPLE 8.6 - OUTPUT OF WHOLE ARRAY
      INTEGER F(10)
      F(1)=1
      F(2)=1
      DO 1 I=1,8
    1 F(I+2)=F(I+1)+F(I)
      PRINT,F
      STOP
      END
```

In this example, the PRINT statement contains only the name of the array F. This is one of the few places an array name may appear in a program without subscripts; the effect of the statement is to print out *all* the elements of the array, i.e., as many elements as are reserved by the dimension. For this example, the two statements

```
PRINT,F
PRINT,(F(I),I=1,N)
```

would produce the same result only if N were equal to 10. Thus, if it is desired that a whole array be printed, we need mention only its name; if part is to be printed, we use an implied DO. The same remarks are true for READ statements which operate on subscripted variables.

Example 8.7 is a program which computes a grocery bill using two arrays. The first array, COST, will contain the cost per item for one hundred different items. The second array, ITEM, will contain the number of units of each item purchased on a trip to the grocery store. The program first reads in the cost for each of the one hundred items, then reads in the corresponding one hundred values for elements of array ITEM and proceeds to compute the bill.

```
C EXAMPLE 8.7 - GROCERY BILL
      DIMENSION COST(100),ITEM(100)
      READ,COST,ITEM
      BILL=0.
      DO 2 I=1,100
    2 BILL=BILL+COST(I)*ITEM(I)
      PRINT,BILL
      STOP
      END
```

It is important to understand how the data cards for this program could be punched. Obviously more than one data card will have to be punched to contain the two hundred values which are to be read in. The question is: Will the single READ statement read all the cards? The answer to this is yes; enough data cards will be read until values have been assigned to the one hundred elements of COST and the one hundred elements of ITEM. The successive elements of COST could be punched one after the other on a data card, with an intervening comma or blank to separate the values; a new data card would be started if the next value would not fit into the remaining columns of the current card. The values of ITEM would be punched next, with ITEM(1) following COST(100) or starting a new data card. Note that the values of COST must be punched as real constants, and the values of ITEM as integer constants.

As can be seen, more than one array may be declared in a single DIMENSION statement, with a comma between the various array declarations.

The program would be more efficient if both COST and ITEM were real arrays, since the present version uses mixed-mode arithmetic. This is time consuming, particularly when used in a loop such as is contained in the example. The improved version is Example 8.8.

```
C EXAMPLE 8.8 - IMPROVEMENT OF 8.7
        DIMENSION COST(100)
        REAL ITEM(100)
        BILL=0.
        READ,COST,ITEM
        DO 2 I=1,100
      2 BILL=BILL+COST(I)*ITEM(I)
        PRINT,BILL
        STOP
        END
```

Alternatively, the first two statements could be replaced by

```
        REAL COST(100),ITEM(100)
```

or
```
        DIMENSION COST(100), ITEM(100)
        REAL ITEM
```

or, for that matter,

```
        REAL ITEM
        DIMENSION COST(100)
        DIMENSION ITEM(100)
```

One-dimensional arrays are sometimes called vectors. Mathematicians will note that the DO-loops in Examples 8.7 and 8.8 calculate the scalar or inner product of two vectors.

One final example concludes this section on one-dimensional arrays. The object of the program is to evaluate the polynomial expression

$$a_1x^{n-1}+a_2x^{n-2}+a_3x^{n-3}+\ldots+a_n$$

for given values of n, a_1, a_2, ..., a_n using various values of x which are read in. The program terminates when a zero value for x is read.

109

An efficient way to organize the polynomial for evaluation using a computer is as follows:

$$(\ldots((a_1 x + a_2)x + a_3)x + \ldots + a_{n-1})x + a_n$$

To be specific, we will assume n to be less than or equal to 25.

```
C EXAMPLE 8.9 - POLYNOMIAL EVALUATION
      DIMENSION A(25)
      READ,N,(A(J),J=1,N)
   16 READ,X
      IF(X.EQ.0.)STOP
      POLY=A(1)
      DO 12 I=2,N
   12 POLY=POLY*X+A(I)
      PRINT,X,POLY
      GO TO 16
      END
```

The data deck consists of a value of n followed by the n coefficients a_i on one or more data cards. These are followed by successive data cards, each with a value of x; the final card contains the value zero.

8.3 TWO-DIMENSIONAL ARRAYS

The previous section shows that it is convenient to have variable names which may be used with a subscript. This section introduces the idea of two-dimensional arrays; these involve variables having two subscripts. Their principal use in programs is for working with tables of values. The mathematical equivalent is a matrix, and a similar notation is used.

110

Consider Figure 8.1, where a table of
values is shown. The table consists of the number
of various items that are stocked at several
warehouses belonging to a company.

	Item 1	Item 2	Item 3	Item 4
Warehouse 1	50	0	16	2
Warehouse 2	3	4	0	98
Warehouse 3	0	1	4	220

Figure 8.1

Using this table, it is easy to answer
many questions concerning the company's inventory.
What is the total stock of item 4 on hand? What
is the total number of items stored at Warehouse 2?
Are there any items completely out of stock? Are
there any items out of stock at a particular
warehouse? How many of the fourth item are in
stock at Warehouse 2?

Notice that the data in the table are
organized in three rows and four columns. The
last question above could be paraphrased as: What
is the value in row 2 and column 4? Or, more
generally, what is the value in row i and column j?

In order to use such a table in FORTRAN,
we need only give it a name, say, for this example,
STOCK; then, to refer to a particular element of
the table we append two subscripts, in parentheses,
to the name. Thus STOCK(2,4) is the stock of item
4 on hand in Warehouse 2, i.e., 98. Similarly,

STOCK(3,2) is the stock of item 2 on hand at Warehouse 3, i.e., 1. The first subscript *always* refers to the row number in the table; the second *always* refers to the column number; a comma *always* separates the two subscripts. Thus STOCK(I,J) refers to the entry in row I and column J of the table (or matrix or two-dimensional array) named STOCK.

Let us proceed to write programs which answer some of the questions mentioned above. Example 8.10 is a program to compute the total stock of item 4. It reads in the table, sums down column 4, and prints out the resulting sum.

Again we use a DIMENSION statement to declare the array for the same reasons given under one-dimensional arrays. However, the particular DIMENSION statement in the example supplies one additional piece of information. It informs the compiler that the variable named STOCK has *two* dimensions and will be used with *two* subscripts throughout the program. Note that 12 locations are set aside for STOCK, since it has 3 rows and 4 columns.

```
C EXAMPLE 8.10 - STOCK ON HAND OF ITEM 4
      DIMENSION STOCK(3,4)
      INTEGER STOCK
      DO 2 I=1,3
    2 READ,(STOCK(I,J),J=1,4)
      NUMBER=0
      DO 25 I=1,3
   25 NUMBER=NUMBER+STOCK(I,4)
      PRINT,NUMBER
      STOP
      END
```

The method of reading in the table requires a brief explanation. A DO statement controls a READ statement containing an implied DO. Since I, the index of the DO statement, is used as row designator for STOCK in the READ statement, the implied DO has the effect of reading in the values across a row of the table. The looping action of the DO statement causes all three rows to be read in. The data could consist of three cards, each containing the four values in a row of the table.

The foregoing remarks virtually explain the action of the second DO statement as well. Since the column designator for STOCK in the statement numbered 25 is the constant 4, computation within the DO loop is confined to values in that column. Thus the sum of all values in column 4 is calculated.

As before, the two declaration statements at the start of the program could be replaced by the single statement

                    INTEGER STOCK(3,4)

Example 8.11 is a program which determines the total number of articles in stock at each warehouse, and stores these values in the vector AMOUNT.

The READ statement

        READ,((STOCK(I,J),J=1,4),I=1,3)

introduces the concept of nested implied DO's; the inner implied DO is performed for each application of the outer DO. Thus, one statement reads in the twelve values of STOCK, by rows; they could be punched on one card as:

        50,0,16,2,3,4,0,98,0,1,4,220

```
C EXAMPLE 8.11 - AMOUNT IN WAREHOUSES
      INTEGER STOCK(3,4),AMOUNT(3)
      READ,((STOCK(I,J),J=1,4),I=1,3)
C ZERO OUT VECTOR AMOUNT FOR SUMMING
      DO 1 I=1,3
    1 AMOUNT (I)=0
C SUM ACROSS ROWS OF STOCK
      DO 2 I=1,3
      DO 2 J=1,4
    2 AMOUNT(I)=AMOUNT(I)+STOCK(I,J)
      PRINT,AMOUNT
      STOP
      END
```

The READ statement above could read the data cards for Example 8.10, since any trailing blanks on a card are skipped over by the READ mechanism in its search for enough values to satisfy the READ.

Note that comment statements may be included anywhere in a program; they can serve a valuable documentary purpose.

Although the double DO-loop ending on statement 2 performs the proper row summations for each row, a slightly more efficient program could be obtained by writing the loops in the following fashion:

```
      DO 26 I=1,3
      NUMBER=0
      DO 2 J=1,4
    2 NUMBER=NUMBER+STOCK(I,J)
   26 AMOUNT(I)=NUMBER
```

114

Notice that this modification reduces
the number of array references from 36 to 15, a
saving which could mean a significant difference
in execution time, since array referencing, although
convenient, involves many hidden computations of which
the programmer may not be aware.

The PRINT statement outputs the entire
vector AMOUNT by mentioning its name only. Could
we have read the entire array STOCK by mentioning
only its name in the READ statement? The answer
to this question is yes, but, before giving an
example, a few details concerning storage of arrays
in FORTRAN must be explained.

A one-dimensional array or vector is
stored in the computer's memory with successively
numbered elements in successively higher numbered
adjacent storage locations. The linear ordering
of vector elements is well adapted to the
conventional linear ordering of computer memory
elements.

Two-dimensional arrays present some
problem of storage in a linearly-ordered memory
but this problem is easily overcome by the convention
that matrices are to be stored by columns, that is,
column 1 is stored linearly, followed by column 2
linearly, etc., for as many columns as the array
possesses. Thus the elements of a table T,
declared by DIMENSION T(3,2), would be stored in
ascending memory locations as follows:

T(1,1) T(2,1) T(3,1) T(1,2) T(2,2) T(3,2)

Ordinarily the programmer need not be

aware of this *storage order* but it allows a very
simple rule for describing what happens when input or
output is done on an array mentioned by name only.
The rule is this: All elements of the array are
read or printed in storage order.

Thus the statement

READ,STOCK

causes elements of STOCK to be read by columns.
This statement is used in Example 8.12 which is
merely a modification of 8.11.

```
C EXAMPLE 8.12
C READING AN ENTIRE MATRIX COLUMNWISE
      INTEGER STOCK(3,4),AMOUNT(3)
      DO 6 I=1,3
    6 AMOUNT(I)=0
      READ,STOCK
      DO 2 I=1,3
      DO 2 J=1,4
    2 AMOUNT(I)=AMOUNT(I)+STOCK(I,J)
      PRINT,AMOUNT
      STOP
      END
```

This time, the data would be punched as:

50,3,0,0,4,1,16,0,4,2,98,220

Thus, it can be seen that there are several ways
to read or print an array. All or part of the
array can be read or printed by rows or by
columns, using implied DO's. Or the *whole* array can
be read or printed in storage order merely by
using its name without subscripts.

It is a company policy to send a shipment
of an item to restock a warehouse if the quantity

116

on hand drops below 10. Example 8.13 is a program
that scans the entries in the stock table to detect
such items and prints the warehouse, item, and
quantity on hand for shipment planning purposes.

```
C EXAMPLE 8.13 - SCAN FOR SHIPMENT LEVEL
      INTEGER STOCK(3,4),W
      READ,STOCK
      DO 1 W=1,3
      DO 1 I=1,4
    1 IF(STOCK(W,I).LT.10)PRINT,W,I,STOCK(W,I)
      STOP
      END
```

The final example on two-dimensional
arrays is a program which reads in an n by k
matrix A, a k by m matrix B, forms the matrix
product A × B, and prints the result. For this
example the values of n, k, m, will be read in from
a separate data card with the data for A, and B
following. To be specific, let us assume that each
of k, m, n, will be less than or equal to 25.

```
C EXAMPLE 8.14 - MATRIX MULTIPLICATION
      DIMENSION A(25,25),B(25,25),C(25,25)
      READ,N,K,M,((A(I,J),I=1,N),J=1,K)
      READ,((B(J,I),J=1,K),I=1,M)
      DO 1 I=1,N
      DO 1 J=1,M
      C(I,J)=0.
      DO 1 L=1,K
    1 C(I,J)=C(I,J)+A(I,L)*B(L,J)
      PRINT,((I,J,C(I,J),J=1,M),I=1,N)
      STOP
      END
```

Note that both A and B are read by columns, but that C is printed by rows. The row and column designators are printed for each matrix element, since they are also within the parentheses of the implied DO's.

If N, K, and M are, in fact, less than 25, only part of the storage reserved for the arrays is used during execution of the program. This is indicated by the shaded portion of Figure 8.2.

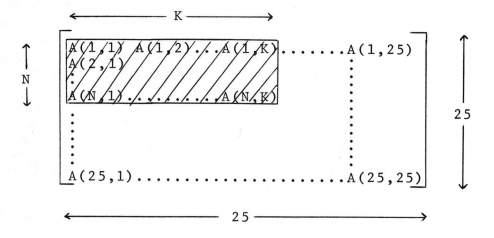

Figure 8.2

Storage Used for Array A, Example 8.14, if N,K<25.

8.4 HIGHER-DIMENSIONAL ARRAYS

FORTRAN allows arrays with more than two dimensions, and essentially the same rules carry over. For example,

DIMENSION X(5,4,7),M(3,3,5,2)

declares a three-dimensional array X and a four-dimensional array M. Storage reserved is 140

118

elements for X and 90 elements for M. The array
X so declared may be imagined as a collection of
7 parallel blackboards, each containing a matrix
of 5 rows and 4 columns. Thus, the element X(3,2,4)
refers to the element in row 3, column 2, of the
fourth blackboard.

Arrays with up to seven dimensions may
be declared in FORTRAN programs, but those with
more than three dimensions are difficult to depict
physically.

The storage order for arrays is defined
as follows. Arrays are stored in ascending memory
locations with the value of the first subscript
increasing most rapidly and the value of the last
subscript increasing least rapidly. The range of
each subscript is from one to the declared dimension
corresponding to that subscript.

The reader may verify that the simple
rules given in Section 8.2 for vectors and matrices
are particular applications of this general rule.

The concept of storage order is important
for an understanding of COMMON and EQUIVALENCE statements, which are discussed in later chapters.

8.5 SUMMARY

This section summarizes in point form
most of the important rules about the use of subscripted variables.

(i)   An array must be declared by including
its dimension in a DIMENSION or type-

declaration statement before it is used in a program. The dimensions of an array are declared only once. Programmers commonly place all array declarations near the beginning of a program for convenience.

(ii) An array may have from one to seven subscripts, but the number of subscripts must remain the same within a program. Thus, if a variable is declared to be two-dimensional, when that variable is used with subscripts, two subscripts must be given - no more, no fewer.

(iii) A subscript may be any integer-valued or real-valued expression always in the range from one to the value of the dimension declared for the subscript position. If the subscript value is real; it is converted to an integer by truncating any fractional part.

(iv) Array names may appear without subscripts in I/O statements. The I/O operation is performed on the elements of the array in storage order.

8.6 EXERCISES

8.1 Write a program that inputs 15 positive real values and stores them in a vector. Determine the largest and smallest value. Print the entire vector and the two computed values. Use the implied DO in any input and output statements.

8.2 Consider a set of 41 data cards, each of which contains a student's number and his mark in a certain course. Write a program to do the following.

(i) The 41 cards are to be read. The student numbers are to be stored in a vector, and the corresponding marks are to be stored in another vector.

(ii) The marks are to be scanned to determine the maximum mark. This is to be printed, together with the corresponding student number. Then this mark is set equal to a negative quantity.

(iii) Step (ii) is then repeated for each student; thus the second-highest, third-highest, etc., marks are located and printed.

The effect of the overall-program is to print the class record as a descending sequence of examination marks.

8.3 Modify the program for Exercise 8.2 so that the results are not printed, but are stored in two new vectors, one for the student numbers and one for associated marks. These new vectors reflect the rank of the students in the subject.

Further modify the program in order to compute the class average and the class median. The median is defined as the mark obtained by the student who is in the

middle-ranking position of the class, in
this case, the 21st. (If the class had an
even number of students, the median would
be the average of the two marks at the
half-way point.)

Print the class record in *ascending*
sequence, with the class average and the
class median adjacent to each student
mark.

8.4   Suppose the 41 data cards for Exercise
8.2 were each to contain a student's
number and his marks for each of six
subjects.

Write a program which reads these
data into an integer array of 41 rows
and seven columns. The first column
contains the student numbers. The program
is to do the following.

(i)   Compute the average for each student,
and store it in a new vector of 41
elements.

(ii)   Compute the average for each course,
and store it in a new vector of 6
elements.

(iii) Compute the class average in two
ways – by averaging the student marks,
and by averaging the course marks.

(iv)   Finally, print all computed results.

8.5   With reference to Exercise 8.4, arrange to
print the examination results, in descending
order by average, for each student. The
final line of output contains the average

for each course.

8.6 Modify the programs for Exercises 8.4 and
8.5 in the following way. The average
for each student is to be computed by
using only his five best marks. Thus,
the minimum mark must be determined, and be
eliminated from the averaging process.

8.7 Using the table described in Figure 8.1,
write programs to answer the following
questions concerning the company's inventory

   (i)   Which items are completely out of
stock at warehouse i, where the value
of i is read in as data?

  (ii) Which of the items are completely out
of stock at any of the warehouses?
Your output should be the warehouse
numbers and item numbers.

 (iii) What is the total number of items
on hand in all the warehouses

8.8 Consider Example 8.11 which is concerned
with the total numbers of various items
in various warehouses. Suppose the cost
of each item is recorded in a real vector
named COST. Write a program which computes
and prints the following quantities.

   (i)   the total cost of each item in each
warehouse

  (ii) the total cost of inventory in each
warehouse

 (iii) the total cost of each item for all
warehouses

 (iv) the grand total cost of inventory.

8.9   When a customer places an order for a
      particular item from the company, an
      order card is punched containing the item
      number and the quantity ordered. Write
      a program which uses the information in
      Figure 8.1, and which reads in the order
      card and checks if there is enough of the
      item in stock at any warehouse. If there
      is enough, the table should be updated
      to reflect the order. If there is not
      enough in any single warehouse, the order
      has to be filled by taking the items from
      a number of warehouses. Again, the table
      should be updated. If the total number
      of items at all warehouses is insufficient
      to fill the order, this should be indicated.

8.10 Write separate programs to perform the
      following operations upon vectors. The
      data consist of the dimensions of the vectors
      and the values of the vector elements.
      Read the data from cards, and check the
      dimensions to ensure they are appropriate
      before calculation takes place.
      (a)   Compute the length of any vector.
      (b)   Compute the inner product of any
            two vectors.
      (c)   Compute the angle between any two
            vectors.

8.11 Write separate programs to perform the
      following matrix operations. Where
      necessary, read the data from cards, and
      check the dimensions to ensure they are

appropriate before calculation takes place. The data consist of the matrix dimensions and values for the matrix elements.

(a) Add two matrices.

(b) Multiply two matrices.

(c) Invert a matrix.

(d) Compute the largest element in a matrix.

(e) Initialize a square matrix to be the identity matrix.

(f) Initialize any matrix of given dimensions to be the zero matrix.

(g) Find the sum of the squares of the diagonal elements in any square matrix.

8.12 Write a program which:

(i) reads the coefficients of a polynomial and stores them in an array. (The program should handle polynomials of degrees up to and including 20.)

(ii) evaluates the polynomial for any values of the independent variable that are read in from cards.

8.13 Write a program which:

(i) reads the coefficients of a polynomial, as in Exercise 8.12

(ii) evaluates the first derivative of the polynomial for any values of the independent variable that are read in from cards.

8.14 Write a program which determines prime
     numbers in the following way.
  (i)   Set up a vector M which has 200
        elements, and initialize these elements
        so that M(I)=I for I=1,2,3,...,200.
  (ii) Print out the contents of M(2). This
        is the first prime, namely, the
        integer 2.
  (iii) Then proceed through the vector, and
        replace all multiples of 2 by zero.
  (iv) Beginning at the position of the last
        prime which has been printed scan
        along the vector until the first non-
        zero element is found. Print this
        as the next prime. Then proceed through
        the vector, replacing by zero all
        multiples of this prime that are found.
  (v)   Repeat step (iv) as long as there are
        non-zero elements remaining in the vector.

8.15 Table 8.1 consists of the quantities of
     various items that are stocked at several
     warehouses belonging to a company. As
     has been seen, this form of table is useful
     for answering questions about the company's
     inventory. However, a company would probably
     like to insert other information about
     its inventory in the table. For example,
     the number of items sold to date from
     each warehouse in the current year - the
     current-year total - might be a requirement.
     These additional data could be inserted by
     changing the table from a two-dimensional

array to a three-dimensional array. The
first row of the following diagram is
the first row of the STOCK table. A
second row is added to contain the current-
year totals.

	700	651	453	54
50	0	16	2	

In the previous examples, the value 50
was referred to as STOCK(1,1), and the
value 16 as STOCK(1,3). If we use a
three-dimensional array, the value 50
will be referred to as STOCK(1,1,1) and the
value 16 as STOCK(1,3,1). Then, the value
700, representing the current number of
the first item shipped from warehouse 1,
would be referred to as STOCK(1,1,2), and
the value 453 as STOCK(1,3,2).

Write a program which answers the
following questions. (Assume that the
price of items 1, 2, 3, and 4 is $5.00,
$6.00, $4.26, and $2.42, respectively;
furthermore, assume these are stored in a
vector called COST. The current-year

127

totals, in storage order, are 700, 3500, 62, 651, 73, 57, 453, 962, 459, 54, 5763, 492.)

(i)   What is the total stock and value of item 2 shipped in the current year?

(ii) What is the total value of all inventory on hand?

(iii) What is the total value of all items shipped in the current year?

8.16 Improve the efficiency of the program in Example 8.14 by using the artifice described on page 114 for Example 8.11.

CHAPTER 9

BASIC FORMAT

All examples prior to this chapter have used format-free input and output. The programmer has had little or no ability to control the appearance or precision of information printed. However, it is desirable for the programmer to have some means of controlling the manner in which results are printed. The FORMAT statement provides this facility.

Furthermore, it is desirable to be able to read data cards which are punched in a manner not suited to format-free input. Again, the FORMAT statement provides the necessary flexibility to allow this.

The purpose of this chapter is to introduce some of the immediately useful features of *format*. Later chapters will expand upon the material as the need arises.

9.1 A SIMPLE EXAMPLE

We have already observed that the sequence of statements

```
X=32.125
PRINT,X
```

will produce the following printed line.

```
0.3212500E 02
```

The following sequence of statements
prints the same value using a FORMAT statement.

```
      X=32.125
      PRINT27,X
   27 FORMAT('0',F7.3)
```

This time, the printer will double-space,
and print the more readable line

32.125

The FORMAT statement has a statement
number, in this case, 27. This statement number
also appears in the PRINT statement immediately
following the word PRINT. It serves to associate
the FORMAT statement with the PRINT statement.

The word FORMAT is followed by a list
of *format codes*, contained in parentheses. In
this case, the list is

'0',F7.3

The first code, '0', causes the printer
to double-space, and prepares it to print a new
line[†]; this code is referred to as the printer
control character. The second code, F7.3, specifies
that (i) a real number, in this case X, is to be
printed using the first available 7 print positions;
these positions are referred to as a *field*, in this

---

† The Model 026 key-punch does not have the quote
  mark as one of its characters; the @ sign is used
  instead of a quote.

```
   27 FORMAT(@0@,F7.3)
```

130

case, of width 7; (ii)   the real number is to be
printed with 3 decimal places; (iii)   the value
printed is to be right justified in the 7-position
field.

Thus the FORMAT statement is a coded set
of rules indicating the precise form in which
information is to be printed. Many format codes
are available, and these are described in detail
in this and future chapters.

9.2   CONTROL CHARACTERS

The control character is used to
determine line spacing on the printer. It appears
as the first entry in the format list, and is
required only when printing. The following table
gives the valid control characters and their
associated actions:

'b'	single spacing
'0'	double spacing
'-'	triple spacing
'1'	skip to the top of a new page
'+'	do not space to a new line

Notice that the letter b is used to denote a blank
space.

Examples (i), (ii), and (iii) below
demonstrate single, double, and triple spacing of
printer output.

Should the programmer want output to
start at the top of a new printer page, the control
character '1' may be used.

            (i)   123456789
                   123456789
           (ii)   123456789

                   123456789
          (iii)   123456789

                   123456789

9.3   PRINTING REAL VALUES

          The F format code is used to print real
values when no exponent is desired. In general, the
format code has the form Fw.d, where 'w' refers to
the next available w print positions and 'd' refers
to the number of decimal positions which are to
appear to the right of the decimal point.

```
          C EXAMPLE 9.1 - DEMONSTRATE F FORMAT
                X=7.639
                Y=-66.93745
                PRINT3,X,Y
              3 FORMAT(' ',F11.3,F14.5)
```

          In Example 9.1, the printer would single-
space and print the following line (the letter b
is used to indicate blanks or spaces).

            bbbbbb7.639bbbbb-66.93745

               F11.3   F14.5
                 X   Y

The format code F11.3 informs the computer that X
is to be printed in the next available 11 print
positions; it is to be printed with 3 decimal places.

Then F14.5 indicates that the *next* 14 print positions are to be used for Y, with 5 decimal places to be printed.   In each case, the value printed is to be placed right justified in the field.   Notice that there is a one-to-one correspondence between the variables in the PRINT list and the format codes.

$$X \leftrightarrow F11.3$$
$$Y \leftrightarrow F14.3$$

Example 9.2 demonstrates the effect of F format in a number of special cases.

```
C EXAMPLE 9.2 - SOME MORE F FORMAT
      A=6.50
      B=-256.496
      C=1.03239
      D=62345.67
      PRINT9,A,B,C,D
    9 FORMAT(' ',F10.5,F7.3,F12.4,F5.2)
```

The following line would be printed

```
bbb6.50000*******bbbbbb1.0324*****
```

| F10.5 | F7.3 | F12.4 | F5.2 |
| A | B | C | D |

Since the number of digits of A following the decimal is less than the 5 specified by the format F10.5, zeros are supplied on the right.

The value for B requires eight positions (six digits, the sign, and the decimal point), and, since only seven are specified, an error condition is indicated by placing *'s in the field.   Similarly, D is too large to fit into five print positions, and again *'s are used to fill the field.   When this happens, either the *field width* w must be increased, or the required number of decimal places, d, must be decreased, if the real number is to be printed using the F format code.

The format code for C specifies four decimal places, but C has five. In this case, the value is rounded before printing.

In some cases, unexpected results can be obtained using F format codes. For example, the sequence of statements

```
      A=123.665
      PRINT15,A
   15 FORMAT('0',F16.7)
```

would cause the value 123.6649000 to be printed. This is because the computer stores the value 123.665 in hexadecimal notation, and the conversion is not exact. Furthermore, only seven digits are retained by the computer.

The E format code provides another means of printing real numbers. It is generally used when the magnitude of numbers is large or unknown at the time the program is written. The general form is Ew.d, and again w refers to the width of the field to be printed. However, in this case d refers to the *total* number of significant decimal digits which are to be printed. Example 9.3 demonstrates the use of the E format code.

```
C EXAMPLE 9.3
C DEMONSTRATE E FORMAT
      X=725.6975
      Y=-.0005239
      Z=76.599
      A=-16.5E7
      PRINT7,X,Y,Z,A
    7 FORMAT(' ',E14.7,E13.5,E14.3,E7.5)
```

The following line would be printed.

b0.7256975Eb03b-0.52390E-03bbbbb0.766Eb02*******

E14.7	E13.5	E14.3	E7.5
X	Y	Z	A

Each field contains a zero, a decimal point, the first d significant digits, an E, and a signed two digit exponent. The field starts with a minus sign if the number is negative. If the sign of the exponent is plus, the sign is replaced with a blank. Notice that format-free output of real values appears as if produced by an E16.7 format code.

The example shows X printed with seven significant digits, as requested, and Y with five significant digits.

The format code for Z specifies only three significant figures; in this case, rounding occurs.

The value for A cannot fit into the seven-digit field which is specified; hence, asterisks are used to indicate the format error. Note that every value printed with the E format code starts with s0. and ends with Esnn where s is either the minus

135

sign or a blank. Thus seven print spaces should
be available over and above the d significant digits.
This means that the relationship w≥d+7 should hold
for E format codes.

Finally, the values are always placed
right justified in the fields.

9.4   PRINTING INTEGER VALUES

The I format code is used to output
integer values. Since there is no fractional part,
a decimal point is not required. The format code
is of the form Iw, where 'w' refers to the next w
print positions. The value printed is placed right
justified in the field. Example 9.4 illustrates I
format.

```
C EXAMPLE 9.4
C DEMONSTRATE I FORMAT
      L=39
      M=72654
      N=-256
      PRINT17,L,M,N
   17 FORMAT('0',I4,I12,I8)
```

The printer would double-space, and print the
following line.

bb39bbbbbbb72654bbbb-256

    I4   I12   I8

    L   M   N

Again there is a one-to-one correspondence between
the list to be printed and the list of codes in
the FORMAT statement.

$$L \leftrightarrow I4$$
$$M \leftrightarrow I12$$
$$N \leftrightarrow I8$$

If the same example were used with L = 76543, the following line would be printed.

****bbbbbbb72654bbbb-256

Note that L requires five print positions; but four positions are the maximum specified by the format code I4. This is considered an error and, as an indication, *'s are placed in the field.

9.5 SPACING

Often the programmer wishes to insert blanks between values printed on one line. The format code nX causes n spaces or blanks to be printed. Example 9.5 shows how the X code can be used.

```
C EXAMPLE 9.5
      I=J=156
      PRINT6,I,J
  6 FORMAT(' ',I6,3X,I4)
```

bbb156bbbb156

I6   3X   I4

Notice that the statement

```
  6 FORMAT(' ',I6,I7)
```

would accomplish the same purpose, since values are always printed right justified in the field, with blanks inserted to the left. Many programmers

137

make the field width larger than required, both
for spacing of results and also for safety, in case
numbers become larger than expected.

9.6 HOLLERITH CODES

On many occasions, alphabetic information
is desirable for headings and identifications.
Example 9.6 demonstrates how this can be accomplished.

```
C EXAMPLE 9.6 - HEADINGS
      PRINT25
   25 FORMAT('1','THIS IS A HEADING')
      PRINT13
   13 FORMAT('0',4X,'X',10X,'F(X)')
```

The printer would skip to a new page, and print the
following lines:

THIS IS A HEADING

bbbbXbbbbbbbbbbbF(X)

4X   10X

A set of characters enclosed in quotes
is referred to as a *Hollerith string*. Notice that
the quotes are not printed.

The PRINT statements used in Example 9.6
do not have a list of variables. As will be
seen in Section 9.8, it is possible to intersperse
Hollerith strings with values to be printed.

Any character may be placed in a Hollerith
string. A quote which is required as part of the
output must be duplicated, i.e. to print IT'S the
string 'IT''S' would be used.

The format code nH may be used instead
of quotes when constructing Hollerith strings.
In this case, the n characters following the H are
printed.

```
25 FORMAT(' ',17HTHIS IS A HEADING)
```

Care should be taken to ensure that the character
count n is correct for the particular string. The
quote-type Hollerith is usually more convenient, and
requires no counting of characters. Early versions
of FORTRAN did not use the quote-type Hollerith
string.

It has probably been noted that the
control character is a Hollerith string of one
character, but it is never printed. The first
position of the print line is reserved for printer
control. Control characters may be inserted by
any permissible format code. The following ways
of obtaining the control character blank are valid,
and perform the same action.

```
1 FORMAT(' ',...
1 FORMAT(1X,...
1 FORMAT(1H ,...
```

Failure to provide a control character
can lead to unexpected results. For example, the
sequence of statements

```
I=12345
PRINT3,I
3 FORMAT(I5)
```

would cause the printer to skip to a new page and
print the incorrect result 2345. This is because
the first character of the first field is used as

the control character.

      If, under any circumstances, an invalid control character is used, it is replaced by a blank, with the result that single spacing occurs.

9.7   CONTINUATION CARDS

      When FORMAT statements are punched, or when *any* FORTRAN statement is punched, it may not be possible to punch the complete statement on one card.   FORTRAN permits the programmer to overcome this difficulty by means of a *continuation card*. If a statement is too long for one card, it may be continued on successive cards by placing any character other than blank or zero in column 6 of each continuation card.   The first card of the statement must have a blank or zero in column 6. For example,

```
      IF(STOCK(I,J).LE.10)PRINT,W,I,J,
     1((STOCK(I,J),I=1,3),J=1,4)
```

The programmer can determine the maximum number of continuation cards allowed by referring to his installation's operating manual.

9.8   COMBINING CODES

      The reader has now seen some of the basic format codes available in FORTRAN.   In most examples presented so far, only one type of code was employed.

      Any of the types of format codes may be mixed within a FORMAT statement.

```
      C EXAMPLE 9.7
      C MIXING FORMAT CODES
            X=14.753
            I=-156
            PRINT9,X,I
          9 FORMAT(' ','X=',F8.3,3X,'I=',I5)
```

Example 9.7 would print the following line

$$X=\underbrace{bb14.753}_{F8.3}\underbrace{bbb}_{3X}\underbrace{I=b-156}_{I5}$$

      The variables X and I are matched
respectively with the format codes F8.3 and I5.
The Hollerith strings and blanks are placed in the
required positions in the output line. It is
important that the format code be appropriate for
the type of the corresponding variable, that is,
I format must be used for integer values and E or
F format must be used for real values. Violation
of this rule will cause an error message and
termination of the program at execution time.

9.9   FIELD COUNTS

      On many occasions, it is desirable to print
several values using the same format code. This
is particularly true when dealing with arrays.
Example 9.8 reads in ten integer values and seven
real values, and prints them on one line.

```
      C EXAMPLE 9.8
            REAL A(7)
            INTEGER N(10)
            READ,(N(I),I=1,10),(A(I),I=1,7)
            PRINT6,(N(I),I=1,10),(A(I),I=1,7)
          6 FORMAT(' ',10I6,7F10.2)
```

141

The 10 preceding I6 and the 7 preceding F10.2 are called *field counts*; they specify that the format code I6 is to be used ten times for the ten elements of N, and that F10.2 is to be used seven times for the elements of A. Alternatively, we could have written the FORMAT statement as

6 FORMAT(' ',I6,I6,...,I6,F10.2,F10.2,...,F10.2)

             10 times   7 times

If we had wished to print the first four values of N under I4 and the last six values under I6, the following FORMAT statement could have been used.

6 FORMAT(' ',4I4,6I6,7F10.2)

Field counts must be positive non-zero constants. Thus, the following example contains an invalid field count.

```
C INCORRECT USAGE OF A FIELD COUNT
      M=10
    7 FORMAT('0',MI6)
```

Field counts may be used with I, E, or F format codes, and may not be used with Hollerith and X codes.

9.10 SOME RULES

There are many rules concerning format codes, and some of these have been presented in the previous sections. The following rules apply to the FORMAT statement in general, and should be studied carefully before using this feature.

(i) FORMAT statements are *non-executable* statements and may only be referred to by input or output statements.

```
C INCORRECT USE OF FORMAT
      GO TO 15
   15 FORMAT(' ','THIS IS BAD NEWS')
```

(ii) More than one I/O statement may refer to a particular FORMAT statement.

(iii) FORMAT statements may be placed almost anywhere in a program. Some programmers prefer to place all their FORMAT statements at the beginning or end of the program, while others like to keep I/O and FORMAT statements together.

(iv) It must be remembered that a printer has a maximum number of print spaces per line   (120, 132, 144, etc. Check with your installation). Since FORMAT is used to print lines, the total number of print positions requested by the list of format codes may not exceed this maximum value. The statement

```
25 FORMAT(' ',6I10,4X,4F10.2,4E11.3)
```

requires 148 print positions; this would be too many for most printers.

(v) The format code must be appropriate for the type of the variable to be printed. If this is not the case, an error message is issued, and the program is terminated.

```
           C THIS IS NOT ALLOWED
                PRINT256,I
           256 FORMAT(' ',F16.8)
```

(vi)   Commas which separate format codes may
be omitted, unless ambiguity would
result. For example, the statement

    FORMAT(' 'I5'ANSWER'F36.2,2I7)

is equivalent to

    FORMAT(' ',I5,'ANSWER',F36.2,2I7)

Note that all commas except the last
have been omitted. If the last comma
were omitted, the sequence F36.22I7 would
be ambiguous. (F36.22 instead of F36.2)
Note also that two adjacent quote-type
Holleriths must be separated by a comma.
The statement

      FORMAT('ABC''DEF')

has only one hollerith string, namely,

      ABC'DEF

(vii) Blanks may be placed in the format list
to improve readability.

(viii) Values used for n, w, d, and field counts
must be positive non-zero integer constants,
and may not exceed 256. Using the FORMAT
statement as described to this point, the
programmer does not have the ability to
change or define these values at execution
time. Another feature that allows this
flexibility is described in Chapter 19.

9.11 FURTHER FEATURES OF FORMAT

The sequence of statements

```
     X=13.25
     Y=-16.3
     PRINT3,X,Y
   3 FORMAT('0',F7.2,F7.2,F7.2)
```

would cause the following line to be printed

        bb13.25bb-16.3

Note that the number of format codes is greater than the number of variables to be printed. In this case, the extra format code is not used. However, if the FORMAT statement had been

```
   3 FORMAT('0',F7.2,F7.2,6X,'HELLO',F7.2)
```

the following line would have been printed

        bb13.25bb-16.3bbbbbbHELLO

The rule is that the computer processes the format codes in sequence, from left to right, matching format codes with variables to be printed. If a format code requiring an entry in the print list is encountered after all items in the print list have been processed, the action is terminated.

If the list of variables has not been completely processed when the end of the list of format codes is reached, processing will continue by returning to the beginning of the format list, and a *new* print line will be started. For example, the statements

```
     PRINT12,(X(I),I=1,12)
  12 FORMAT(' ',5E16.7)
```

would print three lines; the first two lines would each contain five elements of X, and the third line would contain two elements. This feature is useful when printing arrays, but can cause problems in certain cases. Consider the statements:

```
      N=6
      PRINT22,N,(X(I),I=1,N)
   22 FORMAT(' ',I3,5E16.7)
```

The above statements attempt to print X(6) using the format code I3; this, of course, is an error. Chapter 19 will introduce a method for handling this type of situation.

A final example is given to demonstrate the flexibility of format. Example 9.9 calculates the squares of the integers from 1 to 15, and prints a table of values.

```
C EXAMPLE 9.9
C CALCULATE SQUARES OF THE NATURAL NUMBERS
C FROM 1-15 AND PRINT RESULTS
      INTEGER N(15)
      DO 1 I=1,15
    1 N(I)=I**2
      PRINT13,(J,N(J),J=1,15)
   13 FORMAT(' ', 'N(' ,I2, ')=' ,I5)
      STOP
      END
```

The output from this example is

```
N( 1)=      1
N( 2)=      4
N( 3)=      9
N( 4)=     16
N( 5)=     25
N( 6)=     36
N( 7)=     49
N( 8)=     64
N( 9)=     81
N(10)=    100
N(11)=    121
N(12)=    144
N(13)=    169
N(14)=    196
N(15)=    225
```

9.12   FORMAT WITH PUNCHED OUTPUT

Example 9.10 shows how data cards can be punched by a program using the PUNCH statement.

```
C EXAMPLE 9.10
C USE A PUNCH STATEMENT
      A=924.625
      B=890625.
      J=762
      PUNCH19,A,B,J
   19 FORMAT(F7.3,4X,E14.6,I3)
```

The PUNCH statement is similar to the PRINT statement, with the exceptions that only 80 digits and/or characters may be punched on the output card, and no control character is required. The PUNCH statement may be used under the format-free scheme, or may refer to a FORMAT statement in the conventional manner.

9.13 INPUT WITH FORMAT CODES F, E, I, AND X

Format may also be used with READ statements to input data values. This is useful if a
program is to be written to process data decks
pre-punched by someone other than the programmer.
Furthermore, the use of format allows more data to
be punched on one card, since the data item
separators are not required.

For example, suppose a questionnaire
were given involving 80 questions with answers of
a true or false variety. The results could be
punched on cards, with zero representing false and
one representing true. Using format-free input,
at least two data cards would be required for each
reply to the questionnaire, i.e., 40 answers per
card, each value followed by a blank or comma.
However, it would be more convenient to place all
80 answers on one card, and, in this case, a FORMAT
statement would be required to read it.

These problems show that on occasion it
would be convenient to associate FORMAT with a
READ statement in order to define the sizes of the
input fields. Example 9.11 shows how this is
accomplished.

```
C EXAMPLE 9.11
C READ STATEMENT WITH FORMAT
      READ47,A,B,J
   47 FORMAT(F7.3,4X,E14.6,I3)
```

The X code can be used to space over columns to be
ignored.

If the data card

```
924.625JUNKbbb.890625E 06762
```
```
F7.3    4X        E14.6      I3

A                 B          J
```

were read, the values 924.625, .890625E+06, and 762
would be assigned to A, B, and J respectively.
Notice that no control character is used for input.

To make the punching of data cards more
convenient, certain of the rules have been relaxed,
and these are now described.

For all three format codes - I, F, and E -
any blanks within the field are interpreted as
zeros. A field consisting entirely of blanks is
treated as zero.

$$7b5 \rightarrow 705$$
$$7.9b \rightarrow 7.90$$
$$63.5bEb5 \rightarrow 63.50E05$$
$$bbbbb \rightarrow 0 \text{ or } 0.0$$

Hence, for the I format code, the integer constant
should be placed right justified in the field.
Input of the digit 5 using the format code I5
would cause values to be assigned as described
in the following table

$$bbbb5 \rightarrow 5$$
$$bbb5b \rightarrow 50$$
$$bb5bb \rightarrow 500$$
$$b5bbb \rightarrow 5000$$
$$5bbbb \rightarrow 50000$$

With the F format code, the decimal point can be included anywhere in the field, and overrides the position indicated by the 'd' portion of Fw.d. If the decimal point is omitted, the 'd' is used to determine the position of the decimal point. We present several examples using the format code F7.3:

$$b72.76b \rightarrow 72.760$$
$$72.76bb \rightarrow 72.7600$$
$$bb72.76 \rightarrow 72.76$$
$$bb7276b \rightarrow 72.760$$
$$7276bbb \rightarrow 7276.000$$
$$7.0E+05 \rightarrow \text{ERROR (invalid characters)}$$

In the last example, the field contains an E and a plus sign, which are considered invalid characters when read using F format.

With the E format code, considerable flexibility is allowed in the exponent part. The exponent may be punched in any one of the following forms:

$$E+06 = E6 = E+6 = E06 = Eb06 = +6 = +06$$
$$E-02 = E-2 = -2 = -02$$

If the E is omitted, the plus or minus sign must be present.

If a decimal point is punched in the fractional portion, it overrides the position indicated by the 'd' portion of Ew.d. If the decimal point is omitted, the d is used to determine the position of the decimal point. Finally, the exponent may be omitted completely,

in which case the rules for Fw.d are used instead
of Ew.d. The following examples using E12.4 should
clarify the use of E format with input.

$$bbb7.345E+01 \rightarrow 7.345 \times 10^1$$
$$bbbbb7.345E1 \rightarrow 7.345 \times 10^1$$
$$-bbbb7.345E1 \rightarrow -7.345 \times 10^1$$
$$bb-7.345E+01 \rightarrow -7.345 \times 10^1$$
$$bbb76522E+02 \rightarrow 7.6522 \times 10^2$$
$$bbbbb76522E2 \rightarrow 7.6522 \times 10^2$$
$$bbbbbb7654-3 \rightarrow .7654 \times 10^{-3}$$
$$bbbb16.75bbb \rightarrow 16.75000$$
$$bbbb1675bbbb \rightarrow 1675.0000$$
$$bbbb1.23E+5b \rightarrow 1.23 \times 10^{50}$$

9.14 HOLLERITH INPUT

An H-type or quote-type Hollerith string in
a FORMAT statement can be modified by reading
character data. The information read is inserted
into the Hollerith string of the FORMAT statement,
and can be printed if the FORMAT statement is
referenced in a subsequent PRINT statement. The
value 'n' of nH or the number of positions between
quotes is used to determine how many characters
are to be inserted. Example 9.12 uses this feature
to read and print the first 21 columns of ten data
cards.

```
C EXAMPLE 9.12
C READ HOLLERITH DATA
      DO 1 I=1,10
      READ7
    7 FORMAT('THIS WILL BE REPLACED')
    1 PRINT7
```

151

Notice that the example uses the same FORMAT
statement for reading and printing. Note also
that the contents of column 1 of the data card
will ultimately determine the spacing of the
printer.

9.15 EXERCISES

   9.1 Write a program which sets up and initializes
        a vector X of 10 elements so that each
        element contains the same real value, namely,
        3.456789. Then, print this vector by using
        the statement

              PRINT6,(X(I),I=1,10)

        with each of the following FORMAT statements:
        (i)   6 FORMAT('0',6F10.6)
        (ii)   6 FORMAT('0',F10.5,F10.4,F10.3,F10.2,
                 *   F10.1,F10.0)
        (iii) 6 FORMAT(' ',6F10.8)
        (iv)   6 FORMAT(' ',6F5.4)
        (v)   6 FORMAT(' ',F15.3,6X,F15.2)
        (vi)   6 FORMAT('0',4E15.7)
        (vii) 6 FORMAT('0',E15.6,E15.5,E15.4,E15.3,
                 *   E15.2)
        (viii) 6 FORMAT('0',5E12.8)
        (ix)   6 FORMAT('0',E17.4,F17.4)

        It is instructive for the reader to predict
        what the results will be, before the
        program is run on the computer.

   9.2 Write a program which sets up and initializes
        a vector I of 10 elements so that each
        element contains the same integer value,

namely, 123456. Then, print the vector by using the statement

        PRINT8,(I(J),J=1,10)

with each of the following FORMAT statements.

  (i)   8 FORMAT('0',6I10)
 (ii)   8 FORMAT(' ',I10,I9,I8,I7,I6,I5)
(iii)   8 FORMAT(' ',10I6)
 (vi)   8 FORMAT('0',3I8,3X,2I8)
  (v)   8 FORMAT(' ',I20)
 (vi)   8 FORMAT(' ',10F13.6)

It is instructive for the reader to predict what the results will be before actually running the program on the computer.

9.3 Modify your program for Exercise 2.8 to replace the codes 0, 1, 2, 3, 4, with the following messages:

         0   NOT A QUADRATIC, NO ROOTS
         1   NOT A QUADRATIC, ONE ROOT ONLY
         2   EQUAL ROOTS
         3   DISTINCT REAL ROOTS
         4   COMPLEX ROOTS

9.4 Modify any program in any of the examples or exercises so that it has descriptive headings and acceptable FORMAT statements. Try to use FORMAT statements, as outlined in Example 9.9, for some of the other problems.

9.5 A test is given which involves 10 questions with answers of a true or false variety. The results are punched on cards in columns six to fifteen; zero is used to represent false, and one is used to represent true. Columns one to five are used for the contestant number. The first data card contains the correct answers for the test. Write a program that reads the data and calculates the mark for each contestant. Your output should include, for each contestant, the contestant number, his answers, and his mark out of 10.

9.6 Write a program that reads and prints the contents of columns ten to sixty-five of 25 data cards. Use Example 9.12 as a guide.

9.7 Write a program which prints a calendar for a particular year. The following specifications should be used.

(i) January 1 is a Wednesday.

(ii) February has 28 days.

(iii) Each month should have its name spelled out in full.

(iv) The days of the week should be printed as alphabetic headings in abbreviated form.

(v) Each month should be printed starting on a new page.

9.8 Given that the horizontal spacing on the printer is 10 characters to the inch, and that the vertical spacing is six lines to the inch, write a program which uses asterisks to outline an 8-inch-square checkerboard.

CHAPTER 10

SUBPROGRAMS

Some programs are of such a general nature that they can be used over and over by the same programmer, or indeed by any programmer. Examples are:

(i)   determine the largest element in an array

(ii)   sort the elements of a vector into an ascending sequence

(iii)   calculate a sine, cosine, etc.

(iv)   perform a table look-up

(v)   solve a polynomial equation

(vi)   solve a system of linear equations.

When such programs have been written and tested, they should be available in a computer library so that all programmers can have access to them. These library programs are usually referred to as *subprograms*. A program which is not a subprogram is referred to as a *main program*. FORTRAN has statements such as CALL, SUBROUTINE, COMMON, and RETURN which make communication possible between a main program and subprograms or among subprograms.

The use of subprograms has other advantages which will be discussed at the end of this chapter. In the meantime, the following sections discuss the details of defining and using subprograms.

10.1   SUBROUTINE SUBPROGRAMS

We will begin by describing a main program which will subsequently be converted to a subprogram. Example 10.1 is a program designed to find the arithmetic maximum of N real constants, after they have been read in from N data cards and stored in an array.   In addition to determining the maximum, the program uses a pointer J to indicate which of the input data cards actually contains the maximum value.   The program will function for any number of data cards up to 100, since the array size has been chosen to be 100.

```
C EXAMPLE 10.1
C COMPUTE MAXIMUM OF N REAL NUMBERS
      REAL X(100),LARGE
      READ,N,(X(I),I=1,N)
      LARGE=X(1)
      J=1
      IF(N.EQ.1)GO TO 7
      DO 6 I=2,N
      IF(X(I).LE.LARGE)GO TO 6
      LARGE=X(I)
      J=I
    6 CONTINUE
    7 PRINT,J,LARGE
      STOP
      END
```

The program initializes LARGE to X(1) and the pointer J to 1.   If N is one, there is only one card, and the value of LARGE is then the maximum; hence, control is transferred to the statement numbered 7, for printing.   If N≥2, control proceeds through the DO-loop.   Here LARGE is replaced by any one of the X(I) which is greater than the current value of LARGE.

At the same time J, the pointer, is updated. When the DO-loop is satisfied, the value of LARGE is the maximum value, and it and the pointer J are printed.

The program accepts a vector X and an integer N as input. It performs the required calculation and ultimately assigns the results to J and LARGE as output. This can be represented schematically, as in Figure 10.1. X and N are referred to as the input; J and LARGE are referred to as the output.

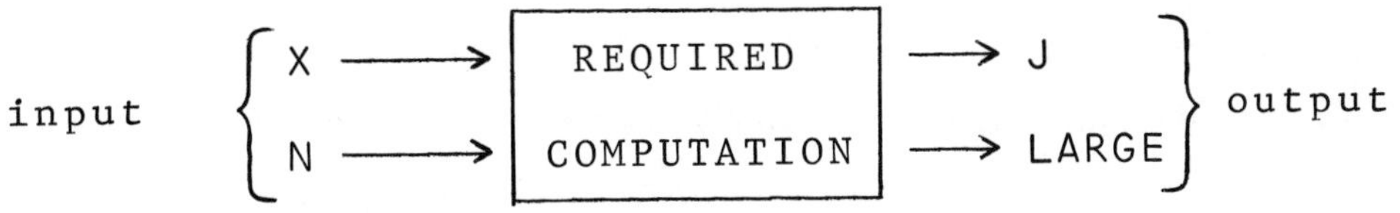

Figure 10.1

Example 10.2 shows how this program can be rewritten as a *subroutine subprogram*.

```
C EXAMPLE 10.2
      SUBROUTINE MAX(N,X,J,LARGE)
      REAL X(100),LARGE
      LARGE=X(1)
      J=1
      IF(N.EQ.1)GO TO 7
      DO 6 I=2,N
      IF(X(I).LE.LARGE)GO TO 6
      LARGE=X(I)
      J=I
    6 CONTINUE
    7 RETURN
      END
```

Note that the following statements, which were in the main program, are no longer present.

```
    READ,N,(X(I),I=1,N)
  7 PRINT,J,LARGE
```

Their input-output function has been assumed by the new statement

SUBROUTINE MAX(N,X,J,LARGE)

This statement identifies the program as a subroutine subprogram. Furthermore, it assigns the name MAX to this particular subprogram. The name MAX is followed by a list of *input-output parameters*, separated by commas and contained in parentheses. There is no explicit designation as to which of the parameters is input and which of them is output. The subprogram clearly requires values for X and N before it can function; hence, they are implicitly assumed as input parameters. On the other hand, the operation of the subprogram causes assignments to be made to J and LARGE; hence, they are implicitly assumed as output parameters.

Note also that the STOP statement in Example 10.1 has been replaced by the RETURN statement in the subprogram. It is usual to employ the RETURN statement in a subprogram wherever a STOP statement would occur in a main program.

We will now consider a trivial main program which makes use of the subprogram called MAX.

```
C EXAMPLE 10.3
      REAL X(100),LARGE
      READ,N,(X(I),I=1,N)
      CALL MAX(N,X,J,LARGE)
      PRINT,J,LARGE
      STOP
      END
```

Example 10.3 causes a number of values,
determined by the variable N, to be read into an
array X. Then the following statement is encountered.

CALL MAX(N,X,J,LARGE)

This causes control to transfer to the first
executable statement in the subprogram called MAX.
It also defines the *input-output arguments* using
an *argument list* similar to the *parameter list* in
the subprogram.

The subprogram MAX performs its calculations,
and ultimately encounters the RETURN statement.
This statement causes control to be transferred back
to the statement immediately following the CALL
statement in the main program. This happens to be
PRINT,J,LARGE and, consequently, the results appear
as printed output.

The example, simple though it may be,
demonstrates some of the basic ideas common to all
subprograms. For example, the subprogram is a
separate entity and has a special statement,
SUBROUTINE, as its first statement. Furthermore,
the subprogram has a distinct name and a list of
parameters. As for the main program, it *calls* the
subprogram using the special statement CALL, which
names the required subprogram and gives a list of

159

arguments. Control is transferred to the subprogram for it to perform its function. When a RETURN
is encountered, control is returned to the first
executable statement following the CALL in the
main program.

Figure 10.2 outlines in pictorial form
the flow of control between the main program and
the subprogram.

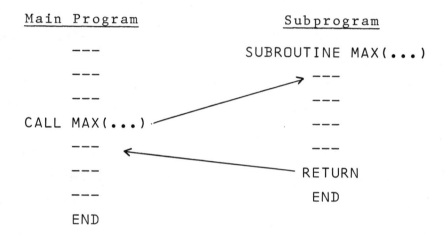

Figure 10.2

The above discussion outlines the basic
philosophy concerning subprograms. They possess
considerable flexibility, and have many other features.
These will be described in the examples which
follow.

Example 10.4 is exactly the same as
Example 10.3 except that the variable names in the
main program have been changed.

160

```
C EXAMPLE 10.4
      REAL A(100)
      READ,K,(A(I),I=1,K)
      CALL MAX(K,A,N,ANS)
      PRINT,N,ANS
      STOP
      END
```

This illustrates that the names of the
entries in the CALL argument list need not be the
same as those in the SUBROUTINE parameter list.
All that is required is that they correspond
exactly in number and type. The parameters in the
SUBROUTINE statement are merely *dummies* which are
replaced by their true names when the CALL statement
is executed.

$$
\begin{array}{c}
\text{CALL} \\
\text{argument list}
\end{array}
\left\{
\begin{array}{l}
K \rightarrow N \\
A \rightarrow X \\
N \rightarrow J \\
ANS \rightarrow LARGE
\end{array}
\right\}
\begin{array}{c}
\text{SUBROUTINE} \\
\text{parameter list}
\end{array}
$$

Figure 10.3

Figure 10.3 illustrates the relationship
between the CALL argument list and the SUBROUTINE
parameter list. Thus we see that N takes on the
value of K, X is the same array as A, and, when
LARGE and J are assigned, it is really ANS and N
which are assigned. This points out the fact that
arrays declared in subprograms should have the

161

same dimensions as those in the main program, since
they are the same arrays. It is a common error to
assign different array sizes in the main program
and in the subprograms.

It should be further pointed out that all
variable names used in a subprogram are *local* to
that subprogram. In other words, these names are
defined only in the subprogram, and are not known
outside the subprogram. This means that it is
perfectly acceptable, and in fact common practice,
to use the same variable names in subprograms as
those in other subprograms or in the main program,
even though they have a completely different use.
This is illustrated in Example 10.4, where the
variable N in the main program has a use different
from that of the variable N used in the subprogram
MAX which was called.

Statement numbers are likewise local to
subprograms. They can be identical with those in
other subprograms or the main program, and no
problems arise.

Note that a subprogram always has an
END statement as its final statement. In order to
have a complete *job*, all the subprograms required
by the main program must be placed either before
or after the main program, in any order. Then
the $JOB and $ENTRY control cards are placed
respectively before and after this combined deck,
and any data cards follow the $ENTRY control card.
A typical job deck is illustrated in Figure 10.4.
Each of the subprograms, as well as the main program,
is referred to as a *program segment*. Note that each

job has one and only one main program, but can have
as many subprograms as required.


```
          $JOB

               _____
               _____

               _____
               END
               SUBROUTINE MAX(N,X,J,SMALL)

               _____
               _____

               _____
               END
          $ENTRY

               _____

               _____           Data Cards

               _____
```


Figure 10.4

It is possible to place subprograms in
a library stored on the random-access storage
devices of the computer. If this is the case, they
need not be placed with the job deck as in Figure
10.4. The WATFOR compiler will locate them automatically. Whether programs are housed in the library
is a matter of personal preference, and this will vary
from installation to installation. The programmer
should consult his installation's operating manual

for details.

Example 10.5 illustrates some additional features of subroutine subprograms. It is a main program which uses MAX as a subprogram. Its function is to read in a vector of N real constants, and print them out in descending order.

```
C EXAMPLE 10.5
      REAL A(100),LARGE
      READ,N,(A(I),I=1,N)
      DO 6 I=1,N
      CALL MAX(N-I+1,A,J,LARGE)
      PRINT,LARGE
    6 A(J)=A(N-I+1)
      STOP
      END
```

The effect is to call the MAX subprogram, and print out the largest element. This element is then replaced by the last element in the array. This means that only N-1 elements remain to be considered, and they occupy the first N-1 positions of the array. This fact allows us to call the subprogram MAX again, this time specifying N-1 elements, rather than N. The largest element among the N-1 is determined and printed. Then, it is replaced by the second-last element in the array. This process continues in the DO-loop until all elements have been printed in descending order.

Note that the arguments in the list for the CALL need not be simple variables. They can be any expressions which, when evaluated, yield a result of the proper type. The type is determined according to the type of the corresponding dummy variable in the parameter list of the SUBROUTINE statement. Thus, N-I+1 is an acceptable expression in the CALL argument list, since it yields an integer value corresponding in type to the integer N in the SUBROUTINE parameter list. On the other hand, the second argument in the CALL must be an array name, as the corresponding entry in the SUBROUTINE parameter list is X, an array name. It would be invalid to use an expression for this argument, since an expression cannot yield an array name as its value.

This example also illustrates the fact that statement numbers are local to subprograms. The statement number 6 is used in both the main program and the subprogram.

It should be noted that the action of the main program causes the original contents of the vector A to be destroyed. This happens because of the statement

$$A(J)=A(N-I+1)$$

If this is undesirable, the vector should be copied before the main part of the execution begins.

Since programs which sequence or sort data are generally useful, it seems appropriate to modify the example to be a subprogram. This is illustrated in Example 10.6.

The subroutine SORT accepts as input a vector A with N components. The effect of the computation is to shuffle the elements of A into ascending sequence.

```
C EXAMPLE 10.6
      SUBROUTINE SORT(N,A)
      REAL A(100),LARGE
      DO 6 I=1,N
      CALL MAX(N-I+1,A,J,LARGE)
      A(J)=A(N-I+1)
    6 A(N-I+1)=LARGE
      RETURN
      END
```

The example illustrates that a subprogram
can call a second subprogram. The second subprogram
can call a third subprogram, etc., with one restriction.
A subprogram may never call *itself*, either directly
or indirectly. In other words, the same subprogram may
not be called again until its RETURN is executed.

10.2   SUBROUTINE SUBPROGRAM SUMMARY

It is appropriate at this point to
summarize and expand upon the major ideas which
have been introduced concerning subroutine subprograms.

(i)   Each subroutine subprogram has a
SUBROUTINE statement as its first statement and an END statement as its last
statement.

(ii) The general form of the SUBROUTINE
statement is as follows
      SUBROUTINE NAME(param1,param2,...,paramn)
The NAME can be any FORTRAN symbolic name.
The parameter list may contain any non-
subscripted variable name or array name.
These parameters are referred to as dummy

variables. No expressions are allowed in
the parameter list. In the next chapter,
we will see that subprogram names and *'s
are also valid entries in the parameter
list. We will also see that no parameter
list is necessary.

(iii)   The subroutine subprogram is referenced
by the CALL statement, which has the
following general form.

CALL NAME (arg1,arg2,...,argn)

When executed, this has the effect of
transferring control to the first executable
statement in the subroutine subprogram,
called NAME. The list of arguments must
agree in number with the list of parameters
in the SUBROUTINE statement. Wherever the
corresponding parameter is a simple variable,
the argument can be an expression of the
same type. If the parameter is an array
name, the calling argument must also be an
array name.

(iv)   Whenever the subprogram uses one of its
dummy variables, it is in actual fact using
the value of the corresponding variable or
expression in the calling argument list.
When one of the dummy variables in the
parameter list is assigned a value in that
subprogram, the effect is to assign the
value to the corresponding argument in
the CALL list. Thus the argument and parameter lists provide a two-way means of

communication between the calling program segment and the called subprogram.

- (v) When a RETURN statement is executed, control is transferred back to the calling program segment. Transfer of control is to the first executable statement following the CALL.

- (vi) All variable names or statement numbers used in a subroutine subprogram are local to that subprogram.

- (vii) A subroutine subprogram can call other subprograms, provided it does not call itself either directly or indirectly.

- (viii) Subroutine subprograms can be in a library, or can be inserted in a job deck as program segments.

10.3   FUNCTION SUBPROGRAMS

Function subprograms are very similar to subroutine subprograms. Example 10.7 is used to point out the differences. This subprogram is designed to accept a real vector X and its dimension N as input, and to compute the sum of the components of the vector.

```
C EXAMPLE 10.7
      FUNCTION SUM(N,X)
      REAL X(100)
      SUM=0.
      DO 6 I=1,N
    6 SUM=SUM+X(I)
      RETURN
      END
```

At first glance, the only difference appears to be the use of the word FUNCTION rather than SUBROUTINE. However, one major difference is that the name, SUM, of the subprogram appears as a *variable* in the subprogram, and is assigned a value. This is always the case with function subprograms, and is never the case in subroutine subprograms.

The other major difference between the two types is the way in which they are called. Whereas subroutine subprograms are always called using the CALL statement, function subprograms never are. Example 10.8 is a main program which calls the subprogram SUM.

```
C EXAMPLE 10.8
      REAL A(100),B(100)
      READ,N,(A(I),I=1,N),M,(B(I),I=1,M)
      AVG=(SUM(N,A)+SUM(M,B))/(M+N)
      PRINT,AVG
      STOP
      END
```

This program reads two vectors with real components, and computes their composite average, AVG. Note that the function subprogram is called in the same manner as SIN or COS, using its name followed by the argument list contained in parentheses. Thus, function subprograms are useful when a single value is to be returned, since the call is included as part of an expression rather than as a separate statement.

Since the name of the function subprogram is treated like a variable, it must be declared according to type in both the calling program and the subprogram. In Examples 10.7 and 10.8, this was unnecessary, since SUM begins with the letter S and is therefore real by default, in the absence of other declarations.

Suppose, however, that the subprogram SUM were designed to compute the integer-valued sum of an array of integers. It would be written as in Example 10.9.

```
C EXAMPLE 10.9
      INTEGER FUNCTION SUM(N,X)
      INTEGER X(100)
      SUM=0
      DO 6 I=1,N
    6 SUM=SUM+X(I)
      RETURN
      END
```

Note that the subprogram name, SUM, is declared to be of integer type by placing the word INTEGER at the beginning of the FUNCTION statement. In fact, this is the only way the type of a function subprogram name can be declared explicitly in the subprogram. The following two statements, although they would seem to have an equivalent effect, are, in fact, illegal.

```
      FUNCTION SUM(N,X)
      INTEGER SUM,X(100)
```

Furthermore, in the calling program, SUM must be declared as an integer by using the INTEGER declaration statement.

10.4　FUNCTION SUBPROGRAM SUMMARY

　　　　The rules for subroutine subprograms in
Section 10.2 generally apply to function subprograms,
when the obvious changes of wording are taken into
account. Only the exceptions and additional rules
will be summarized here.

　(i)　A function name has a type which is
　　　　declared explicitly as in

　　　　　　REAL FUNCTION MAX(P,Q)

　　　　or by default.

　(ii)　A function subprogram must have at least
　　　　one parameter in the parameter list.
　　　　Asterisks (*) may not appear as parameters.

　(iii)　The function subprogram is called by using
　　　　the name of the subprogram followed by an
　　　　argument list in parentheses. The name
　　　　and argument list always appear as a
　　　　component in any legal expression. When
　　　　the name is encountered, control is
　　　　transferred to the first executable
　　　　statement in the function subprogram.
　　　　When the function subprogram reaches a
　　　　RETURN statement, control is returned to
　　　　the point in the expression which contains
　　　　the name and argument list. The name
　　　　assumes the value assigned to it in the
　　　　subprogram, and computation of the expression
　　　　is resumed.

　(iv)　Function subprograms normally return one
　　　　value to the calling program. However,

they may return several by assigning
values to the dummy variables, just as
is the case for subroutine subprograms.

(v) The name of the function subprogram is
defined in any calling program. Hence,
it is not local to the subprogram, as is
the case for other variables used in the
subprogram.

10.5 STATEMENT FUNCTIONS

The *FORTRAN statement function* is a
highly specialized feature which permits the
programmer to define a function by using a single
statement. Its use is illustrated in Example 10.10.

```
C EXAMPLE 10.10
      AREA(A,B,C)=SQRT(S*(S-A)*(S-B)*(S-C))
      SUM=0.
      DO 8 I=1,10
      READ,X,Y,Z
      S=(X+Y+Z)/2.
    8 SUM=SUM+AREA(X,Y,Z)
      PRINT,SUM
      STOP
      END
```

The first statement is known as a
statement function definition which, in this
case, defines the function AREA with three dummy
variables A, B, and C as parameters. This function
evaluates the area of a triangle with sides of
lengths a, b, and c, by using the formula

$$\text{Area} = \sqrt{s(s-a)(s-b)(s-c)}$$

$$\text{where } s = \frac{a+b+c}{2}$$

The first executable statement in the example is SUM=0.. The effect of the program is to read the lengths of the sides of ten triangles into the computer and calculate the total of the areas of these triangles. In the statement numbered 8, the function, AREA, is referenced. Note that the arguments agree in order, number, and type with the dummy variables in the function definition statement. Also note that the expression

SQRT(S*(S-A)*(S-B)*(S-C))

contains dummy variables A, B, and C, as well as a variable S which is assigned in the course of computation. It also contains a reference to a built-in function.

10.6 FORTRAN STATEMENT FUNCTION SUMMARY

The following points summarize the rules for the use of the FORTRAN statement function.

(i) In general, the statement function definition has the form

NAME(list of dummy variables) = expression

The name can be any valid FORTRAN symbolic name. The name must be declared according to type in a statement prior to that of the statement function definition; other-wise, the default declaration is used.

(ii) The list of dummy variables can contain any FORTRAN symbolic name. These variables are local to the *single* statement in which they appear.

(iii) The expression can be of any type, but should not contain subscripted variables. If other statement functions are referenced in the expression, they must be defined by using earlier statement function definitions. The expression can use variables defined anywhere in the program segment, as well as the dummy variables.

(iv) Statement function definitions should be placed in the program prior to the first executable statement.

(v) The argument list in a reference to the function must have arguments which agree in number, order, and type with the dummy variables. These arguments may be expressions.

(vi) Statement functions are defined only in the program segment in which they appear. They cannot, under any circumstances, be referenced from other segments.

10.7 ADVANTAGES OF SUBPROGRAMS

As has been pointed out, subprograms make it possible to store debugged routines in a library so that they are available to all users. They have other obvious advantages worth mentioning. They permit the programmer to write his total program in segments which are easy to debug and document. This expedites the programming and testing, and makes the final product easier for another programmer to understand. Since variables and statement numbers are local to each program segment, they can be repeated at will from segment to segment. This saves a good deal of book-keeping, and reduces errors. The same feature allows several programmers to handle different segments of the same project with a minimum of consultation with each other.

10.8   EXERCISES

10.1   (a)   Convert the subprogram of Example 10.2 to a function subprogram.

(b)   Convert the main program of Example 10.3 to use the function subprogram of (a).

10.2   Write a subprogram to do each of the following:

(a)   Compute the average of the elements of a one-dimensional array.

(b)   Find the maximum value of the elements of a one-dimensional array.

10.3   Write a main program which reads in a two-dimensional array containing marks for several students in each of various courses. Use the subprograms of Exercise 10.2 to assist in the production of a class list, printed in descending order of student averages.

10.4 Write a subroutine subprogram which accepts any positive integer as input, and determines whether or not it is prime. A variable should be set to one if the integer is prime, and to zero otherwise.

10.5 Suppose we have a one-dimensional array, X, of ten elements.

(a) Write a subroutine SUMS, with parameters X, S, S2, which computes the sum, S, and the sum of squares, S2, of the ten elements of the array X.

(b) Write a main program which reads the elements of a 10 by 10 array A. Then, the program should use SUMS on each row of A to form two new vectors of 10 elements each. Use SUMS on these vectors to produce an over-all sum and sum of squares of elements in A.

10.6 (a) Write a function subprogram which evaluates a polynomial, given the coefficients in array form and a value for the independent variable.

(b) Modify the function subprogram in part (a) so that it evaluates the derivative as well as the function. In the process, change it to a subroutine subprogram.

10.7 Write a subprogram to compute the median of a set of n integers, regardless of the sequence in which they appear.

10.8   Write subprograms which accomplish the
       matrix operations outlined in Exercise
       8.11. Include careful documentation
       with your subprograms, so that other
       programmers could use them.

10.9   Write subprograms which accomplish the
       vector operations outlined in Exercise
       8.10. Include careful documentation
       with your subprograms, so that other
       programmers could use them.

10.10 Write a subprogram which computes the
       greatest common divisor of two positive
       integers.

10.11 Write a subprogram which computes all
       of the prime factors of a given positive
       integer. These factors are to be returned
       to the main program, stored in an array.

10.12 The FORTRAN language does not have
       built-in functions for secant and cose-
       cant. Write statement-function
       definitions for each of these. In a
       main program, use the statement functions
       to tabulate the two functions over a
       convenient range.

10.13 (a) Write a subprogram which will
            convert any non-negative integer,
            less than 500, to the corresponding
            binary integer. The binary integer
            should be stored using an integer
            variable.

(b) Write a subprogram which will
convert any non-negative binary
integer, of 10 or fewer digits, into
the equivalent decimal integer.
The binary integer should be input
to the subprogram as an integer
constant consisting only of ones
and zeros.

CHAPTER 11

SUBPROGRAMS - ADDITIONAL FEATURES

In Chapter 10 we discussed the basic
ideas involving the use of subroutine and function
subprograms. There are many other features of
these subprograms; as well, there are other
facilities in the FORTRAN language which tend to
make the use of subprograms easier and more
flexible. The purpose of this chapter is to
describe some of these additional features.

11.1 COMMON BLOCKS

It has been noted that variables used
in a main program or in a subprogram are local
to that program segment. COMMON statements provide
a means of declaring selected variables to be in
a *common* area in the memory of the computer, and
thus accessible to all program segments. This
common area is referred to as a *common block*,
because all variables in the area are adjacent
to one another in memory. Consider Example 11.1,
which is a reprogramming of Example 10.3 and
its associated subprogram, Example 10.2.

```
C EXAMPLE 11.1
      REAL A(100)
      COMMON K,A,M,ANS
      READ,K,(A(I),I=1,K)
      CALL MAX
      PRINT,M,ANS
      STOP
      END

      SUBROUTINE MAX
      REAL X(100)
      REAL LARGE
      COMMON N,X,J,LARGE
      LARGE=X(1)
      J=1
      IF(N.EQ.1)GO TO 7
      DO 6 I=2,N
      IF(X(I).LE.LARGE)GO TO 6
      LARGE=X(I)
      J=I
    6 CONTINUE
    7 RETURN
      END
```

The statement

COMMON K,A,M,ANS

declares that the variables K, A, M, and ANS,
referenced in the main program, are to be located
in the common block. Since A is a subscripted
variable of 100 elements, the block requires 103
storage locations. The subroutine contains a
similar statement,

COMMON N,X,J,LARGE

which declares that the variables N, X, J, and
LARGE used within it are in the common block.
Since there is only one common block, the effect
is to have K and N use the same storage location

in computer memory. Similarly, the arrays A and X occupy the same memory locations, as do the variables M and J and the variables ANS and LARGE.

The statement

SUBROUTINE MAX

has no list of dummy variables, and, similarly, the CALL statement has no argument list. The CALL merely transfers control to the first executable statement in MAX which is

LARGE = X(1)

When the subprogram is dealing with variables N, X, J, and LARGE, it is, in fact, dealing with the corresponding variables K, A, M, and ANS in the common block. When the RETURN is executed, control is, as usual, returned to the statement following the CALL. Hence, the values of M and ANS are printed.

The use of a common area has eliminated the need for a parameter list in the SUBROUTINE and CALL statements. There has been an *implicit* transfer of variables between the subprogram and its calling program.

It is not necessary to eliminate all the variables in the SUBROUTINE and CALL lists. Some of the variables could be placed in COMMON; the remaining ones could be passed explicitly, using arguments in the CALL. The use of common blocks is a matter of personal preference, and provides an extra degree of freedom to the

programmer. However, there is one important rule;
variables cannot appear both in the parameter list
and in the common list.

It should be noted that variables in the
two COMMON statements are in exact one-to-one
correspondence according to type and number. For
the moment, this should be accepted as the rule.
However, it may be legally violated, as will be
discussed in Chapter 20.

As an extra convenience to the programmer,
the dimensions of subscripted variables can be
declared in the COMMON statement. For example, if
the COMMON statement in the main program had
been written as

COMMON K,A(100),M,ANS

the need for the statement

REAL A(100)

would have been eliminated. In fact, the presence
of both statements would create a redundant condition
which would be signalled as an error.

If more than one COMMON statement appears
in a single program or subprogram, the effect is
cumulative; the variables in the first COMMON
statement are the first variables in the common
block, and are followed by those in the second,
etc. This means that the statements

COMMON A,B,C
COMMON D

are equivalent to the single statement

COMMON A,B,C,D

Example 11.1 has illustrated the use of
COMMON statements associated with the main
program and a single subprogram. If several subprograms were used, the COMMON statement could be
used in all of them, or in any subset of them.
In fact, the COMMON statement can be used in some
of the subprograms, and not appear in the main
program at all.

11.2   LABELLED COMMON

As an added convenience to the programmer,
the common area can be extended to include as many
labelled or *named* common blocks as desired.   The
statement

COMMON /AREA1/ A,B,C

would set up a separate common area called AREA1
containing the variables A, B, and C.   COMMON
statements in various program segments would use
the identical name AREA1 to place their variables
in the same labelled common area.   These names can
be any valid FORTRAN symbolic name.

The unlabelled common area used in the
last section is known as *blank common*.   Labelled
common areas and associated COMMON statements are
used according to the same rules as are their
blank common counterparts.   One set of program
segments can have as many common areas as is
convenient to the programmer.

A single COMMON statement can define
variables as members of both blank common and

labelled common areas.

The statement

COMMON A,B/AREA1/C,D/AREA2/E,F

defines A and B as members of blank common, C and D as belonging to the common block named AREA1, and E and F as belonging to AREA2. An equivalent form of the same statement is

COMMON /AREA1/C//A,B/AREA1/D/AREA2/E,F

Note that blank common is defined using two consecutive slashes. A further rule is that a comma never immediately precedes or follows a slash. This example illustrates the general flexibility in setting up common areas using the COMMON statement.

The reader may wonder why named common is available. One use of named common is to provide "private" common areas between program segments. Suppose we wanted several subprograms in the library to form an integrated set. They undoubtedly would share common areas for data. On the other hand, the user might not need to know about these common areas. However, he might wish to use common areas for his own purposes. In this case, the subprograms would use specific labelled common blocks, and the other common blocks would be left to the user. All he must know is the names of the labelled common blocks so that he does not use them again.

11.3 EXECUTION-TIME DIMENSIONING OF ARRAYS

It has been pointed out that an array whose name appears in a subprogram parameter list should have the same dimension specifications in both the calling program and the subprogram. This means that both the calling program and the subprogram must be modified if a different array size is to be used. This is frequently a nuisance, especially since the subprogram is probably in a library, and thus not readily available to the programmer for him to make changes. Furthermore, changes of this type to the library would be disastrous, since many people are using the library simultaneously.

To overcome this difficulty, a way has been provided to permit the calling program to include the dimension information as part of its input to the subprogram; thus, the dimension in the subprogram is assigned at execution time, rather than at compile time. Example 11.2 incorporates this feature into the subroutine MAX of Example 10.2.

```
C EXAMPLE 11.2
      SUBROUTINE MAX(M,N,X,J,LARGE)
      REAL X(M),LARGE
      LARGE=X(1)
      J=1
      IF(N.EQ.1)GO TO 7
      DO 6 I=2,N
      IF(X(I).LE.LARGE)GO TO 6
      LARGE=X(I)
      J=I
    6 CONTINUE
    7 RETURN
      END
```

The changes are

(i) The declaration statement has become

REAL X(M),LARGE

with the variable M replacing the
constant 100.

(ii) The parameter list has one more parameter,
namely, M, an integer variable.

Declaration statements of this type can
occur *only* in subprograms, and never in the main
program.

Example 11.3 shows the modification
necessary to solve the same problem as Example 10.3.

```
C EXAMPLE 11.3
      REAL X(100),LARGE
      READ,N,(X(I),I=1,N)
      CALL MAX(100,N,X,J,LARGE)
      PRINT,J,LARGE
      STOP
      END
```

Note that, since the array X is of size
100 in the calling program, the corresponding
parameter in the CALL statement is set at 100 to
ensure that the subprogram receives the proper
dimension information. As before, the dimension
in the called program must be identical with the
dimension in the calling program.

The following additional points should
be kept in mind when using execution-time dimensioning
of arrays.

(i)   Dimensions can be assigned at execution
        time in both function and subroutine
        subprograms.

(ii)   Only arrays which appear as elements in
        the parameter list of the FUNCTION or
        SUBROUTINE statement can have variable
        dimensions. Thus, they cannot be contained
        in any common blocks.

(iii)   The integer variables which indicate the
        dimensions of the array are usually
        members of the parameter list, and have
        their values assigned when the subprogram
        is called. Alternatively, they can be in
        a common block.

(iv)   The integer variables which indicate the
        dimensions of the array should not be
        reassigned new values in the course of
        execution of the subprogram.

11.4   MULTIPLE ENTRIES

Sometimes two subprograms are similar in
that the statements in one are identical with a subset of the statements in the other. In situations
like this, it is desirable to combine the two in some
way, in order to save memory space. One way is to use
only the larger subprogram, and have *multiple entry
points* to it. Then, if the whole program is needed,
the normal entry point is used; if only the subset
is needed, an alternate entry point is used. This
use of multiple entries will be illustrated in
Example 11.4 below.

```
C EXAMPLE 11.4
      SUBROUTINE CLINP(X,N)
      REAL X(20,20)
      DO 6 I=1,20
      DO 6 J=1,20
    6 X(I,J)=0.
      ENTRY INP(X,N)
      DO 7 K=1,N
    7 READ,I,J,X(I,J)
      RETURN
      END
```

If the subprogram is called using the
statement

CALL CLINP(A,K)

control transfers as usual to the first executable
statement following the SUBROUTINE statement, in
this case, the first DO. The effect is to set all
elements of array A equal to zero, and to read N new
elements into the array. (The ENTRY statement is
non-executable, and so can be ignored.) If, however,
the subprogram is called using the statement

CALL INP(A,K)

control transfers to the first executable statement
following the ENTRY statement, since the ENTRY
statement defines the *entry point* INP. The effect
is to read N new elements into the array A without
initializing it to zero, as happens in a call to
CLINP.

Another common use for multiple entries
is to allow segmentation of processing in the subprogram. For example, the calling program may
enter the subprogram only to pass certain values

to it; the RETURN is then executed immediately.
Subsequently, the subprogram is re-entered at an
alternate entry point, and the former values are
still available for computation. This will be
further discussed in Chapter 20.

As many entry points as desired can be
set up using ENTRY statements. Each one must have
a distinct name in order to reference it. The
entries in the list of dummy parameters of the ENTRY
statement must correspond to the entries in the
calling list according to order, type, and number,
as is the case for SUBROUTINE and FUNCTION statements. However, the lists in the ENTRY statements
do not have to correspond to each other, or to the
lists in the SUBROUTINE or FUNCTION statements.
All that is required is that the variables to be
manipulated in the part of the subprogram that is
used be assigned values prior to their use. This
could be done in many ways, including the use of
COMMON statements and previous calls to the same
subprogram.

When ENTRY statements are used within
function subprograms, the entry point name is
treated like a variable, and so must be declared
according to type if necessary. The FUNCTION
name and ENTRY names can be of differing types.

The following additional points about
ENTRY statements should be kept in mind.

(i) The ENTRY statement can be used only in
     subroutine and function subprograms.
     It can never appear in the main program.

(ii)   The ENTRY statement cannot appear within
       the range of a DO.

(iii) If statement function definitions are
       used in a subprogram which has ENTRY state-
       ments, these definitions should be placed, as
       usual, prior to the first executable
       statement in the total subprogram.

11.5   MULTIPLE RETURNS FROM SUBROUTINE SUBPROGRAMS

When a RETURN statement in a subroutine
subprogram is executed, control is returned to the
statement immediately following the CALL statement
in the calling program. However, it is possible
to return control to other statements in the calling
program by using the multiple return feature, as
illustrated in Example 11.5.

```
C EXAMPLE 11.5
      SUBROUTINE TEST(ARG,A,*,B,*)
      INTEGER A(100),B(100),ARG
      DO 8 I=1,100
      IF(ARG.EQ.A(I))RETURN1
    8 IF(ARG.EQ.B(I))RETURN2
      RETURN
      END
```

The subroutine TEST accepts an integer
ARG and two integer vectors A and B as input. Its
function is to scan the elements in A and B in a
search for ARG. If ARG is found in A, the
subprogram uses the statement RETURN1 to exit;
if ARG is found in B, the subroutine uses the
statement RETURN2 to exit. If ARG is not found, the
normal RETURN statement is executed. The asterisks

in the list of dummy variables provide the means of communication of statement numbers from the CALL statement to the subroutine subprogram. For example

CALL TEST(STUDNO,CLASS1,&10,CLASS2,&20)

will test to see whether a certain student having student number STUDNO is in class 1, class 2, or neither. If he is in class 1, control is returned to statement 10 in the calling program. If he is in class 2, control is returned to statement 20 in the calling program. If he is in neither class, control is returned to the statement following the CALL. Note that the *alternate returns* to statement numbers 10 and 20 are indicated by inserting &10 and &20 in the appropriate places in the calling argument list[†]. The appropriate places are those corresponding to the *'s in the associated parameter list of the subroutine subprogram. The first * is associated with RETURN1, the second * with RETURN2.

The subprogram can be set up to have as many alternate returns as are required. Normally, these returns are numbered consecutively, beginning with RETURN1, RETURN2, etc. Whenever the subprogram encounters the statement RETURNn, it uses the nth return. This return is defined using the nth asterisk (*) in the parameter list of the SUBROUTINE

---

† The & is not available on the 026 key-punch; a 12-8-6 multipunch must be used.

statement. This asterisk will correspond to an
entry in the argument list of the CALL statement.
This entry is always of the form &s, where s is a
statement number in the calling program.

The n in RETURN n can be an integer
variable, provided its value is appropriate, i.e.,
a positive integer having the required magnitude.

The multiple return feature is used
only in subroutine subprograms. It makes no sense
to use it in function subprograms, nor can the
main program use the statement RETURNn.

11.6 EXTERNAL STATEMENTS

Example 11.6 is a function subprogram
for approximating the integral

$$\int_a^b f(x)\ dx$$

using the trapezoidal rule. The formula employed
is

$$\int_a^b f(x)\,dx \approx \frac{h}{2}[f(a)+2f(a+h)+2f(a+2h)+$$

$$\ldots+2f(a+(n-1)h)+f(b)],$$

where $h = \dfrac{b-a}{n}$, and n is the number of trapezoids.

```
C EXAMPLE 11.6
      FUNCTION TRAP(A,B,N,FX)
      H=(B-A)/N
      SUM=0.
      K=N-1
      DO 6 I=1,K
    6 SUM=SUM+FX(A+I*H)
      TRAP=(FX(A)+FX(B)+2.*SUM)*(H/2.)
      RETURN
      END
```

The subprogram TRAP calls another function subprogram FX which defines the function which is the integrand of the integral. The name of this function, FX, appears as one of the entries in the parameter list, and therefore must be supplied by the calling program, just as any other parameter would have to be supplied. We illustrate this in Example 11.7, which is designed to approximate

$$\int_0^{.4} \sin x^2 \, dx + \int_{.1}^{.3} \cos x^2 \, dx$$

using TRAP with 5 trapezoids.

```
C EXAMPLE 11.7
      EXTERNAL FX1,FX2
      APPROX=TRAP(0.,.4,5,FX1)+TRAP(.1,.3,5,FX2)
      PRINT,APPROX
      STOP
      END

      FUNCTION FX1(X)
      FX1=SIN(X**2)
      RETURN
      END

      FUNCTION FX2(X)
      FX2=COS(X**2)
      RETURN
      END
```

The example consists of the main program
and two function subprograms to define the integrands.
The function subprogram names FX1 and FX2 appear
in the calling argument lists when TRAP is used in
the main program. However, an additional statement

EXTERNAL FX1,FX2

becomes necessary in the calling program. This is
a special declaration which must be used in every
calling program which passes the name of a subprogram or built-in function to another subprogram.
This is the only circumstance when the EXTERNAL
statement is used.

11.7 EXERCISES

11.1 Modify any of the programs for the
       examples or exercises in Chapter 10 so
       that one or more of the parameters of
       the subprogram list are in COMMON.

11.2 Write a real-valued function subprogram
       named J35 which computes

$$\sqrt{1 - [f(x)]^2}.$$

       The parameter list should include the
       variable X and the function name FX. Test
       J35 by tabulating it for f(x) = sin x
       and x = 0, .1, .2, .3, ..., 1.0. Compare
       the results with the corresponding values
       of cos x.

11.3   Convert the subprogram in Exercise 10.4
       to have two returns, one if the integer
       is prime, the other if it is not.   In
       this case, it is not necessary to use the
       variable which indicates whether or not
       the integer is prime.

       A main program reads data cards
       containing integer values.   Use the sub-
       program to test the integer values to
       determine whether or not they are prime.
       Print a list of the input integers with
       the words PRIME or NOT PRIME adjacent
       to them.

11.4   Consider the following two subprograms.
       (i)   The subprogram A is to accept an array
             X as input and compute the median
             value, Y, of the elements of X.
       (ii) The subprogram B is to accept an
             array X as input and compute the
             median value, Y, of the squares of
             the elements of X.
       In each case, the original contents of
       the array X are to be left unchanged.
       Thus, a work area could be provided in
       which to store, in ascending sequence, the
       elements of X or their squares, prior to
       calculating the median value, Y.

       The two subprograms can be organized
       to use the same work-area, and thus save
       space.   Accomplish this in the following
       two ways.

(a) Write the two subprograms so that they share the same labelled common block for work space.

(b) Combine the two subprograms into one with two entry points. By employing the same variable names, the same work space can be used for each problem. As well, with careful planning, parts of one program can be overlapped with parts of the other, to save program space.

11.5 Predict the output of the following program.

```
      CALL ONE(3)
    3 CALL THREE(&1,&2,J,&2)
      PRINT,J
    2 CALL TWO(J,&3,&3)
    1 STOP
      END
      SUBROUTINE ONE(I)
      RETURN
      ENTRY TWO(K,*,*)
      I=K-1
      ENTRY THREE(*,*,L,*)
      PRINT,I
      L=I
      RETURN I
      END
```

Verify your prediction by running the program on the computer.

CHAPTER 12

LOGICAL OPERATIONS

In many of the examples in previous chapters, we have used the logical IF statement. This has a logical expression embedded within it, and, to this point, we have treated such expressions rather casually. All we have noted is that they yield a result which is either true or false. The purpose of this chapter is to introduce logical computations more formally.

12.1 LOGICAL CONSTANTS

There are only two *logical constants* and they are represented in FORTRAN as .TRUE. and .FALSE..

12.2 LOGICAL VARIABLES

Variables capable of being assigned values which are logical constants are said to be *logical variables*. A logical variable can be any valid FORTRAN symbolic name which is declared in a LOGICAL declaration statement. For example, the statement

        LOGICAL A,B,SAM,T(10),D

declares each of A, B, SAM, and D to be logical variables and T to be a logical one-dimensional array.

12.3 LOGICAL OPERATORS

Since logical variables and constants are not arithmetic quantities, they cannot be manipulated using the arithmetic operators +, -, *, /, and **. Three special *logical operators* are available; they are .AND., .OR., and .NOT..

Suppose X and Y are logical variables. The following statements define .AND., .OR., and .NOT..

(i)   The expression

X.AND.Y

has the value .TRUE. if and only if both X and Y have the value .TRUE.. Otherwise, it has the value .FALSE..

(ii) The expression

X.OR.Y

has the value .TRUE. if either or both of X and Y have the value .TRUE.. Thus the expression has the value .FALSE. if and only if both X and Y are .FALSE..

(iii) The expression

.NOT.X

has the value .TRUE. if X is .FALSE. and .FALSE. if X is .TRUE..

These definitions can be summarized in tabular form as follows.

X	Y	X.AND.Y	X.OR.Y	.NOT.X
.TRUE.	.TRUE.	.TRUE.	.TRUE.	.FALSE.
.TRUE.	.FALSE.	.FALSE.	.TRUE.	.FALSE.
.FALSE.	.TRUE.	.FALSE.	.TRUE.	.TRUE.
.FALSE.	.FALSE.	.FALSE.	.FALSE.	.TRUE.

12.4   RELATIONAL OPERATORS

There are six *relational operators* available in FORTRAN. Most of these have been encountered in examples used in previous chapters.

Operator	Meaning
.EQ.	equal to
.NE.	not equal to
.LT.	less than
.LE.	less than or equal to
.GT.	greater than
.GE.	greater than or equal to

These operators are binary operators which have two arithmetic expressions as operands; the result of the binary operation is always a logical value. Consider the following examples.

Examples (i) and (ii) have integer-valued expressions as operands. Examples (iii) and (iv) have real-valued expressions as operands, and (iv) illustrates that functions and subscripted variables can be used in the expression. Finally, Example (v) illustrates that mixed-mode arithmetic can be used;

in this case, one of the operands is an integer
expression and the other is a real expression.

	FORTRAN	Algebra
(i)	I.GT.4	$i > 4$
(ii)	(I+2*J).LT.K	$i + 2j < k$
(iii)	(A+2*X).EQ.6.4	$a + 2x = 6.4$
(iv)	(X+COS(X)).NE.T(I)	$x + \cos x \neq t_i$
(v)	(I+4).GE.((X+J)/3)	$i + 4 \geq \dfrac{x+j}{3}$

Each of the examples is an assertion
which is either true or false. We can paraphrase
the expression I.GT.4 as follows: The current
value of I is greater than four; this assertion
is either true or false. Thus the expression
I.GT.4, when computed, yields the result .TRUE.
or .FALSE., depending on the current value of I.
Similar explanations can be given for the other
examples.

12.5 LOGICAL-VALUED EXPRESSIONS

Any expression which, when evaluated,
produces a logical result is said to be a *logical-
valued expression*, or, more briefly, a *logical
expression*. Assuming that A, B, and X are variables
of integer or real type, and that U, V, and W are
of logical type, the following are examples of
logical expressions.

```
  (i)    .TRUE.
 (ii)    A.GT.B
(iii)    A.GT.6.4
 (iv)    .NOT.(A.GT.6.4)
  (v)    ((X+3.2).LT.(SIN(A**2+1.))).AND.(B.EQ.3.)
 (vi)    U
(vii)    .NOT.U.OR.V.AND.W
(viii)   V.OR..TRUE.
 (ix)    X.LE..5
```

When arithmetic operators were introduced, the notion of operator priority was discussed. In a similar way, priorities for logical and relational operators have to be established. The complete operator list of FORTRAN, in order of diminishing priority is as follows.

```
function evaluations
**
* and /
+ and - (including unary + and -)
.EQ.,.NE.,.LT.,.LE.,.GT., and .GE.
.NOT.
.AND.
.OR.
```

Thus the logical expression (v) could be written as follows

```
X+3.2.LT.SIN(A**2+1.).AND.B.EQ.3.
```

and would have exactly the same meaning, because of the rules of priority. This illustrates the fact that parentheses, while sometimes redundant, are

nevertheless useful to help clarify the meaning
of an expression. The expression (vii) might be
more clearly understood if written in the equivalent
form

$$(.NOT.U).OR.(V.AND.W)$$

12.6 LOGICAL ASSIGNMENT STATEMENTS

The general form of a *logical assignment
statement* is

logical variable = logical expression

Examples are:

```
X=.TRUE.
Y=A.GT.B.OR.Y
Z=U.AND.V.OR.W
```

where X, Y, Z, U, V, and W are logical variables,
and A and B are of real or integer type.

The computer first evaluates the
logical expression, then assigns the result to the
logical variable to the left of the equals sign.

Extended assignment statements can be
used to assign more than one logical variable in
a single FORTRAN statement. For example, the
statement

```
U=V=W=.TRUE.
```

would assign the constant .TRUE. to each of the
logical variables U, V, and W.

12.7 LOGICAL IF STATEMENT

In the chapter entitled "Control Statements", we defined and illustrated the use of the logical IF statement. It remains to be said that the logical expression used in the logical IF statement can be more flexible than has been illustrated in any examples to this point. The logical IF might look like any of the following:

```
  (i)   IF(A.EQ.X+3.)GO TO 7
 (ii)   IF(A.LT.1.0.AND.B**2.GT.25.)PRINT,A
(iii)   IF(X*SIN(Y).GT.0.)A(I)=B(I)
 (iv)   IF(.NOT.(A.EQ.B))CALL SUBR(X,Y)
```

12.8 EXAMPLES USING LOGICAL OPERATIONS

Suppose TABLE is an array containing integer variables. Example 12.1 illustrates a subprogram for determining if a specific integer ARG is a member of the array. The logical variable RESULT will be .TRUE. if ARG is in the table; otherwise, RESULT will be returned as .FALSE..

```
C EXAMPLE 12.1
      SUBROUTINE LOOK (ARG,TABLE,SIZE,RESULT)
      INTEGER ARG,SIZE,TABLE(SIZE)
      LOGICAL RESULT
      RESULT=.FALSE.
      DO 6 I=1,SIZE
      IF(ARG.NE.TABLE(I))GO TO 6
      RESULT=.TRUE.
      RETURN
    6 CONTINUE
      RETURN
      END
```

Example 12.2 is identical with Example 12.1, except that a function subprogram is used instead of a subroutine subprogram.

```
C EXAMPLE 12.2
      LOGICAL FUNCTION LOOK(ARG,TABLE,SIZE)
      INTEGER ARG,SIZE,TABLE(SIZE)
      LOOK=.FALSE.
      DO 6 I=1,SIZE
      IF(ARG.NE.TABLE(I))GO TO 6
      LOOK=.TRUE.
      RETURN
    6 CONTINUE
      RETURN
      END
```

Note that the variable LOOK, which is also the name of the function subprogram, is declared as logical in the first statement of the subprogram. This variable must also be declared as logical in the calling program.

Logical variables can be useful in time-tabling and scheduling problems. Suppose that an institution operates on a schedule of 50 one-hour periods per week, and that 100 courses numbered 1 to 100 are taught. The time-table might be represented as in Figure 12.1.

The symbol T, representing true, indicates the periods at which the particular course meets. For example, course 3 meets in periods 2 and 50, but not in periods 1, 3, 4, and 49. This information could be stored as a two-dimensional table with logical entries, set up with the declaration statement

```
LOGICAL TTABLE(100,50)
```

204

The time-table would probably be read into the
computer from data cards.

Period Course	1	2	3	4	.	.	49	50
1	T	F	F	T			F	F
2	F	F	F	F			T	F
3	F	T	F	F			F	T
4	F	F	F	F			F	F
.								
.								
99	T	F	F	F			F	F
100	F	F	T	F			T	F

Figure 12.1

Assuming the time-table is stored in
memory, Example 12.3 shows how a subprogram could
be written to detect whether or not a conflict would
arise as a result of the selection of a particular
set of courses. The set of N selected courses is
assumed to be stored in the vector called COURSE.

The inner DO-loop employs the variable
USED to indicate the availability of time period J.
The first course which requires time period J causes
USED to assume the value .TRUE. as a result of the
statement numbered 7. If a subsequent course also
requires time period J, the IF statement causes a
transfer, and RESULT assumes the value .TRUE.,
indicating a conflict. If, after moving over all

time periods using the outer DO-loop, no conflict is found, the subprogram returns RESULT as .FALSE.

```
C EXAMPLE 12.3
      SUBROUTINE CNFLCT(TTABLE,COURSE,N,RESULT)
      LOGICAL TTABLE(100,50),RESULT,USED
      INTEGER COURSE(10),N
      RESULT=.FALSE.
      IF(N.EQ.1)RETURN
      DO 6 J=1,50
      USED=.FALSE.
      DO 7 I=1,N
      IF(USED.AND.TTABLE(COURSE(I),J))GO TO 8
    7 USED=USED.OR.TTABLE(COURSE(I),J)
    6 CONTINUE
      RETURN
    8 RESULT=.TRUE.
      RETURN
      END
```

This example also illustrates the use of a subscripted variable used as a subscript, i.e., the variable TTABLE(COURSE(I),J).

12.9   FORMAT-FREE I/O OF LOGICAL VALUES

Whenever a logical variable appears in the list of a format-free PRINT statement, its value is printed as T or F depending on whether it has the value .TRUE. or .FALSE. Thus, the sequence of statements

```
LOGICAL U,V,W
X=3.25
I=4
U=V=.TRUE.
W=.FALSE.
PRINT,U,X,V,W,I
```

would cause the following line to be printed.

```
      T      0.3250000E 01      T      F      4
```

Entire arrays of logical values can be printed, just as is the case for real or integer arrays. Consider the following examples with reference to the time-table described above.

```
  (i)    PRINT,TTABLE
  (ii)   PRINT,((TTABLE(I,J),I=1,100),J=1,50)
  (iii)  PRINT,((TTABLE(I,J),J=1,50),I=1,100)
```

The first statement causes the entire time-table to be printed in storage order, which is column by column. The second statement uses a pair of nested implied DO's, and accomplishes exactly the same result as the first. The third statement causes the time-table to be printed row by row.

It is legal to use logical expressions in format-free PRINT or PUNCH statements. Thus the sequence of statements

```
      U=.TRUE.
      I=3
      J=4
      PRINT,I,J,I.GT.J,.NOT.U,.FALSE.
```

would cause the following line to be printed.

```
      3      4      F      F      F
```

Example 12.4 illustrates the use of format-free output of logical variables and also shows how logical operations can be useful in problems involving set theory. Suppose three sets A, B, and C are defined as follows:

A: All points inside or on the circle
$$x^2+y^2 = 25$$
B: All points inside the ellipse
$$\frac{x^2}{36} + \frac{y^2}{16} = 1$$
C: All points (x,y) which satisfy the condition $y > 1 - x$

The program in Example 12.4 causes a data card containing the coordinates of a point (x,y) to be read; it then determines whether or not (x,y) is a member of each of the following sets:

U: $A \cap B \cap C$

V: $\bar{A} \cap B \cup A \cap C$

W: $\bar{A} \cap (B \cup C)$

```
C EXAMPLE 12.4
      LOGICAL EA,EB,EC,EU,EV,EW
      READ,X,Y
      EA=(X**2+Y**2).LE.25.
      EB=(X**2/36.+Y**2/16.).LT.1.
      EC=Y.GT.(1.-X)
      EU=EA.AND.EB.AND.EC
      EV=.NOT.EA.AND.EB.OR.EA.AND.EC
      EW=.NOT.EA.AND.(EB.OR.EC)
      PRINT,X,Y,EU,EV,EW
      STOP
      END
```

Logical constants can be read using the format-free input statement READ. They can be punched as T or F, or as .TRUE. or .FALSE., or as any combination of these representations. Each constant must be separated from the next by a comma or by at least one blank column. Thus an input data card might be punched as follows.

        T   F .TRUE. .TRUE.,T .FALSE.,F T

The rules for READ are otherwise identical with
those outlined in the chapter entitled "Simple
Input and Output".

12.10   FORMAT FOR I/O OF LOGICAL VALUES

The format code used for logical variables
is Lw, where w denotes the width of the field. On
output, the letter T or F is printed, depending
upon whether the value is .TRUE. or .FALSE.. The
T or F is right justified in the field, For example,
the statements

```
          LOGICAL U,V
          U=.TRUE.
          V=.FALSE.
          I=3
          J=760
          PRINT5,I,U,J,V
        5 FORMAT('0',I5,L7,I4,L4)
```

would cause the following line to be printed.

bbbb3bbbbbbTb760bbbF

I5	L7	I4	L4
I	U	J	V

On input, a field of width w which
consists of the next w columns of the card is
scanned from left to right until T or F is
encountered, and, correspondingly, .TRUE. or .FALSE.
is assigned to the variable. For example, the
time-table in Example 12.2 could be punched into
100 cards, one for each course. Columns 1 to 3

would contain the course number and columns 4 to 53 would contain T's or F's depending upon the time-table for the particular course. These cards could be read as follows:

```
      DO 5 K=1,100
    5 READ6,I,(TTABLE(I,J),J=1,50)
    6 FORMAT(I3,50L1)
```

If the input field is blank, the value .FALSE. is assigned to the corresponding variable.

12.11   EXERCISES

12.1   Suppose a data deck contains forty cards, each of which contains a student number and his marks in three examinations. These numbers are recorded as integers. Write a program which does the following:

(i)   reads the cards, and stores the student numbers and marks in four separate vectors.

(ii)   scans the mark vectors, and sets up three logical vectors of forty elements each. These vectors reflect whether or not the student passed or failed the particular subject by using .TRUE. if the mark is greater than or equal to 50 and .FALSE. otherwise.

(iii) prints these logical vectors.

12.2   This is a continuation of Exercise 12.1. Use the three logical vectors as data to determine the total number of students

210

who

(i)   passed each course, (that is, add
up the number of "trues" in each
vector).

(ii)   passed all three courses

(iii)   passed at least two courses

(iv)   passed at least one course

(v)   passed courses one and two, failed
course three

(vi)   passed course one or course two,
failed course three

(vii)   did not pass any courses

(viii)   did not pass course one.

12.3   Write a logical-valued function subprogram called ODD which accepts an
integer value as input, and determines
whether or not it is odd. If it is odd,
the function returns a value of .TRUE.;
otherwise, the function returns a value
of .FALSE.. The subprogram should work
for negative, zero, or positive integers.

12.4   The values for the elements of a two-
dimensional array of integers are read into
the computer from data cards. Use the
function subprogram ODD, written in
Exercise 12.3, to help solve the following
problem.

(a)   The program is to compute the total
number of odd integers in the array.

(b)   Write a second program which determines
the number of pairs of odd integers in
each column of the array. A pair of

211

odd integers is defined as two
consecutive elements, both of which
have odd values. Thus, if the
column had ten elements, all of
which are odd, it would have nine
pairs.

12.5 With reference to Example 12.4, write a
program which reads several data cards,
each containing a pair of co-ordinates
defining a point (x,y). Determine how
many of the points are in each of the
following sets.

(i)   A ∪ B ∪ C

(ii) $\bar{A}$ ∪ $\bar{B}$ ∪ C

(iii) $\overline{A ∪ B}$ ∩ C

12.6 Test the subroutine CNFLCT used in
Example 12.3 by punching some data for a
time-table, storing it, and reading
in further data for students' selections
of courses. To reduce the volume of data,
it is probably best to reduce the number
of courses and periods to 20 and 15,
respectively.

12.7 Suppose each course were offered in two
sections, with each section at two different
time periods. Thus, if a conflict existed
for one time period, it might not for the
other. Re-program the subroutine CNFLCT
to reflect this extension of the problem.
Note that this is not just a trivial
modification of CNFLCT, but requires a
complete re-thinking of the various aspects

of the problem. For example, how will
the time-table be stored? Also, when no
conflict is found, how are the appropriate
sections indicated?

The problem can be further extended
by allowing a variable number of sections
for each course, some of which may be
at the same time period.

12.8 Use format statements whenever input-
output is required in the above problems
if you have not already done so. For
example, the time-table data could be
punched in consecutive columns of the
card, thus saving space on the card.

12.9 Given a square array of points, connection
between points is defined by horizontal
and vertical lines.

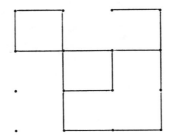

One way of representing a connection
between two points is to define two
arrays to represent horizontal and vertical
connections of points. For example, the
element HOR(I,J) of a logical array has
a value .TRUE. if, in row I, the Jth point
starting from the left is connected to the

to the $(J+1)^{st}$ point. Thus, in the
following diagram

HOR(1,1)   HOR(1,2)   HOR(1,3)

HOR(2,1)   HOR(2,2)   HOR(2,3)

HOR(1,1), HOR(1,3), and HOR(2,2) would
have value .TRUE.,and HOR(1,2), HOR(2,1),
and HOR(2,3) would have value .FALSE..
A similar technique could be used to
define vertical connections using a
logical array, VER, say.

Write a program which reads in a set
of connections between n^2 points, which
represents internally the required figure
(assume $2 \le n \le 5$), and which determines the
number of squares formed by the connections.
(e.g., for the given figure there are two
squares of size 1, and 1 square of size 2).
Your program should print the number of
squares of each size.

CHAPTER 13

DOUBLE PRECISION

It is often desirable to do computations
using real arithmetic, but with more significant
digits than the seven allowed using real constants.
When this need arises, it is convenient to employ
the *double-precision* features of the FORTRAN language.
It should be noted that these features should not be
used indiscriminantly, since more memory space is
required in the computer, and the computations
usually proceed more slowly.

13.1 DOUBLE-PRECISION CONSTANTS

Double-precision constants are similar to
real constants except that each of them occupies
double the physical space in the computer's memory.
As a consequence, over 16 significant digits are
recorded. The range of magnitude remains between
10^{-78} and 10^{75}, approximately. Note that, while the
term "double precision" implies a doubling of the
precision, in actual practice, more than a doubling
is achieved. This is because of the nature of the
hardware in the IBM 360 computer. Since the
precision is not really doubled, this feature is
frequently referred to as *extended precision*
rather than double precision. Now that we have
introduced double precision, it will be convenient

215

to refer to the other real constants and variables as having *single precision*.

Examples of double-precision constants are as follows:

(i)   12.3456789
(ii) 12.3456789D-11
(iii) 1.25D2
(iv) 0.D0
(v)   12345678.12345678D6

Note that the constant (i) has more than seven digits, and so is automatically taken to be in double precision. In Example (ii), the letter D is used to denote exponentiation (recall that E was used in real constants). Example (iii) shows that the constant can have fewer than eight digits and still be a double-precision constant, because of the presence of the D. Example (iv) shows how zero can be written as a double-precision constant.

The following are examples of invalid double-precision constants.

(i)   1.2D+362   (magnitude out of range)
(ii) 3,865D3   (comma not allowed)
(iii) 3   (no decimal - this is an integer
                   constant)

13.2 DOUBLE-PRECISION VARIABLES

Variables capable of being assigned values which are double-precision constants are said to be *double-precision variables*. A double-precision variable can be any valid FORTRAN symbolic

name which is declared in a DOUBLE PRECISION
declaration statement. For example, the statement

DOUBLE PRECISION A,B,C(18)

declares A and B to be double-precision real
variables, and C to be an array with the 18 double-
precision elements, C(1), C(2), C(3), ..., C(18).

13.3 DOUBLE-PRECISION EXPRESSIONS

Any expression which, when evaluated,
produces a double-precision result is said to be
a *double-precision expression*. If variables
have been declared using the statements

```
DOUBLE PRECISION A,B,C
REAL X,Y,Z
INTEGER I,J,K,L,M,N
```

the following are examples of double-precision
expressions.

(i)   1.3D20
(ii)   A
(iii) (.1D0*A+B)/(C**A-8.2D0)
(iv)   (A+X+I+L)/(A*X-I**L)
(v)   A+.1D0
(vi)   A+.1

Examples (i) and (ii) illustrate the
simplest of double-precision expressions.

Example (iii) illustrates the fact that
the arithmetic operators can be used in a double-
precision expression, with the usual rules of
priority applying.

Examples (iv), (v), and (vi) show that it is completely acceptable to mix modes between real, integer, and double-precision operands. In general, the resulting expression is a double-precision expression. Evaluation proceeds from left to right, taking into account priority of operators and parenthesized expressions. Whenever a binary operator has only one of its operands in double precision, the other is converted to double precision. This conversion is done by

    (i)   filling out single-precision constants with zeros and

  (ii)   converting integers exactly.

Thus the expressions A+.1D0 and A+.1 do not produce the same result. In the first case, .1D0 is a double-precision constant, accurate to 16 figures; in the second case, .1 is converted to a double-precision value but the converted value is accurate only to seven figures. This illustrates that care must be taken when using mixed-mode expressions.

To complete this section, it is in order to mention that logical expressions of the type A.GT.X or A.LE.I are allowed. In other words, the expressions used as the two operands can be of different types, including double-precision.

13.4 DOUBLE-PRECISION ASSIGNMENT STATEMENTS

The general form of a *double-precision assignment statement* is

double-precision variable = any arithmetic expression

Assuming A, B, and C to be of double-precision, examples are:

   (i)   A=1.2D10
  (ii)   B(10)=A**2+3
 (iii)   B(J)=B(J-1)
  (iv)   A=D
   (v)   A=.1

The computer first evaluates the arithmetic expression, then assigns the result to the double-precision variable to the left of the equals sign. If the arithmetic expression is not of double precision, the result is converted to double-precision using the same rule stated for evaluation of mixed-mode arithmetic expressions. Thus, in Example (v) the variable A would not be assigned the double-precision version of .1; it would be assigned the single-precision version filled out with zeros.

13.5   DOUBLE-PRECISION BUILT-IN FUNCTIONS

Many double-precision built-in functions are available. For example, DSQRT(d) will evaluate the double-precision square root of a double-precision expression d. Similarly, we can evaluate the double-precision sine, cosine, arctan, exponential, logarithm, and absolute value, using DSIN(d), DCOS(d), DATAN(d), DEXP(d), DLOG(d) and DABS(d). A complete list of available built-in functions can be consulted in Appendix A.

All function names, including built-in functions, must be declared to be in double-precision,

using a DOUBLE PRECISION statement. For example,
if a program used X and Y as double-precision
variables, and also used the DSQRT built-in function,
a declaration statement equivalent to the following
would be necessary.

DOUBLE PRECISION X,Y,DSQRT

The functions DBLE(r) and SNGL(d) deserve
special comment. DBLE(r) takes the calculated value
of a real expression r and converts it to a double-
precision result. This is done by filling out the
single-precision constant with zeros. SNGL(d)
converts the value of the double-precision expression
d to single precision by truncating the extra digits;
rounding does not take place. Note also that SNGL
is a single-precision real function.

13.6   EXAMPLE

Extended precision is useful, and often
necessary, in many types of computations. Most
examples require a specialized understanding of
the numerical properties of the particular problem
being considered, and so are not of general interest.
In order to give an illustration of the mechanics
of using double precision, the following problem is
considered.

Each term of the Fibonacci sequence

1, 1, 2, 3, 5, 8, 13, 21, 34, ...

is formed by taking the sum of the previous two
terms. Thus, if the sequence is written as

$$f_1, \ f_2, \ f_3, \ f_4, \ \ldots, \ f_n, \ \ldots$$

it can be defined using the rule

$$f_1 = f_2 = 1$$

$$f_{n+2} = f_{n+1} + f_n \qquad \text{for } n \geq 1, \ n \text{ integral}$$

Mathematicians have discovered that the ratio of consecutive terms approaches the constant value $\frac{1+\sqrt 5}{2}$, as n approaches infinity. In mathematical notation

$$\lim_{n \to \infty} \frac{f_n}{f_{n-1}} = \frac{1+\sqrt 5}{2}$$

Consider the problem of calculating $\frac{1+\sqrt 5}{2}$ as accurately as possible using double precision, and of determining how large n must be in order to have the ratio f_n/f_{n-1} at least as accurate. A program to do this could be written as in Example 13.1.

```
C EXAMPLE 13.1
C FIBONACCI PROBLEM
      DOUBLE PRECISION CONST,DSQRT,RATIO,DABS
      DOUBLE PRECISION FNM2,FNM1,FN
      CONST=(1.D0+DSQRT(5.D0))/2.D0
      PRINT,CONST
      N=3
      FNM2=1.D0
      FNM1=1.D0
    3 FN=FNM1+FNM2
      RATIO=FN/FNM1
      IF(DABS(CONST-RATIO).LT.1.D-15)GO TO 6
      FNM2=FNM1
      FNM1=FN
      N=N+1
      GO TO 3
    6 PRINT,N,RATIO
      STOP
      END
```

The output for Example 13.1 is illustrated below, and shows that one must go as far as the 38th term of the sequence in order to produce the constant $\frac{1+\sqrt{5}}{2}$ to 16 digits by taking the ratio of consecutive terms.

```
      0.1618033988749894D 01
   38          0.1618033988749894D 01
```

13.7   FORMAT-FREE I/O OF DOUBLE-PRECISION VALUES

Whenever a double-precision variable appears in the list of a format-free PRINT statement, its value is printed with 16 digits of precision using the D exponent. As is the case for single-precision variables, entire arrays can be printed by using the array name in the PRINT list. Also, double-precision expressions can appear in the PRINT list, and their computed values are printed.

It is possible to assign values to double-precision variables by using the READ statement. In this case, the double-precision constants are punched on data cards, and are separated by a comma or at least by one blank column. They can be punched in D exponent form, or as real constants without exponents. For example, .1 can appear on the data card; when assigned to a double-precision variable by using a READ statement, it will be converted with 16 digits of precision, just as if it had been punched as .1D0.

13.8   FORMAT FOR I/O OF DOUBLE-PRECISION VALUES

Double-precision values can be printed using either D format or F format; E format cannot be used.

D format works exactly like E format, except that more significant digits can be printed, and the symbol D is used to denote exponentiation. as seen in the output from Example 13.1. The format code Dw.d specifies that the variable whose value is to be printed is of double precision, and is to be printed right-justified in the next w print positions, with a precision of d significant digits. In general, the output will be according to the following pattern.

$$\underset{-}{+}0.\underbrace{xxxxxxxxxx}_{\text{d digits}}D\underset{-}{+}xx$$

Thus it follows that, unless $w \geq d+7$, a format error will occur.

When double-precision values are printed using F format, the rules are identical with those for real variables.

For input, double-precision values are read using the F and D format codes. The rules are essentially the same as those for reading single-precision values using the F and E format codes, as outlined in the Chapter 9.

13.9   EXERCISES

13.1 (a) Write a program to compute n! (n factorial) for n = 0, 1, 2, ..., 18. Note that double-precision real

arithmetic is the easiest way to
achieve accurate results.

(b)   Modify the program so that it becomes
a subprogram, FACT, which stores the
nineteen values in an array.

(c)   Write a subprogram, COMB, designed
to compute the number of combinations
of n things taken r at a time using
the formula

$$\binom{n}{r} = \frac{n!}{r!(n-r)!}.$$

This subprogram should use the array
formed by the previously written subprogram.

(d)   Write a main program which reads data
cards containing values for n and r,
and uses COMB and FACT to compute $\binom{n}{r}$.
Note that FACT should be executed
only once, i.e., it is an initializing
subroutine.

13.2   In the computation of compound interest, it
is important to have tables of the function

$$(1+i)^n,$$

where i is an interest rate, and n is an
integer indicating a number of time periods.
These tables are often required to eight
or more decimal places. Write a program
to compute this function for i = .0025
and n = 1, 2, 3, ..., 50. Each answer
should be rounded to eight decimal

places. Printing should be controlled,
by using format, to produce only eight
decimal places.

13.3 The mathematical functions sine, cosine,
and exponential can be evaluated using
the following series.

$$\sin x = \frac{x}{1!} - \frac{x^3}{3!} + \frac{x^5}{5!} - \frac{x^7}{7!} + \dots$$

$$\cos x = 1 - \frac{x^2}{2!} + \frac{x^4}{4!} - \frac{x^6}{6!} + \dots$$

$$e^x = 1 + \frac{x}{1!} + \frac{x^2}{2!} + \frac{x^3}{3!} + \dots$$

Write a program which evaluates each of
these functions, using both the extended-
precision built-in functions and the above
series. Determine, for x = .1, the
number of terms of the series which are
required, in each case, to produce the
same precision as the built-in function.

13.4 In Exercise 3.11, we wrote a program to
do extended-precision multiplication with
integers. Suppose we now consider extended-
precision division. The dividend has 16
significant digits, and is stored as two
integer constants, the first set of eight
digits as one integer, and the second set
of eight digits as the other.

(a) Write a program which divides an
extended-precision integer by another

integer of up to eight digits of
precision. The result is to be a
quotient of no more than eight digits.
The program should be designed to
reject divisions by zero or divisions
which would result in a quotient of
more than eight digits.

(b) Make the necessary modifications to
your program for part (a) so that
it computes the eight-digit remainder
as well.

(c) Try the program on the computer for
various values of the dividend and
divisor. Check to see that it
handles all possible combinations of
signs.

CHAPTER 14

COMPLEX OPERATIONS

FORTRAN permits arithmetic computations with complex numbers. This is accomplished by defining complex constants, complex variables, and complex functions, and using them in the appropriate FORTRAN statements. It is also possible to do complex arithmetic in extended precision.

14.1   COMPLEX CONSTANTS

In mathematical textbooks, complex numbers are usually written in the form a+ib where a and b are real numbers and $i^2 = -1$. At times, they are written in vector form as (a,b), with the first component "a" representing the real part and the second component "b" representing the imaginary part. This latter technique is used in FORTRAN. Thus typical complex constants would be

```
(1.24, -6.8)
(0., 0.)
(.2456E-8, -7.3)
```

Note that both components are real constants, they are separated by a comma, and the pair is enclosed in parentheses. Illegal forms follow.

```
(1, 2)      integer constants must not be
            used
(2.68, X)   a variable must not be used.
```

227

14.2 COMPLEX VARIABLES

Variables capable of being assigned values which are complex constants are said to be *complex variables*. A complex variable can be any valid FORTRAN symbolic name which is declared in a COMPLEX declaration statement. For example, the statement

COMPLEX A,B(25),K

declares A and K to be complex variables, and B to be an array of 25 complex elements.

14.3 COMPLEX-VALUED EXPRESSIONS

Any expression which, when evaluated, produces a complex result is said to be a *complex-valued expression*, or, more briefly, a *complex expression*. If A and B are complex variables, the following are legal complex expressions.

(i)   A+B
(ii)   A−B
(iii)   A*B
(iv)   A/B
(v)   (A+B)**2−A/(2.0,3.0)*B
(vi)   2*A+3.6*B+5
(vii)   CSQRT(A*B)

Examples (i), (ii), (iii), and (iv) illustrate how complex numbers can be added, subtracted, multiplied, or divided. Of course, the rules of complex arithmetic are used, and the result is a complex constant.

Example (v) illustrates the use of all possible arithmetic operators in a single expression. The established rules of priority apply to complex operations. It is important to note that exponentiation of complex expressions is permitted, but the exponent *must* be an integer expression. Furthermore, complex expressions can never be used as exponents of any type of expression.

Example (vi) illustrates that mixed-mode arithmetic is permitted. As the expression is evaluated, the constants 2, 3.6, and 5 are converted to the complex constants (2.0, 0.), (3.6, 0.0), and (5.0, 0.0), and the final result is complex.

Example (vii) includes a complex built-in function which will be explained later.

14.4   COMPLEX ASSIGNMENT STATEMENTS

A complex variable can be assigned a value using a *complex assignment statement* of the form

complex variable = expression

If the expression is complex, the complex variable assumes this value. If the expression is not complex, its value is converted to a complex value before assignment takes place; the value of the expression is assigned to the real part and zero is assigned to the imaginary part. Of course, the expression cannot be logical-valued.

Assuming A, B, and C to be complex, the following are valid assignment statements.

```
A = (2.0,-4.8)
B = (A+3)*B
C(I,3) = (A+B)**2
B = 6
A = 0
```

14.5 COMPLEX BUILT-IN FUNCTIONS

Many of the commonly used mathematical routines are available as built-in functions. For example, CSQRT(c) will compute the square root of the value of a complex expression c. Of course, the result is, in general, another complex number. Some other available functions are CSIN(c), CCOS(c), CEXP(c), and CLOG(c), to calculate the sine, cosine, exponential, and logarithm, respectively. A complete list is given in Appendix A.

All complex function names must be declared as of complex type, even though they may be built-in functions. Thus, a program using the complex variables X and Y, and the functions CSQRT and CLOG, must have a declaration statement equivalent to the following.

COMPLEX X,Y,CSQRT,CLOG

It is worth underlining the usefulness of the function $CMPLX(r_1,r_2)$. It has already been pointed out that it is illegal to write a complex constant as

(X, 3.4)

where X is a real variable or real expression. This is accomplished by using the function CMPLX as follows:

CMPLX(X, 3.4)

The function CMPLX is used extensively in the examples which follow.

It is also worth noting that, while most functions used with complex numbers yield complex values as their result, some of them produce real values. For example, CABS(c) produces $\sqrt{a^2+b^2}$, where a+ib is the complex constant produced when c is evaluated. In a similar fashion, REAL(c) produces the real number a (the real part of c); and AIMAG(c) produces the real number b (the imaginary part of c).

14.6 EXAMPLES

Example 14.1 tabulates the function

$$w = 1+z+z^2$$

for z = x+iy

x = 0, .1, .2, ..., 1.0;

and y = 0, .2, .4, ..., 3.0

```
C EXAMPLE 14.1
      COMPLEX W,CMPLX,Z
      Y=0.
    4 X=0.
    3 Z=CMPLX(X,Y)
      W=1.+Z+Z**2
      PRINT,Z,W
      X=X+.1
      IF(X.LE.1.)GO TO 3
      Y=Y+.2
      IF(Y.LE.3.)GO TO 4
      STOP
      END
```

This example uses mainly real arithmetic, but changes to complex arithmetic in the statement numbered 3 just in time to do the complex arithmetic and print the results. The loops are controlled using the real and imaginary parts of the complex independent variable.

The same problem can be solved using the built-in functions REAL and AIMAG as illustrated in Example 14.2.

```
C EXAMPLE 14.2
      COMPLEX Z,W,CMPLX
      Z=0.
    3 W=1.+Z+Z**2
      PRINT,Z,W
      Z=CMPLX(REAL(Z)+.1,AIMAG(Z))
      IF(REAL(Z).LE.1.)GO TO 3
      Z=CMPLX(0.,AIMAG(Z)+.2)
      IF(AIMAG(Z).LE.3.)GO TO 3
      STOP
      END
```

Note that REAL and AIMAG are not declared as complex functions,because they produce real results. Also REAL and AIMAG do not have to be declared as REAL,because any variable or function name beginning with letters other than I to N inclusive is automatically real, unless declared otherwise.

Example 14.3 illustrates how the function

$$\bar{w} = \cos(1 + \sqrt{z} + z^2)$$

could be tabulated in the circular region

$$|z| < 1$$

```
C EXAMPLE 14.3
      COMPLEX Z,W,CONJG,CMPLX,CCOS,CSQRT
      Z=(-.9,-.9)
    4 IF(CABS(Z).GE.1.)GO TO 3
      W=CONJG(CCOS(1.+CSQRT(Z)+Z**2))
      PRINT,Z,W
    3 Z=CMPLX(REAL(Z)+.1,AIMAG(Z))
      IF(REAL(Z).LE..9)GO TO 4
      Z=CMPLX(-.9,AIMAG(Z)+.1)
      IF(AIMAG(Z).LE..9)GO TO 4
      STOP
      END
```

To illustrate the use of a complex FUNCTION subprogram, we will write a routine called MAX which is designed to find the complex number of largest magnitude in an array of complex numbers.

```
C EXAMPLE 14.4
      COMPLEX FUNCTION MAX(N,A)
      COMPLEX A(N)
      MAX=A(1)
      IF(N.EQ.1)RETURN
      DO 7 I=1,N
      IF(CABS(A(I)).LE.CABS(MAX))GO TO 7
      MAX=A(I)
    7 CONTINUE
      RETURN
      END
```

Note that the function name MAX is declared complex in the statement

```
      COMPLEX FUNCTION MAX(N,A)
```

Furthermore, MAX must be declared as complex in the calling program segment.

14.7 EXTENDED PRECISION WITH COMPLEX NUMBERS

Any complex constant can have extended precision, provided *both* of its real components have double precision. Examples are

(1.0D0,-8.D11)

(.123456789,0.D0)

Extended-precision complex variables can be declared in a COMPLEX*16 declaration statement. For example

COMPLEX*16 A,B,C(8),D

declares A, B, and D as extended-precision complex variables and declares C to be an array with 8 extended-precision complex elements.

Complex double-precision expressions are those which give a computed result which is of complex double precision. All the rules for single-precision complex expressions apply in a similar fashion to complex double-precision expressions. Furthermore, it is permissible to mix modes between single-precision complex, extended-precision complex, real, double-precision, and integer expressions. In all cases, the output of an expression is re-typed to suit the type of arithmetic which is to be done, and, wherever possible, precision is not reduced. Remember that it is never possible to have a complex number, either with single or extended precision, in an exponent. Also, exponents of complex expressions can only be integer expressions.

As an illustration of one of the rules for mixed-mode arithmetic, consider the expression:

$$1.2D6 + (1.0,6.3)$$

The result would be an extended-precision complex constant. This is because the constant 1.2D6 is first converted to the extended-precision complex constant (1.2D6,0.D0); then the constant (1.0,6.3) is converted to extended precision by filling out the real and imaginary components with zeros. Finally, the two extended-precision complex constants are added together.

A set of extended-precision complex built-in functions is available. For example, CDSQRT(epc) computes the square root of the computed result of the extended-precision complex expression epc. The result is an extended-precision complex number. The complete list of built-in functions is in Appendix A. These function names must be declared according to type whenever they are used.

14.8   FORMAT-FREE I/O OF COMPLEX VALUES

Whenever a complex variable appears in the list of a format-free PRINT statement, its value is printed as two real constants side by side. If the variable is of single precision, the two constants are printed with seven digits of precision and use the E exponent; if the variable is of extended precision, the two constants each have 16 digits of precision and use the D exponent. An entire array of complex constants can be printed by placing its name in the PRINT list. Complex expressions can appear in the PRINT list, and their computed values are printed.

When format-free READ is used with complex

235

variables, the complex values must be punched on
the data cards in the same manner they would appear
in a FORTRAN program. Thus, they must be pairs
of real constants, separated by a comma, and enclosed
in parentheses. If more than one complex constant
is punched on a single data card, a comma or at least
one blank column must separate each from its successor.

14.9   FORMAT FOR I/O OF COMPLEX VALUES

There is no special format code for
handling complex values. Since every complex
number is really a pair of real numbers, we use
either a pair of E or a pair of D format codes,
depending upon whether single or extended precision
is needed. For either precision, a pair of F codes
can be used instead of the E or D codes, or a
combination of F and E or F and D is acceptable.

For example, consider the statements:

```
     X = (1.0,-8.6)
     PRINT5,X
   5 FORMAT('0',E20.8,E20.8)
```

The printer would double-space, and the two components
1.0 and -8.6 would be printed, using the E20.8 code.
Alternatively, the FORMAT statement could have been
any of the following:

```
   5 FORMAT('0',F20.4,E18.6)
   5 FORMAT('0',2F20.6)
   5 FORMAT('0',E14.5,F18.6)
```

On input, complex numbers are punched as
two real constants, both having either single or double
precision. They are read in using any combination

of E and F for single precision, and any combination
of D and F for double precision.

14.10 EXERCISES

14.1 Write a program which reads in two complex
numbers, A and B, using format-free input.
Perform the following computations.

(i)   C=A+B

(ii)   C=A−B

(iii) C=A*B

(iv)   C=A/B

Verify that the results are consistent
with the rules of complex arithmetic.

14.2 Write programs which tabulate the following
functions. Here, $i^2 = -1$.

(a) $f(x)=(1+i)x^2+(7+3i)x+5-6i$

for x = 0, −1, −2, ..., −8.

(b) $f(z) = z^3+3z+y$

where z=x+iy

for x = 0, 1, 2, ..., 7;

and y = −3, −1, 1, ..., 9,

for each value of x.

(c) $f(z)=e^z+\sqrt{\sin z}$

where z = x+iy

for x = 0, .8, 1.6, ..., 4.0;

and y = 0, .5, 1.0, ..., 3.0,

for each value of x.

(d) $f(x)=(x^2+3x+6)+i(2x^2+7)$

for x = 0, 1, 2, ..., 10.

14.3 It is well known that sin x and e^x can be
represented by the following series:

237

$$\sin x = x - \frac{x^3}{3!} + \frac{x^5}{5!} - \frac{x^7}{7!} + \dots$$

$$e^x = 1 + \frac{x}{1!} + \frac{x^2}{2!} + \frac{x^3}{3!} + \dots$$

The series can also be used if x is a complex number.

(a) Write a program that evaluates sin x and e^x, where x = a+ib

for a = 1, 2, 3, ..., 5;

and b = -2, -1, 0, 1, ..., 4,

for each value of a. Use both the series (ten terms) and the built-in functions CSIN and CEXP. Compare your results.

(b) How many terms of the series are required to compute the real and imaginary parts of sin x and e^x to five decimal places for x = 1+i.

14.4 The quadratic equation

$$ax^2 + bx + c = 0,$$

where a, b, and c are real values, has complex roots when $b^2 < 4ac$. Write a program which uses complex arithmetic to compute the roots of any quadratic equation (note that a≠0) regardless of whether the roots are complex or not. Test your program using the following values of a, b, and c:

a	b	c
5	5	4
2	4	2
1	0	16
3	0	37
1	2	0
3	0	0

14.5 Calculate the modulus and complex conjugate of the function

$$f(z) = z^2 + \sin z + e^z$$

for x = y, where z = x+iy. Use the values 0, 1, 2, ..., 10, for x.

14.6 Write a program which does the following:

(a) Generate a 3 by 3 matrix A, with complex entries, such that

$$A_{jk} = j + ki \qquad i^2 = -1$$

(b) Print out the matrix.

(c) The complex conjugate, $\bar{A}$, of A has elements

$$\bar{A}_{jk} = j - ki$$

Calculate the complex conjugate $\bar{A}$, and print it out.

(d) Multiply the 2 matrices A and $\bar{A}$, using complex arithmetic, and print out the product.

14.7 Develop a logical-valued statement function, called TEST, designed to take, as inputs, two complex numbers X and Y. This statement function is to have the value .TRUE. if

239

$|x^2 + y^2| < \sqrt{2}$, .FALSE. otherwise. Using *one* program, test your statement function on the following two cases:

(i) X = 1 + i

     Y = 2 - i

(ii) X = $\frac{1}{2} + \frac{1}{5}$i

      Y = $\frac{3}{10} - \frac{1}{4}$i

Your program should print (using FORMAT statements) the values for X and Y, as well as the word .TRUE. or the word .FALSE., depending upon the value yielded by TEST.

14.8 Write a subroutine subprogram, called TEST, designed to accept as input, a square matrix A, with complex numbers for elements. Determine if the matrix A satisfies both of the following properties:

(i) A_{kk} = k + ik   k = 1, 2, ..., N (i^2=-1)

(ii) A_{kj} = 0   k≠j k,j = 1, 2, ..., N

                       (N ≤ 25)

The output from the subroutine should be a logical-valued variable having the value .TRUE. if the input matrix satisfies both of the conditions above, .FALSE. otherwise.

CHAPTER 15

HARDWARE-DEPENDENT FEATURES

It has often been said that languages such as FORTRAN are machine-independent, that is, programs written in FORTRAN are capable of being processed on any computer for which a compiler exists. Although this would be ideal, in actual fact there are many variations of FORTRAN. These differ slightly, because any particular computer for which a compiler has been created will have its own special features. Consequently, programs written in FORTRAN may require some modification if they are to yield the same results when run on different computers.

This chapter is meant to outline features of the IBM 360 computer which, to some extent, affect the results obtainable by FORTRAN programs written to be processed using WATFOR. It will also put the reader in a better position to understand those features of FORTRAN, peculiar to the IBM 360, described in succeeding chapters.

15.1 MEMORY AND ADDRESSING

The memory of the IBM 360 is composed of eight-bit modules called *bytes*. The size of the memory on a particular machine depends on the 360 model used, and on the economic resources of the

241

installation. Memory sizes vary from several
thousand to several million bytes. However, a
programmer may not have all the memory of a
particular machine at his disposal, since he may
have to share it with other programs which are
in the computer at the same time. Machines which
use WATFOR have at least 128K bytes, where K equals
1024.

Each byte is assigned a reference number
called its *address*; addresses always start at zero,
and increase by unity to the number of bytes in
the memory. Machine-language instructions gain access
to a particular byte in memory by specifying the
address of that byte.

Certain machine-language instructions
operate on adjacent groups of bytes which are
referred to as *half words*, *full words*, and *double
words*. These consist of two, four, and eight bytes
respectively. Often a full word, or four bytes, is
called a *word*, for brevity. The address of a group
of bytes is the address of its farthest left or lowest-
numbered byte. An address which is a multiple of
2, 4, or 8 is called a half-word, full-word, or
double-word *boundary*, respectively. Note that all
double-word boundaries are also full-word boundaries
and half-word boundaries, but not vice-versa. The
360 has been designed so that when a half word in
memory is referenced, the half word must be stored
aligned on a half-word boundary. Similarly, full-
word and double-word operands must be properly
aligned in memory on their corresponding boundaries.

The FORTRAN programmer usually need not concern himself with proper boundary alignment, since the compiler takes care of storage allocation for variables, and automatically provides the alignment. The exception is that the programmer can construct a common block which can force invalid boundary alignment for some variables in the block. The compiler diagnoses this, however, and provides a warning message. Furthermore, if the block is not reconstructed to provide the proper alignment, the compiler, at execution time, will move invalidly aligned operands, when referenced, to valid boundaries before performing any operations on them. This, of course, slows the execution of the program, and should be avoided when possible.

15.2 INTEGER VARIABLES

A FORTRAN integer variable occupies a full word of memory. Positive values are stored in true binary form, and negative values in twos-complement form. The farthest-left bit in the word is taken as the sign, with zero representing plus, one representing minus. This storage procedure restricts integer values to the range from -2^{31} to $2^{31}-1$, i.e., -2147483648 to 2147483647.

In a previous chapter, we warned the reader that it was the programmer's responsibility to ensure that results of computations with integers do not fall outside this range, since the compiler gives no indication of such occurrences. If, for example, two integers such as 2147483645 and 129 are added, the result cannot be stored in a full word; the result *overflows* a word, or a *fixed-point overflow* is said to occur. The computer ignores the over-flowed part of the result, and proceeds with the part that will fit into a word. This can lead to unexpected results. The term *fixed-point* constant is also used as a synonym for integer constant.

The 360 has machine-language instructions for doing integer arithmetic with half-word operands. The farthest-left bit of the half word is used as the sign; positive values are in true binary and negative values in twos-complement notation. Thus, the range of values is from -2^{15} to $2^{15}-1$, i.e., -32768 to 32767. Half-word integers allow a saving in space at the expense of a decrease in precision of values that may be used. Also, fixed-point overflow can occur with improper use of half-word integers.

15.3 REAL VARIABLES

A FORTRAN real variable occupies a full word of memory, and is stored according to the notation for single-precision normalized *floating-point* numbers in the 360. This means that a word contains both a fraction and an exponent which specify the value of the number. A different notational system - hexadecimal - is used for arithmetic, and a few words might be said about this notation.

The base used in hexadecimal arithmetic is 16, and hence 16 symbols are required to express numbers to this base. For convenience, the

characters 0, 1, 2, 3, 4, 5, 6, 7, 8, 9, A, B, C,
D, E, and F are used as hexadecimal digits. A
number expressed in hexadecimal notation can be
expressed in binary notation by expanding each
hexadecimal digit to an equivalent four-bit binary
number (see Figure 15.1). Thus, the decimal number
156 has hexadecimal representation 9C or binary
representation 10011100, since 1001 and 1100 are
binary representations of hexadecimal digits 9 and
C, respectively. Similarly, any binary integer can
be expressed in hexadecimal form by grouping the
bits into groups of four from the right, and replacing
each group by the equivalent hexadecimal digit.

0	1	2	3	4	5	6	7
0000	0001	0010	0011	0100	0101	0110	0111

8	9	A	B	C	D	E	F
1000	1001	1010	1011	1100	1101	1110	1111

Figure 15.1

Hexadecimal Digits and Binary Equivalents

Figure 15.2 (b) shows the internal format
of a floating-point number in the IBM 360, corresponding to a number written symbolically as $.f \times 16^e$.
Here f represents a hexadecimal fraction different
from zero, and e represents the exponent of the base
16. For example, $.A4 \times 16^1$ is equivalent to the
decimal number $.1025 \times 10^2$. The fraction f is stored as

245

six hexadecimal digits, $h_1h_2h_3h_4h_5h_6$, in the three farthest-right bytes of the word; the sign of f is the first bit of the farthest-left byte, and is zero for positive and one for negative. Normalized numbers always have h_1 greater than zero. To allow for positive and negative exponents, *excess-64* notation is used, that is, the *characteristic* is obtained by adding 64 (= 40, hexadecimal) to the exponent e, and this is stored in the seven farthest-right bits of the first byte.

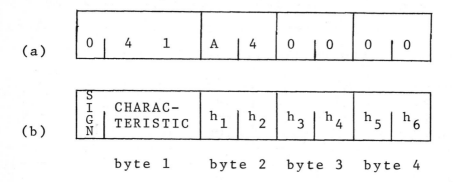

(a)

(b)

byte 1   byte 2   byte 3   byte 4

Figure 15.2

Single-Precision Floating-Point Word

A seven-bit characteristic allows for a range of from 0 to 127, with a corresponding range of exponent from -64 to 63. Thus, the largest real number which can be represented in this format is $.FFFFFF \times 16^{63}$, or approximately $.7237005 \times 10^{76}$ in decimal notation. The smallest in magnitude (except for zero, represented as a full word of zero-bits) is $.1 \times 16^{-64}$, or approximately $.5397605 \times 10^{-78}$ in decimal notation.

246

An attempt to compute a non-zero value
with magnitude greater than $.7237005 \times 10^{76}$
or less than $.5397605 \times 1^{-78}$ results in an
exponent overflow or *exponent underflow* respectively,
since the resulting exponent cannot be stored in
the seven bits allotted to it.   This situation
is usually considered a program error, and the
program is terminated, since further calculations
involving the invalid result are usually meaningless.

The hexadecimal integer FFFFFF is
equivalent to $2^{24}-1$ or 16,777,215 (decimal). For
this reason, WATFOR prints out at most seven
significant decimal digits for a real value,
although computations proceed with slightly more
accuracy, using about 7.2 decimal digits.

15.4   DOUBLE-PRECISION VARIABLES

A FORTRAN double-precision variable
occupies a double word of memory, and is stored
in double-precision floating-point notation.
This differs from the single-precision form only
in that the extra four bytes are used to supply eight
additional hexadecimal digits of precision to
the floating-point fraction.   Figure 15.3 shows
the internal format of such numbers.

S I G N	CHARAC- TERISTIC	h_1	h_2	h_3	h_4	h_5	h_6

byte 1   byte 2   byte 3   byte 4

h_7	h_8	h_9	h_{10}	h_{11}	h_{12}	h_{13}	h_{14}

byte 5   byte 6   byte 7   byte 8

Figure 15.3

Double Precision Floating-Point Format

Since the exponent is identical with that
used by single-precision numbers, the range of
magnitudes is essentially the same. However, the
hexadecimal integer FFFFFFFFFFFFFF is equivalent
to $2^{56}-1$ or 72,057,594,037,927,935 (decimal). For
this reason, WATFOR prints double precision values
to a maximum of sixteen significant decimal digits;
in fact, computations proceed with the equivalent
of about 16.7 decimal digits.

The details on internal formats of
numbers covered above allow us to discuss the
differences in the numbers 1.3, 1.3D0, and the value
of the built-in function DBLE(1.3). The single-
precision constant 1.3 has internal format equivalent
to $.14\text{CCCD} \times 16^1$; the double-precision constant
has internal format equivalent to $.14\text{CCCCCCCCCCCCC} \times 16^1$;

the value of DBLE(1.3) has internal format equivalent to .14CCCD00000000 × 16^1. The differences just illustrated are important considerations for programs which use mixed-mode calculations.

15.5   COMPLEX VARIABLES

A FORTRAN complex variable occupies two adjacent full words of memory, one for the real part and one for the imaginary part. Both parts are stored as single-precision floating-point numbers with the real part in the farther-left or lower-addressed word.

Extended-precision complex variables are similar, except that the real and imaginary parts occupy adjacent double words.

The address of a complex number is the address of its real part.

15.6   LOGICAL VARIABLES

A FORTRAN logical variable occupies a full word of memory, but in actual fact only the farthest-left byte is used to store the logical value. WATFOR uses a string of eight one-bits to represent .TRUE., and a string of eight zero-bits to represent .FALSE.. The three low-order bytes are ignored in logical calculations.

If a program makes extensive use of logical variables, especially of large logical arrays, considerable memory is wasted. Thus it would be better if the programmer had a means of restricting the size of logical variables to, say, one byte.

This is, in fact, possible, and will be illustrated
in the next chapter.

15.7 EXERCISES

The following exercises are meant to give
the reader an opportunity to familiarize himself
with the ways in which values are stored in the
memory of the IBM 360 computer. No programs are
necessary to complete these exercises; however, the
reader may choose to develop programs to accomplish
some of the conversions.

15.1 (a) Convert the following hexadecimal
numbers to binary numbers using
Figure 15.1.
(i)   00FA1234   (iv)   00000000
(ii)   12345678   (v)   11111111
(iii) FEDCBA98   (vi)   ABCDEFFF

(b) Convert the following sixteen-bit
binary values to their corresponding
hexadecimal representations.

(i)   1010101010101010
(ii)   0111111010110001
(iii) 1111111111111111
(iv)   0000000000000000
(v)   0001001101111111

15.2 (a) Convert the following decimal numbers
to their corresponding (i) binary
representations, (ii) hexadecimal
representations.

(i)	46	(iv)	127
(ii)	32	(v)	32767
(iii)	7632	(vi)	1234567

(b)   Convert the binary values in Exercise 15.1 (b) to their corresponding decimal representations.

15.3   The internal format of a single-precision floating-point constant is illustrated in Figure 15.2.   Convert the following hexadecimal representations of floating-point numbers to their corresponding decimal representations.   Recall that this calculation involves two steps; the first is to calculate the exponent, and the second is to convert the fraction to its decimal representation.

(i)	41100000	(iv)	C2560000
(ii)	41200000	(v)	437F0000
(iii)	41480000	(vi)	A4630500

15.4   Convert the following decimal values to their corresponding hexadecimal representations using normalized floating-point notation.

(i)	1.3	(iv)	1.11
(ii)	10.5	(v)	-6.125
(iii)	1.5	(vi)	256.354

15.5   Perform the following operations which involve hexadecimal values.   Check your answers by performing the operations in decimal arithmetic.

```
(i)    00FF + 0013       (iv)   0080/0010
(ii)   FFFF - 1234        (v)   00E1/000F
(iii)  0012 x 00AB       (vi)   1234 x 1111
```

CHAPTER 16

DECLARATION STATEMENTS

Although the type-declaration statements
INTEGER, REAL, COMPLEX, and LOGICAL have been
introduced in previous chapters, they have some
features not yet discussed. Some of these features
are connected with the hardware-dependent concepts
described in the previous chapter. The new features
will be discussed in this chapter.

In addition, a new declaration statement -
IMPLICIT - is introduced and explained.

16.1 INTEGER DECLARATIONS

The integer declaration statement

    INTEGER I,X(3),MABLE,SOON

declares the symbolic names I, X, MABLE, and SOON
to be integer variables. In addition, the variable
X represents an array of 3 integer values.

If the statement were written as

    INTEGER I/2/,X(3),MABLE/-8/,SOON

the variables would not only be declared as of
integer type, but I and MABLE would have assigned
to them the initial values 2 and -8 respectively.
This means that the programmer could assume that
the variables I, MABLE, would have the values 2, -8,
at the time his program begins execution. These

assignments are made at compile time, and the
process is often referred to as *initialization*.
The statement also shows that all variables
declared need not be initialized.

Example 16.1 shows a program which
computes the sum of squares of the first fifty
integers. The integer variable TOTAL is
initialized to zero, at compile time, to act as
an accumulator.

```
C EXAMPLE 16.1 - USING INITIALIZATION
      INTEGER TOTAL/0/
      DO 43 INT=1,50
  43  TOTAL=TOTAL+INT*INT
      PRINT,TOTAL
      STOP
      END
```

Although initialization is a very useful
feature of the declaration statement, its action
must be understood, for effective use. Example 16.2
will illustrate how this feature can be misused.
It is an attempt at the following problem: Read in
a data card containing the number of students, say
n, in a class. Then read in n cards, each containing
a mark, and calculate the average. Repeat this
process for a number of classes, and terminate when
a value of zero is read for n.

The program produces incorrect results
for all classes but the first, since the value of
SUM is not reset to zero for each class. Thus the
statement SUM=0 should be included, following the
READ statement numbered 75. The point illustrated
is that the initialization in the declaration

statement is performed only once, at compile time.

```
C EXAMPLE 16.2 - CLASS AVERAGES
      INTEGER SUM/0/,STUDNT
   75 READ,N
      IF(N.EQ.0)STOP
      DO 24 STUDNT=1,N
      READ,MARK
   24 SUM=SUM+MARK
      PRINT,SUM/N
      GO TO 75
      END
```

The initialization feature finds its greatest use in initializing variables which remain constant throughout the execution of a program, for example,

INTEGER YEAR/365/,WEEK/7/,DAY/24/

Entire arrays may be initialized in declaration statements, as the following example statement shows.

INTEGER I/2/,X(3)/3*5/,MABLE

This statement declares X to be an integer vector of dimension 3; also, its three elements are all to be initialized to the value 5. The constant 3 in the construction /3*5/ is called a *replication factor*, since it specifies how many times the constant following the asterisk is to be repeated in the initializing process. An alternative form of the statement, which does not use the replication factor, is

INTEGER I/2/,X(3)/5,5,5/,MABLE

255

The initializing of arrays is done in storage order, using the specified constants from left to right. The rule is that there must be exactly as many constants as there are array elements to be initialized, with any replication factors being taken into account. Thus, to initialize a table T as shown in Figure 16.1 the, following statement could be used:

```
INTEGER T(3,4)/50,3,2*0,4,1,16,0,4,2,98,220/
```

50	0	16	2
3	4	0	98
0	1	4	220

Figure 16.1

Initial Values for a 3×4 Table T

The dimensions of arrays can be declared separately in a DIMENSION statement, and the initial values can be specified in the type-declaration statement, e.g.,

```
DIMENSION T(3,4),X(3)
INTEGER T/50,3,2*0,4,1,16,0,4,2,98,220/,X/3*5/
```

There are two more rules which can conveniently be stated at this time, and they apply also to the initialization which will be described in the next three sections of this chapter.

256

(i)   The constant used for initialization must
be of the same type as the variable to be
initialized.   Thus the statement

INTEGER Z/2.38/

is illegal, since 2.38 is not an integer
constant.

(ii) Subprogram parameters and function names
may not be initialized.

The previous chapter mentioned that the
IBM 360 could operate with integers stored in half-
word form. The FORTRAN programmer is able to use
this facility by declaring particular variables as
half-word integer variables. Thus the statement

INTEGER*2 JACK,BALL,Z

has the effect of specifying that variables JACK,
BALL, and Z are of integer type, but occupy only two
bytes of memory rather than the four bytes used for
ordinary integer variables. The use of half-word
integer variables can produce a saving of space, if
this is critical, at the expense of a decrease in
the range of values which can be stored. The range
of half-word integer values is from -32768 to 32767.

Arrays of half-word integers can be
declared, and half-word integer variables can be
initialized. For example, the statement

INTEGER*2 XRAY/28/,VEL(10)/5*3,5*0/,BOB

declares the variables XRAY, VEL, BOB, to be half-
word integers; the '*2' specifies that all variables
named are of length two bytes. VEL is declared as

an array of 10 half-word elements. Furthermore,
XRAY is initialized to the value 28; the first
five elements of VEL are each initialized to 3,
the last five to 0.

Half-word integers may be mixed freely
in programs with full-word integers; the former
may be used in all places in which the latter may
be used, except as index of an assigned GO TO.

Example 16.3 shows a simple program that
mixes the use of integer variables of length two
bytes and of length four bytes.

```
C EXAMPLE 16.3 - MIXED LENGTH INTEGERS
      INTEGER*2 HALF
      INTEGER   FULL
    2 READ,HALF,FULL
      IF(HALF*3.EQ.FULL)STOP
      HALF=HALF+5
      PRINT,HALF,FULL
      GO TO 2
      END
```

The assignment statement

HALF=HALF+5

uses mixed-length arithmetic, since the integer
constant 5 is treated as a full-word operand by
the compiler. The compiler treats *all* integer
constants in this way. The effect is that the
addition of the two integer values is done to
full four-byte precision; then the low-order two
bytes of the resulting value are assigned to the
variable HALF. It is the programmer's responsibility
to make sure that no information is lost in such
operations.

The two declaration statements of
Example 16.3 could be replaced by the single
statement

```
INTEGER HALF*2,FULL*4
```

since the INTEGER statement allows mixed declarations
of this kind. The '*4' appended to FULL specifies
that FULL is to be treated as an ordinary integer
variable occupying a word, or four bytes, of memory.
The values 2 and 4 are called the *length specifications*
of the corresponding variables HALF and FULL. In
fact, the INTEGER statement has an implied default
standard length specification of four bytes, and thus
the following two statements are equivalent:

```
INTEGER A,B(5,3),C/-2/
INTEGER*4 A,B(5,3),C/-2/
```

The last statement emphasizes the fact
that when a length specification is appended to
the type identifier, INTEGER, the said specification
applies to all names which do not have an appended
explicit length. Furthermore, if no length
specification is appended to the word INTEGER, the
standard length of 4 is assumed. Thus, the following
statements all result in the same declarations:

```
INTEGER A*2,B,C*4,D*2
INTEGER*2 A,B*4,C*4,D
INTEGER A*2,B*4,C,D*2
INTEGER A*2,B,C,D*2
INTEGER*4 A*2,B,C*4,D*2
```

The length specification 2 is called the
optional length for integers.

The following statements show that initialization may be done and array dimensions may be declared when length specifications are included in the declaration statement.

(i) INTEGER*2 A/-5/,C*4(5)/1,2,3,4,5/,D(3,3)/9*0/,B*2
(ii) INTEGER*4 X*2/7/,Z,Y*2(3)/1,2*-7/,W*2,U*4,T(2,5)

The statements have the effect of declaring names A, D, B, X, Y, W, to be half-word integer variables, and names C, Z, U, T, to be full-word integers. Furthermore, C and Y are vectors of 5 and 3 elements, respectively; and D and T are matrices of dimensions 3 by 3 and 2 by 5, respectively. Initialization is supplied for variables A, X, and for the elements of C, Y, D. Note that the *2 appended to the name B in (i), and the *4's appended to the word INTEGER and to the name U in (ii), are redundant.

Half-word integer values can be obtained from real values by using the built-in function HFIX, as shown by Example 16.4.

```
C EXAMPLE 16.4 - USE OF HFIX
      INTEGER*2 HFIX,JACK
      READ,X
      JACK=HFIX(X+2.5)
      PRINT,X,JACK
      STOP
      END
```

16.2 REAL DECLARATIONS

Earlier chapters have introduced the REAL and DOUBLE PRECISION declaration statements and the use of variables of these types. In particular,

the previous chapter explained the internal machine
forms of real and double-precision values. There
is little difference between them; real values
occupy four bytes of memory, and double-precision
values occupy eight. For this reason, it is
convenient to consider double-precision values as
merely a variation of real values. In fact, it is
possible to do away with the DOUBLE PRECISION
statement entirely if we agree to consider two
kinds of real variables - those with a standard
length of four bytes, and those with an optional
length of eight bytes.

Thus the declaration statement

REAL*8 B,DSQRT,A

can be used instead of

DOUBLE PRECISION B,DSQRT,A

In addition, the REAL statement has the same
flexibility as the INTEGER statement discussed
in the previous section, that is, real variables
of either length can be declared in the same
statement, and initialization can be specified.

A few examples should suffice, since the
rules for REAL are similar to those for INTEGER.

   (i)   REAL*8 A,B*4,C(25),D*4(6,3),E*4/2.718282/
  (ii)   REAL*4 ROOT2/1.414214/,PI*8/3.141592653589793/
 (iii)   REAL*8 ROOT2*4/1.414214/,PI/3.141592653589793/
  (iv)   REAL ROOT2/1.414214/,PI*8/3.141592653589793/
   (v)   REAL*8 X(5)/5*3.8D0/,Y,Z*4(2,3)/3*.5,3*1./

Note that (ii), (iii), and (iv) achieve the same
result.

16.3   COMPLEX DECLARATIONS

There are two kinds of complex values
in FORTRAN - those with the standard length of eight
bytes and those with the optional length of sixteen
bytes. Examples of both kinds have been given in
an earlier chapter, and the method of declaring
each was described. The previous chapter showed
that a complex value of length eight is really stored
as two adjacent real values of length four, and an
extended-precision complex value is composed of
two adjacent real values of length eight.

Since the COMPLEX declaration statement
has the same properties as the REAL and INTEGER
statements, sample statements only will be given.

```
 (i)  COMPLEX*8 CDSQRT*16,CMPLX,Z*16/(1.5D0,-1.5D0)/,P*8
(ii)  COMPLEX CDSQRT*16,CMPLX,Z*16/(1.5D0,-1.5D0)/,P
(iii) COMPLEX*16 CDSIN,Q5*8(3,3)/9*(0.,1.)/,CDCOS*16
(iv)  COMPLEX*16 D*8(3)/(-1.,1.),2*(1.,-1.)/,EGGMOR
```

Statements (i) and (ii) are equivalent.

16.4   LOGICAL DECLARATIONS

The last section of the previous chapter
mentioned that a variable declared in a LOGICAL
statement occupies four bytes of memory although,
in fact, only one byte of the four is used for
storing the logical value. Logical variables can
be restricted to occupy one byte of storage, with
a resulting saving of space, if they are declared
to have the optional length of one; the standard
length occupied by a logical variable is four bytes.

Thus the following statements are valid, and the rules are similar to those used in the preceding sections.

```
 (i) LOGICAL*1 GIPWAD/.TRUE./,UVZ(2)/.TRUE.,.FALSE./
 (ii) LOGICAL*1 A*4(5)/4*.TRUE.,.FALSE./,FALSE/.FALSE./
(iii) LOGICAL YES/.TRUE./,NO*1/.FALSE./,TV*1(5,5)/25*T/
 (iv) LOGICAL*4 YES/T/,NO*1/F/,TV*1(5,5)/25*.TRUE./
```

Statements (iii) and (iv) are equivalent, since the standard length used for logical values is four bytes. These statements show also that T and F may be used as abbreviations for .TRUE. and .FALSE. when initializing variables.

When logical values of different lengths are combined using the logical operators .AND. and .OR., the result is of length four. Moreover, the logical constants .TRUE., and .FALSE. are considered to be of length four.

16.5 TYPE DECLARATION FOR FUNCTION SUBPROGRAMS

Previous chapters have introduced the statements

```
          FUNCTION
          REAL FUNCTION
          INTEGER FUNCTION
          LOGICAL FUNCTION
          DOUBLE PRECISION FUNCTION
          COMPLEX FUNCTION
```

Each of these statements always appears as the first statement of a function subprogram, and serves the purpose of identifying the name of the function and providing information about its type.

263

The function's parameters are also identified by
including them in a parenthesized list following
the function name. Sample statements follow:

        (i)   FUNCTION SUM(X,N)
       (ii)   REAL FUNCTION MAX(L,V,S)
      (iii)   FUNCTION MOD3(T)
       (iv)   LOGICAL FUNCTION TEST(A,B)

        In (ii) and (iv), the types of MAX and
TEST are explicitly declared to be real and logical,
respectively; in (i) and (iii) the types of SUM and
MOD3 are taken by default as real and integer,
respectively. The length of each name is the standard
for its type.

        It remains only to point out that function
subprogram names, like variable names, can be of
the optional length for a particular type. To
achieve this, the appropriate length specification
is appended to the function name, as the following
examples show.

        (i)   REAL FUNCTION TVAL*8(P,Q)
       (ii)   INTEGER FUNCTION ARGFU*2(N,A,L,S)
      (iii)   COMPLEX FUNCTION HONK*16(Z)
       (iv)   LOGICAL FUNCTION YESRNO*1(IN,OUT)

        Statement (i) could be used to head a
function subprogram named TVAL; the function value,
TVAL, is of real type, and has the appropriate
optional length, 8 bytes. Similar descriptions
could be given for (ii), (iii) and (iv).
        Note that (i) is equivalent to

    DOUBLE PRECISION FUNCTION TVAL(P,Q)

It is important to note the position of the length specification in these statements - it follows the function name. The statement

```
REAL*8 FUNCTION TVAL(P,Q)
```

is not a valid function declaration.

If desired, the standard length specification of a type may be given; for example,

```
REAL FUNCTION VEPROD*4(T,A)
COMPLEX FUNCTION OMEGA*8(V,T)
```

The programmer must declare the type and length, if different from those assigned by default, of the function name in any program segment in which the function is called. The following Example, 16.5, illustrates this for the logical function TEST. The function has one parameter, a positive integer N, and the result of the function is .TRUE. if N is a prime number, and is .FALSE. otherwise. The main program, using TEST, determines and prints all twin primes less than 100.

```
C EXAMPLE 16.5 - FINDING TWIN PRIMES
      LOGICAL*1 TEST
      DO 26 I=3,100,2
   26 IF(TEST(I).AND.TEST(I+2))PRINT,I,I+2
      STOP
      END
      LOGICAL FUNCTION TEST*1(N)
      TEST=N.NE.N/2*2.OR.N.EQ.2
      DO 44 I=3,N,2
      IF(I*I.GT.N.OR..NOT.TEST)RETURN
   44 TEST=N.NE.N/I*I
      END
```

16.6 THE IMPLICIT STATEMENT

The first version of FORTRAN developed in the mid-1950's allowed only two types of variables - integer and real. At that time, the rule was established that variables beginning with the letters I, J, K, L, M, or N were to be integer, all others real; there were no statements for type declaration.

Later versions of FORTRAN allowed variables of complex or logical type, as well as the declaration statements, mentioned in the previous sections, for typing names explicitly. The original "first-letter rule" was maintained, however, for "default" typing of integer and real variables.

Some additional freedom was added with the design of FORTRAN for the IBM 360 by including a very general type-declaration statement, IMPLICIT. This statement essentially allows the programmer to specify his own 'first-letter rule', and to extend it to include all types. Moreover, the rule may be changed in each program segment. Several examples are given to illustrate these ideas.

The statement

```
IMPLICIT REAL*8(D,T-Z),INTEGER*2(M,N),LOGICAL(O-S)
```

specifies that variable names whose first letters are D, T, U, V, W, X, Y, or Z will be real of length 8, by default, that is, in the absence of any explicit declaration statements. Similarly, variable names beginning with letters M or N will be, by default, integer of length 2, and those beginning with the letters O to S will be logical of standard length 4, by default. The conventional FORTRAN first-letter rule will apply for all other letters; that is, variables beginning with I, J, K, or L are integer of standard length 4, and variables beginning with A, B, C, E, F, G, H, or $ are real of standard length 4.

As shown, standard or optional lengths can be given for a letter or range of letters, and the standard length is assumed if not specified. A range of letters is indicated by separating the first and last letters of the range by a minus sign.

The statement

```
    IMPLICIT REAL(A-H,O-Z,$),INTEGER(I-N)
```

is equivalent to the conventional first-letter rule.

Explicit declarations still override implicit typing. For example

```
        IMPLICIT INTEGER*4(A-N)
        REAL*8 ABLE,JACK*4
```

explicitly declares ABLE and JACK to be of type real with lengths 8 and 4 bytes, respectively; if not explicitly so declared, they would both be integer of length 4.

The statement

```
        IMPLICIT REAL*4(A-Z,$)
```

might be used in a program segment which is to do computations in real arithmetic only. This could give the programmer some additional freedom in naming variables. The program could easily be

converted to double-precision arithmetic by replacing
the above statement by

    IMPLICIT REAL*8(A-Z,$)

However, care needs to be taken if the program
uses constants or makes references to built-in
functions. The above statement implicitly types,
for example, SQRT as a name of length 8. Statements
containing calls to the built-in function SQRT could
be repunched to reference DSQRT. To avoid this
we might make use of a statement function defined
as

    SQRT(X)=DSQRT(X)

There are only a few rules that apply to
the IMPLICIT statement.

(i)   At most *one* IMPLICIT statement is allowed
      per program segment, that is, each subprogram
      may have one or none. The regular first-
      letter rule applies in any program segment
      which does not have an IMPLICIT statement.

(ii) The IMPLICIT statement, if used, must be
      the first in the main program and the
      second in any subprogram. Thus, it
      immediately follows the SUBROUTINE or
      FUNCTION statement. In a subprogram, it
      types a function name and any arguments,
      if these are not explicitly typed. Thus,
      for

    FUNCTION THETA(COV,STAR)
    IMPLICIT COMPLEX*16(C),COMPLEX(Q-U)
    REAL STAR

the function THETA is of complex type and
standard length 8, COV is of complex type
and length 16. STAR is explicitly declared
to be of real type and standard length 4.

(iii) The IMPLICIT statement, like all declaration
statements, is not executable, and serves
only as a guide at compile time.

16.7 <u>EXERCISES</u>

16.1 (a) Consider the following sequence of
statements.

```
REAL*8 D,E
INTEGER*2 IH
R=3.0*(1./3.)
D=3.0*(1./3.)
E=3.D0*(1.D0/3.D0)
I=45678+92
IH=45678+92
PRINT,R,D,E,I,IH
```

Predict the values which would be
printed. Verify your prediction by
including the sequence of statements
in a program for the computer.

(b) Given the following declaration
statements,

```
REAL A,B*8
INTEGER I,J*2
COMPLEX C,D*16
```

state the type of each of the
following expressions.

(i)   A+B/I   (iv)   A*I*J
(ii)   C+I+J*A   (v)   C**I+C**J
(iii) D-J

16.2 (a) Using the feature of initialization
         in declaration statements, set up
         the starting, ending, and increment
         values, and tabulate the function

$$f(x) = \sin x + \cos x$$

         for $x = 0, \frac{\pi}{8}, \frac{\pi}{4}, \ldots, \pi$.

    (b) Do Exercise 3.6 using initialization
         to set up the constant values required
         for the various calculations.

    (c) Repeat part (b) using half-word
         integers to store the required
         values.

16.3 Exercises 2.3, 2.5, 2.8, 7.3(d), and 7.3(c)
     involve calculations with single-precision
     real variables, constants, and built-in
     functions. Make use of the IMPLICIT state-
     ment to assist in the conversion of these
     programs to extended-precision real
     arithmetic.

16.4 Exercise 14.3 involves computations with
     single-precision complex quantities.
     Modify the program to perform the
     computations in extended precision.

16.5 (a) Repeat Exercise 10.6 using extended-
         precision arithmetic.

    (b) Write a main program that inputs
         the degree and the coefficients of
         the polynomial

$$f(x) = x^6 + x^3 + x + 1.$$

         The program is to evaluate the poly-
         nomial and its derivative for

x = 10, 11, 12, ..., 25

using the subprograms written for part (a).

16.6 In Exercise 8.14, we determine prime numbers. Re-write the program using half-word integers to store the values. Use it to determine all primes less than 400.

CHAPTER 17

CHARACTER MANIPULATION

The examples to date have dealt mainly with numerical computation. We have occasionally used alphabetic information for headings and identification purposes, using Hollerith strings. However, sometimes alphabetic characters enter into calculations. For example, in order to determine that SMITH follows JONES in alphabetic order, the two alphabetic *strings* must be compared. FORTRAN has some features which make such character manipulation possible. These features will be discussed in this chapter.

17.1 CHARACTER STRINGS

Each byte of the IBM 360 memory is capable of storing one character. Hence, four characters can occupy the space used by an integer variable. In fact, a common way of storing character strings is as values assigned to integer variables. Then the name of the variable becomes the name of the string of four characters.

Let us consider the following declaration statement:

    INTEGER A/'JOKE'/,X/2568/

Here the variables A and X are declared to be of integer type. The variable X is initialized to have

272

the value 2568; the variable A is initialized so that it contains the character string JOKE. Note that this would completely fill the full word, with J as the first byte, O as the second, K as the third, and E as the last. The extremities of the character string are delimited using quote symbols. These symbols, as is usually the case with Hollerith strings, are not part of the string itself.

Suppose the string were longer than four characters, as is the case for CHARLIE. This could be stored using two integer variables as follows:

```
INTEGER A/'CHAR'/,B/'LIE'/
```

Here B has assigned to it a character string LIE, which is not long enough to fill the full word. In cases like this, blank characters are automatically inserted on the right, as necessary.

At this point it would be instructive to consider Example 17.1.

```
C EXAMPLE 17.1
      INTEGER A/'CHAR'/,B/'LIE'/
      INTEGER X/2568/,Y/'2568'/
      PRINT,A,B,X,Y
      STOP
      END
```

The output for the example would be

```
 -1010253351   -741751488      2568   -218761480
```

which might not be what the reader would have expected. This is because the computer has no way of identifying that A, B, and Y contain

273

character strings when it encounters the statement

PRINT, A,B,X,Y

They are treated as integer variables, and hence are assumed to represent integer values. Consequently, apparently meaningless integer values are printed. In a later section, we will see how these variables can be more appropriately printed using the A format code.

The example also emphasizes the fact that the integer constant 2568 takes on quite a different appearance when represented as a character string.

Character strings can also be stored in the other types of variables. For example, a string of sixteen characters can be stored as the value of an extended-precision complex variable.

We are now in a position to describe the various possibilities in detail.

17.2 STORING CHARACTER DATA

Characters may be stored using any of the four types of variables - real, integer, complex, or logical. As seen previously, each integer variable can store a maximum of four characters, whereas each double-precision complex variable can store a maximum of sixteen characters. Figure 17.1 is a table which shows the number of characters that can be stored for each of the various types of variables. The length specification of the type of variable indicates the maximum number of characters which can be stored in it.

Variable Type	Number of Characters
INTEGER*2	2
INTEGER*4 or INTEGER	4
REAL*4 or REAL	4
REAL*8 or DOUBLE PRECISION	8
COMPLEX*8 or COMPLEX	8
COMPLEX*16	16
LOGICAL*4 or LOGICAL	4
LOGICAL*1	1

Figure 17.1

17.3 DEFINING CHARACTER DATA IN DECLARATION STATEMENTS

Declaration statements may be used to initialize character variables prior to execution time. The following examples further demonstrate how character strings can be formed.

(i)   INTEGER A/'LIFE'/,B/'DOGS'/

(ii)   REAL*8 X/8HABCDEFGH/

(iii)   REAL XX(3)/'SUBC','OMMI','TTEE'/

(iv)   LOGICAL*1 Z(5)/'A','B','C','D','E'/

(v)   INTEGER N/'AB'/

(vi)   REAL*8 Q/'HORSE'/,W/'ABCDEFGHIJK'/

(vii)   REAL X(4)/4*'AB'/,Y(4)/'AB','AB','AB','AB'/

Example (i) assigns the character strings LIFE and DOGS to the integer variables A and B, respectively.

Example (ii) illustrates the use of the H-type Hollerith. Usually the quote-type Hollerith is more convenient to use.

Example (iii) illustrates how a relatively large amount of character data can be stored using

275

consecutive elements of an array. Here, the word
SUBCOMMITTEE is segmented into three strings of
four letters each, and they are assigned to the
three elements of the array XX. It is important
to note that the character data *must* be subdivided
into strings of length less than or equal to the
length of the elements in the array. Thus, the
following statement would not produce the desired
results.

REAL XX(3)/'SUBCOMMITTEE'/

It would cause an error message to be produced,
and is another example of the rule that there must
be one piece of data for every element in an array
which is being initialized.

Example (iv) declares Z to be a logical
array with five elements. Each of the elements
occupies one byte; the five elements are initialized
to the character data A, B, C, D, and E, respectively.

In Example (v), we have a situation where
there are only two characters in the string, whereas
the integer variable N is capable of storing four
characters. As has been stated in Section 17.1,
two blanks are inserted on the right. In Example
(vi), we have the opposite situation; the string has
eleven characters, and the variable can store only
eight. In such cases, the string is truncated, and
the farthest-right characters, in this case the
letters IJK, are lost.

Example (vii) illustrates the use of a
replication factor. Here the character string AB,
padded on the right with two blanks, will be repeated

four times, once for each of the elements of the array X. The array Y will be initialized to exactly the same data, but this time no replication factor is used.

17.4 INPUT-OUTPUT OF CHARACTER STRINGS

We have seen how to initialize variables with character data. If we wish to print the values of these variables and have them appear as characters, we must use the A format code. Consider Example 17.2.

```
C EXAMPLE 17.2
      INTEGER A/'CHAR'/,B/'LIE'/
      INTEGER X/2568/,Y/'2568'/
      PRINT6,A,B,X,Y
  6 FORMAT('0',A4,A4,3X,I4,3X,A4)
      STOP
      END
```

The following line would be printed, after double spacing.

```
CHARLIEbbbb2568bbb2568
  A4  A4 3X  I4 3X  A4

  A   B     X      Y
```

The format code Aw assumes that character data is stored in the variable being printed. This data is printed right justified in a field of width w. Thus the letters CHAR are printed in the first four print positions, followed by LIEb in the next four print positions. Three blanks are inserted because of the 3X code, and the integer value for X is printed using the I format code. Finally, three

277

more spaces are left, and the character string 2568
is printed using format code A4.

It would be instructive to consider the
effect of replacing the FORMAT statement in Example
17.2 with the following statement:

```
6 FORMAT('0',A3,A6,3X,I4,3X,A2)
```

In this case the line printed would be

CHAbbLIEbbbb2568bbb25
A3 A6   3X I4 3X A2

A   B   X   Y

Here the format code A3 is used to print A. Since
the field width is three, only the three farthest-left
characters stored in A are printed; the fourth
character is ignored. Thus, whenever the field
width w is less than the number of characters in
the string, only the w farthest-left characters are
printed, and the remainder are ignored.

The format code for B is A6, which means
that the field width has two more character positions
than the string stored in B. Thus, the output is
right justified in the field, with two blanks padded
on the left.

The variable Y is printed under format A2,
and once again only the farthest-left characters are
printed, as was the case for the variable A.

The A format code is also used for input.
Suppose the following sequence of statements was
executed.

```
        INTEGER A,B,C
        READ4,A,B,C
      4 FORMAT(A4,A4,A4)
```

A card would be read, and the first four columns would
be assigned to A as character data, because of the A4
format code.   Similarly, the characters in columns 5
to 8 would be stored in B, and the characters in
columns 9 to 12 would be stored in C.   Thus, if the
input data card contained the following characters
in columns 1 to 12 inclusive,

X$*AB123+9Z@

then the integer variables A, B, and C would have
assigned to them the character strings X$*A, B123
and +9Z@, respectively.

Suppose that the FORMAT statement were
replaced by

4 FORMAT(A6,A2,A4)

and the same input data card were read.   In this
case, the first six columns are considered as the
field associated with the integer variable A; since
A can store only four characters, the four farthest-
right characters in the field are assigned.   Thus A
has assigned to it the character string *AB1.

The integer variable B has its input
controlled by the format code A2.   Only a two-digit
field is involved, namely, the contents of columns
7 and 8; however, the integer variable B is capable
of storing four characters.   In this case, the two
characters are stored left justified, and blanks are
inserted on the right.   Thus, B has assigned to it

the character string 23bb.

Example 17.3 illustrates the use of the
A format code with both input and output. The
example is designed to read a deck of 50 cards, one
at a time, and output their contents on the printer.

```
C EXAMPLE 17.3
      INTEGER CARD(20)
      DO 13 I=1,50
      READ21,CARD
   21 FORMAT(20A4)
   13 PRINT22,CARD
   22 FORMAT('0',20A4)
      STOP
      END
```

The integer array CARD has 20 elements, and
each of these has assigned to it the characters
contained in four consecutive columns of the input
data card. The characters in columns 1 to 4 are
stored in CARD(1), the characters in columns 5 to
8 are stored in CARD(2), etc. Note that the format
code A4 has a field count of 20 to satisfy the
requirements of the whole array.

For each card read, a line is printed.
This line contains the entire contents of the
vector CARD, printed using the A format code. Exactly
80 print positions are used, with the result that the
contents of all 80 columns of each of the previously
read input cards are printed.

It would be appropriate to summarize the
rules for using the Aw format code.

(i) On output, if the number of characters
     stored in the string being printed is less

than the field width w, the field is padded
on the left with blanks. If the number of
characters in the string exceeds the field
width, only the w farthest-left characters are
printed to fill out the field.

(ii)   On input, if w exceeds the length
specification, s, of the variable which is
to store the string, only the s farthest-right
characters in the field are stored. If w
is less than s, the entire field is stored
left-justified in the variable, and blanks
are inserted on the right.

17.5   COMPARISON OF CHARACTER STRINGS

The previous sections were concerned with
the assignment and printing of character strings.
It is important to be able to do comparisons with
character strings, as illustrated in Example 17.4.

Example 17.4 reads a single data card
which contains an English sentence, beginning
in column one. The individual words in the sentence
may have any length, up to a maximum of ten characters.
The words are separated by single blanks, with a period
terminating the sentence. The program determines
the number of words having one letter, the number
of words having two letters, ..., the number of
words having ten letters.

```
C EXAMPLE 17.4
      INTEGER BLANK/' '/,DOT/'.'/
      INTEGER CHAR(80),COUNT(10)
      READ22,CHAR
   22 FORMAT(80A1)
      DO 1 I=1,10
    1 COUNT(I)=0
      NUMBER=0
      DO 2 I=1,80
      IF(CHAR(I).EQ.DOT)GO TO 3
      IF(CHAR(I).NE.BLANK)GO TO 4
      COUNT(NUMBER)=COUNT(NUMBER)+1
      NUMBER=0
      GO TO 2
    4 NUMBER=NUMBER+1
    2 CONTINUE
    3 COUNT(NUMBER)=COUNT(NUMBER)+1
      PRINT23,CHAR
   23 FORMAT(' ',80A1)
      PRINT24,(COUNT(I),I,I=1,10)
   24 FORMAT(' ',I3,'WORDS OF LENGTH',I3)
      STOP
      END
```

The program reads the data card, and places
each character of the sentence in a separate element
of the vector CHAR. The elements of the array COUNT
are used as word length counters, and NUMBER is used
as the character counter. All of these counters are
initialized to the value zero. A DO-loop is used to
control the scanning of the characters. The scan
consists of testing for a period or blank. For each
character in a word, unity is added to NUMBER. Each
time a blank is encountered, the appropriate element
of the array COUNT is increased by one, using the
current value of NUMBER as a subscript. Similarly,
when the period is encountered, the appropriate element
of the array COUNT is increased by one. The original
sentence and counts are then printed.

This example is useful to illustrate
several points.

The statements

```
IF(CHAR(I).EQ.DOT)GO TO 3
IF(CHAR(I).NE.BLANK)GO TO 4
```

utilize the comparison of character strings. This
is accomplished by treating the character string
which is assigned to an integer variable as if it
were an integer value; these integer variables may
then be used in arithmetic expressions and assignment
statements. Thus if CHAR(13) has the character
string .bbb assigned to it, there will be a true
result for the logical expression

```
CHAR(13).EQ.DOT
```

since the integer variable DOT has been initialized
to the character string .bbb.

Memory space could have been saved if all
variables used were declared with the INTEGER*2
statement. However, note that the program would not
work if the variables were declared with either of
the LOGICAL or LOGICAL*1 declaration statements.
This is because the expressions

```
CHAR(I).EQ.DOT
CHAR(I).NE.BLANK
```

would not be legal expressions, since logical
expressions may not be used as operands with relational
operators.

Could we have declared the variables to
be of any other type, such as REAL? The answer is
yes for Example 17.4. However, if the example were

slightly different, trouble could arise in certain relatively rare circumstances. This is because of the nature of *normalized* floating-point numbers. A random assignment of data as a character string could result in an unnormalized floating-point number.

Consequently, as a general rule, it is advisable to use integer variables to store character strings whenever these variables are to be used in comparisons or other arithmetic computations.

If a program requires no such operations, any type of variable is suitable. For example, it is usually more convenient to use variables of type COMPLEX*16 when lengthy strings are involved. For instance, the statement

        COMPLEX*16 C/'THIS IS THE DATA'/

is easier to formulate and key-punch than is

        INTEGER*4 N(4)/'THIS',' IS ','THE ','DATA'/

17.6   ALPHABETIC SORTING OF CHARACTER STRINGS

Consider the following two statements

        INTEGER X/'AAAA'/,Y/'AAAB'/
        PRINT,X,Y

The values printed for X and Y would be -1044266559 and -1044266558, respectively. If the two character strings are compared, we have the condition that X is less than Y. This is as we would like it, since AAAA precedes AAAB in alphabetical order. The character representations for all the letters have been chosen in such a way that alphabetic sequence is always reflected in such comparisons. Thus, if the integer variables X and Y each contain character data, the expression

X.LT.Y

will have the value .TRUE. if and only if the character string stored in X precedes, in alphabetical order, the character string stored in Y.

The program in Example 17.5 reads one hundred data cards, each containing a word which consists of four letters, and stores them in the vector WORD. Then it arranges them in alphabetical order.

```
C EXAMPLE 17.5
      INTEGER WORD(100)
      LOGICAL SWT
      DO 1 I=1,100
    1 READ2,WORD(I)
    2 FORMAT(A4)
      N=99
      DO 3 I=1,99
      SWT=.FALSE.
      DO 4 J=1,N
      IF(WORD(J).LE.WORD(J+1))GO TO 4
      ITEMP=WORD(J)
      WORD(J)=WORD(J+1)
      WORD(J+1)=ITEMP
      SWT=.TRUE.
    4 CONTINUE
      IF(.NOT.SWT)GO TO 5
    3 N=N-1
    5 PRINT7,WORD
    7 FORMAT('0',10A6)
      STOP
      END
```

The method used compares successive pairs of four-letter words. Two successive words are interchanged

in the vector if they are not in alphabetical
order, i.e., the first is not "less than" the
second. After the entire vector has been processed,
the last word in alphabetical order has been
"shuffled" to the end of the vector. The vector
is processed again, and, as a result, the "second-
largest" word appears in the second-last position.
After ninety-nine passes over the data in the
vector, the words are arranged in the required
order. The reader might determine the purpose
served by the logical variable SWT.

As a final note, consider Example 17.6,
which illustrates that mixed-mode comparisons
produce unexpected results.

```
C EXAMPLE 17.6
      LOGICAL L
      INTEGER A/'ABCD'/
      REAL B/'ABCD'/
      L=A.EQ.B
      PRINT,L
      STOP
      END
```

The value printed for L is F, representing false.
Since A is an integer variable, its value is
converted to a real number before the comparison
with the real variable B occurs. Thus, even though
the original character strings are identical, one
of them is changed before the comparison is made.
Hence they are not recognized as equal.

17.7 EXERCISES

17.1 Prepare a data deck which contains 40
cards, one for each of 40 students. Each
card contains the student's name and his
mark for a particular course.

(a) Write a program which reads the data
deck and prints the data.

(b) Write a program which reads the data
deck, stores the information in the
computer, and prints a list of student
names and marks in descending sequence
according to marks.

17.2 Consider a data deck of eight cards which
contain some literary text. (For example,
they could contain a poem.) Write a program
which reads all of the text, and stores it
in a one-dimensional array. The array is
then to be scanned to determine

(i) the number of non-blank characters

(ii) the number of occurrences of the
letter A

(iii) the number of words

(iv) the number of occurrences of the
word THE.

17.3 Consider a data deck of twenty cards,
each of which contains a family name of
not more than 10 letters, beginning in
column 1. This deck is in random sequence.
Write a program which reads the cards,
and stores the names in array form. As
each card is read, it should be inserted

in the array to reflect alphabetic
sequence. Thus, the position for the
new name must be determined, and all
previously stored data of higher alphabetic order must be shuffled to make room
for the new name. After all data cards
have been read, print the stored data
to check that it is in alphabetic
sequence.

17.4 (a) Write a program which prints all
           possible three-letter sequences
           involving the five letters A, C, E,
           T, and W. Print these sequences
           five-to-a-line.

      (b) Modify the program in (a) so that
           each three-letter sequence has at
           least one vowel.

17.5 Prepare a data card which contains a
      message consisting of only letters and
      blank spaces. Write a program which reads
      the message, codes it into a "secret message",
      and prints the message. Use the following
      coding rules:

      (i) Any letter is replaced by its
           successor in the alphabet. For
           example, A is replaced by B and S
           by T. The letter Z is replaced by
           A.

      (ii) Blanks are to remain unchanged.

CHAPTER 18

INPUT/OUTPUT FEATURES

The purpose of this chapter is to describe those features of FORTRAN input/output that are implemented in the WATFOR compiler. In particular, the FORTRAN statements oriented to the use of magnetic tapes for input/output of sequential files are described and illustrated.

A brief review of input/output features covered in previous chapters is included in this chapter.

18.1   FORMAT-FREE I/O

Early in Chapter 1 of this book, the reader encountered example programs which required the reading of data values or the printing of results. At that time, he was introduced to the so-called format-free input/output statements of WATFOR, some examples of which follow.

```
READ,X,A,I
READ,(B(K),K=N,M,L),T
PRINT,J,P**2,(B(I),I=1,J)
```

These are the simplest forms of I/O statements available using WATFOR, and are particularly convenient for the beginning programmer, since he need not bother himself with the more difficult FORMAT statement. These statements allow him the ability to input to the computer memory data values punched on cards, and to output values to a printer for examination.

The general form of these statements is

```
READ,list
PRINT,list
```

The 'list' is the means by which the values to be transmitted to or from memory are specified to the I/O mechanism. The list is composed of *list elements*, separated by commas; list elements may be variable names, array names with or without subscripts, or implied DO's containing any of the previous or other implied DO's.

With WATFOR, list elements in output statements may also be any FORTRAN expressions.[†]

Occasionally the programmer has need to obtain output, which is not printed, but instead is punched on cards, possibly to be used as input for another program.

The format-free statement

```
PUNCH,list
```

is available for this purpose. Since values are transmitted to be punched on 80-column cards any list items which will not fit on the first card

---

† An exception is that the expression may not start with a left parenthesis, since this signals an implied DO. Thus PRINT,(X+Y)/2. would be flagged with an error message. However, PRINT,+(X+Y)/2. is valid.

are punched on successive cards. Thus, a single
PUNCH statement may produce more than one card as
output, in the same way that a PRINT statement may
produce more than one line on the printer, if
many values are produced as output.

18.2   FORMATTED I/O

The introduction of FORMAT greatly
increased the flexibility of FORTRAN I/O since,
with it, the programmer could compose print lines
himself, and could also control the editing of
lines and the layout of values on data cards.

The forms of the statements using FORMAT
are:

```
READfmt,list
PRINTfmt,list
PUNCHfmt,list
```

where 'fmt' stands for the statement number of a
format statement which appears elsewhere in the
program. Here 'list' need not contain any elements;
if it does not, the commas are omitted. Examples
are:

```
READ 12,X,A
PRINT 784,(I,SQRT(FLOAT(I)),I=1,25)
PUNCH 13,((B(I,J),I=1,N),J=1,M)
PRINT 26
READ 43
```

18.3   GENERAL READ AND WRITE STATEMENTS

The three statements given in the previous
section provide the FORTRAN user with access to a
card reader, card punch, and printer for I/O. To

avoid the proliferation of statement types that
could occur in permitting access to other kinds of
I/O devices such as magnetic tapes, discs, or drums,
it was decided, in the course of FORTRAN's development,
that uniform input/output statements should be
designed to accommodate all devices. This decision
resulted in the design of two general statements -
one for input and one for output. Their forms are

```
        READ(unit,fmt,END=n,ERR=m)list
        WRITE(unit,fmt)list
```

Here 'unit' is called the *unit number*[†] and n and m
are statement numbers of executable statements.
Rather than explain the full significance of these
statements, we will give examples to illustrate
the various forms they may take.

The first example illustrates the usefulness of the 'END=' feature. Example 18.1 is an
attempt at a program to sum numbers punched one per
data card.

```
        C EXAMPLE 18.1 - READ LOOP
              SUM=0.
           75 READ 2,X
            2 FORMAT(F10.2)
              SUM=SUM+X
              GO TO 75
              END
```

Of course the program is faulty, since it

---

† Sometimes called the data set reference number.

loops continuously while reading cards. One might think that the program would gobble up all cards following it in the card reader - including other persons' programs. To guard against such run-away programs, the card-read mechanism includes an automatic check on the first column of each data card read; if a card is read which contains the special control character[†] that is usually on a control card signalling the start of the next job in the card reader, the program is terminated with an error message. However, a program may take advantage of this check by using the *END return* in a READ statement. Example 18.2 is a program which sums and counts an unspecified number of values, read one per card.

```
C EXAMPLE 18.2 - USES 'END=' PARAMETER
      N=0
      SUM=0.
   75 READ(5,2,END=64)X
    2 FORMAT(F10.2)
      SUM=SUM+X
      N=N+1
      GO TO 75
   64 PRINT,N,SUM
      STOP
      END
```

---

† The control cards mentioned in this book use a $ in column 1. The actual character used at an installation will become apparent the first time you run a program.

The statement

$$READ(5,2,END=64)X$$

might be paraphrased as follows: "Read X on unit
5 according to FORMAT statement 2 with automatic
transfer to statement 64 when a control character
in column 1 is read". Thus if there were seven
data cards following the program, the eighth attempt
at execution of the READ statement would cause
control to transfer directly to statement 64;
the value printed for N would be 7.

The END return has effect only upon the
READ statement it is in. The 'END' comes from the
term 'end-of-file', which will be more fully explained
in the next section.

A few words should be said about the unit
number. The unit number is used by the programmer
to specify which I/O device he wants to associate
with the I/O operation. It is usually[†] the case
that unit number 5 specifies the standard card
reader, and unit numbers 6 and 7 specify the standard
printer and standard punch respectively. Under such
circumstances, the statements

$$READ2,X,A$$
$$READ(5,2)X,A$$

are exactly equivalent, as are

[†] Some installations prefer other numbers for
standard reader, printer, punch units. You
should check before running a program.

```
                    PRINT 25,Y
                    WRITE(6,25)Y
and
                    PUNCH 16,Z**2+3.
                    WRITE(7,16)Z**2+3.
```

WATFOR's format-free versions of READ, PRINT, and PUNCH also use the standard units.

The unit number in the general I/O statements may, in fact, be an integer variable name; for example,

```
            READ(I,25)X,Y
```

Example 18.3 shows part of a program which gives symbolic names to the standard units; this makes it very easy to change the program if it is to be used at an installation with different standard unit numbers.

```
        C EXAMPLE 18.3 - VARIABLE UNITS
                INTEGER READER/5/,PRNTER/6/,PUNCH/7/
                READ(READER,25)X,Y
                -
                -
                -
                WRITE(PRNTER,78)A,B
                -
                -
                -
                WRITE(PUNCH,204)(Z(I),I=1,5)
                -
                -
                -
                END
```

18.4   MAGNETIC TAPE CHARACTERISTICS

The previous section showed that the value of an integer variable could be used to specify a unit number. Are there units other than 5, 6, and 7, and devices other than card readers, printers, and punches, available to the FORTRAN programmer?

The answer to this question depends on the computer installation whose services the programmer uses. Usually it is safe to say that other unit numbers may be used to perform I/O on magnetic tape drives. Tapes are extremely useful for manipulating large volumes of data, because of their speed and data storage capacities. Magnetic tapes provide an extension of the memory capacity of the computer, and may be used by the FORTRAN programmer to store intermediate results of calculations for later use, or as data input or output media. Their use permits the convenient interchange of data between different programs or even different computers.

Since methods of doing I/O on magnetic tapes are somewhat different from methods used with the other devices mentioned so far, a brief description of magnetic tape characteristics is now given.

A computer tape drive is much like a conventional tape recorder, in that a long thin ribbon of oxide-coated plastic material, wound on a reel mountable on the drive, may have information recorded on it in the form of magnetic impressions. The recording takes place by moving the tape past a stationary read/write head on the tape drive while data is transmitted to the head from the computer memory. (This movement is accomplished by winding up the tape on one reel, while allowing it to play off another reel.) Information that

has previously been recorded may be read back into
the computer memory by repositioning the tape so
that the data to be read again move past the read/
write head, this time with the tape drive instructed
to read instead of to write. Material previously
recorded may at any time be destroyed by over-writing
with new data, i.e., the tapes can be used many times.

Reading or writing of the tape takes
place in one direction only, and, at the completion
of an I/O operation, the tape comes to a stop. It
is not possible to read a tape 'backwards' in
FORTRAN, although some modern tape drives allow this
possibility. Hence, instructions must be given to
position the tape to the proper place with respect
to the read/write head before attempting to read
or overwrite previously written information. There
are special FORTRAN statements to control the backward
movement of the tape, as will be seen shortly.

Near the beginning and end of the tape,
there are special markers to indicate the limits
between which recording can be done. The tape drive
can sense these marks, and the one at the beginning
is used to indicate where the first recorded
information starts; the one at the end serves
to prevent the accidental writing of information
beyond the end of the tape.

This description, although it ignores all
the details of the actual recording and the physical
characteristics of any tape drives, should be
sufficient to understand the examples which follow.

18.5 SEQUENTIAL FILES

Example 18.4 is a simple program which illustrates the use of a tape unit. It merely reads in the elements of vector A, punched on cards, and copies them onto the tape on the drive associated with unit number 3.

```
C EXAMPLE 18.4 - WRITING ON TAPE
      DIMENSION A(25)
      REWIND3
      READ(5,27)A
   27 FORMAT(8F10.2)
      WRITE(3)A
      STOP
      END
```

The statement REWIND3 is a new statement. Its effect is to position the tape to the starting marker, so that the first recording on the tape will be in a known fixed position. Failure to do this almost always leads to trouble. If the tape is already in this *rewound* position, the statement has no effect. The programmer should not assume that for his job the tape is in the rewound position since the computer operator who mounts the tape on the drive may not have put it in the rewound position. It is wise to rewind a tape before doing any I/O with it.

Notice that the statement WRITE(3)A contains no reference to a format; the elements of the vector A are transmitted directly to tape unit 3 in the form in which they are stored within the computer. This method of output is termed *writing without format control*, and is the most efficient way of recording data on a tape in terms of both time and space.

The amount of data transmitted by a WRITE statement is called a *logical record* or *record* for brevity. The size of a record, when writing without format control, is determined by the number and lengths of all list elements transmitted. For Example 18.4, the record consists of 25 computer words or 100 bytes.

Example 18.5 shows that it is possible to have records of varying sizes written on a tape; the number of elements of the vector X written each time is not necessarily the same.

```
C EXAMPLE 18.5 - VARYING RECORD LENGTHS
      DIMENSION X(100),Y(100)
      REWIND2
   42 READ(5,63,END=4)N
   63 FORMAT(I3)
      READ43,(X(I),I=1,N)
   43 FORMAT(8F10.3)
      WRITE(2) N,(X(I),I=1,N)
      GO TO 42
    4 BACKSPACE 2
      READ(2)M,(Y(I),I=1,M)
      STOP
      END
```

The program loops reading various vectors from the card reader, and, for each vector, writes the number of elements and the vector on tape 2. When the data cards are exhausted, control transfers to statement numbered 4, namely, BACKSPACE 2. The BACKSPACE statement works something like REWIND, in that tape 2 is moved backwards, but only past the *last* logical record written. Thus, the READ statement following statement 4 effectively reads a copy of N and the N elements of the last vector recorded on tape 2 into variable M and the first M elements of vector Y, respectively.

We can always get to the first record on a tape by doing a REWIND; we can always back up one record by doing a BACKSPACE. A BACKSPACE has no effect if the tape is already rewound.

Example 18.5 potentially writes numerous records on tape. The total collection of records recorded on a particular tape is called a *file*[†]. Specifically, a file on tape is called a *sequential file* since there is an implied ordering to the records. Thus, if the tape is rewound, to read the twelfth record, for example, records one to eleven must be skipped over. This is in contrast to the random order in which records may be retrieved from or written on a direct-access device such as a disc or drum.

It is the usual convention to follow the last record of a sequential file by a special character called an *end-of-file mark* which the tape drive can sense. This is to guard against any attempt to read more information than has been recorded in the file. The statement ENDFILE2 will write an end-of-file mark at the current position of the tape on unit 2.

The reader might guess that the END return of the READ statement may be used to gain control

---

† Sometimes called a data set.

300

when the end-of-file mark is sensed while reading
a sequential file.   Example 18.6 illustrates this.
The program reads various vectors from a tape on
unit 3, and writes them alternately on units 1 and 2;
it repeats this procedure until the end-of-file mark is
sensed on tape 3.   Then tape 3 is rewound, and the
records of tape 1 are copied onto 3, followed by
the records of tape 2.   An end-of-file mark is written
on 3 so that the data on it can be used again.

```
      C EXAMPLE 18.6 - END RETURN FOR TAPE
            DIMENSION X(100)
            REWIND2
            REWIND1
            REWIND3
            J=2
         58 READ(3,ERR=19,END=25)N,(X(I),I=1,N)
            J=J-J/2*2+1
            WRITE(J)N,(X(I),I=1,N)
            GO TO 58
         25 ENDFILE2
            ENDFILE1
            DO 99 J=1,3
         99 REWINDJ
          2 READ(1,END=43,ERR=19)N,(X(I),I=1,N)
            WRITE(3)N,(X(I),I=1,N)
            GO TO 2
         43 READ(2,ERR=19,END=8)N,(X(I),I=1,N)
            WRITE(3)N,(X(I),I=1,N)
            GO TO 43
         19 WRITE(6,61)
         61 FORMAT(' ERROR WHILE READING TAPE')
          8 ENDFILE3
            STOP
            END
```

The READ statements show examples of the
ERR return used to gain control if an I/O device-
error occurs while in the process of reading a

record. This problem can arise occasionally with
tapes,if dust or smoke particles adhere to the
recording surface. If the ERR return were not
present and an I/O error occurred, the program
would be terminated by the compiler. Note that
the positions of the END and ERR returns are
interchangeable if both are present.

The general forms of the tape control
statements are

```
        REWIND i
        BACKSPACE i
        ENDFILE i
```

where i is an integer constant or variable name
representing the unit number.

It is entirely possible to read less
information than has been written in a record,as
the following example will show.

```
C EXAMPLE 18.7 - READING LESS THAN RECORD SIZE
      DIMENSION A(100),I(25),C(10,10)
      COMPLEX*8 D(40)
      READ(5,3)A
    3 FORMAT(8F10.2)
      REWIND1
      WRITE(1)A
      REWIND1
    4 READ(1)X,I
      BACKSPACE1
    5 READ(1)D
      BACKSPACE1
    6 READ(1)C
      STOP
      END
```

The one hundred elements of vector A are
read from cards and written on tape unit 1. This

single record of size 400 bytes is then read by
three different READ statements.

The READ statement numbered 4 places the
first 4 bytes of the record into variable X and
the next 100 bytes into the 25 elements of integer
vector I.   The remaining 296 bytes of the record
are ignored.   The READ statement 5 places the
first 320 bytes of the record into the 40 elements
of the complex vector D.   Thus alternate elements
of A become real and imaginary parts of elements
of D.   Again, the last 80 bytes of the record are
ignored.   The READ statement 6 places the entire
record, by columns, into the 100 elements of matrix
C.

This example emphasizes that the data are
recorded on tape in the exact form in which they are
stored.   When data are retrieved from a record,
as many bytes as required to fill a list item are
moved directly from the record to the memory locations
occupied by the list item.   Thus it is the programmer's
responsibility to ensure that data of type appropriate
for his requirements are read into the variable;
otherwise, erroneous results may be obtained.   The
programmer should be aware of the contents, sizes,
and relative positions of the records he has placed
on a file.

It is, in fact, possible to have a READ
statement with no list, and this is handy for skipping
records in a forward direction.   For example, the
statements

```
          DO 28 I=1,10
       28 READ(4)
```

will skip over 10 records since each execution of
the READ causes the tape drive to read a record;
however, the information in it is ignored.

It is *not* possible to read more
information than has been written in a record.

By convention, records written on tape
must be at least 16 bytes long. This guards
against the accidental acceptance of small stray
magnetic impressions on a tape as valid information;
a record of less than 16 bytes is called a *noise
record*.

To review the ideas given above, consider
Figure 18.1. A program has written m logical
records, followed by an end-of-file mark, on unit
2; has rewound the tape; and has since read three
records. The arrow indicates the current position
of the tape with respect to the read/write head.
(Direction of tape movement for reading or writing
is assumed to be from right to left.)

| | Record1 | Record2 | Record3 | Record4 | Record5 | | Recordm | |

Figure 18.1

The tape is now in a position so that
record 4 may be read, or a new record may be written
over old record 4. If it were desired to read
record 2 back into memory, the tape would first
have to be repositioned by backspacing twice. If
the programmer wishes to skip record 4 and read
record 5, he could execute a READ with no list.

Note that if a file currently contains
m records, numbered from 1 to m, and the
programmer writes a new record j with j<m, he *must*
assume that the file now has only j records and that
records j+1, j+2, ..., m,are no longer accessible.
For Figure 18.1, if the programmer wrote a new
record 4, he has, for all purposes, made records 5,
6, 7, ..., m, along with old record 4, unavailable.

18.6   SEQUENTIAL FILES WITH FORMAT CONTROL

It is also possible to read and write
sequential files *with format control* by including
a reference to a FORMAT statement in the I/O
statement.   Thus

```
     WRITE(2,78)X,Y,Z
  78 FORMAT(F10.2,2E16.7)
```

would write the values of X, Y,and Z onto the tape
on unit 2 according to the formats specified.   The
same record could be read by a statement such as

```
     READ(2,78,END=12,ERR=45)A,B,C
```

The records written with format control
resemble the printer lines that would be created
if the unit number had been that of the standard
printer, except that the first character of each
line is not treated as a carriage control,but is
actually written on the tape.   This is important
to consider if the file is ever to be listed on a
printer.

Sequential files written with format
control are not normally used for storing inter-

mediate results of a program since considerable
computer time is involved in converting values
from internal form to that specified by FORMAT.

For records written without format
control, the record size was specified by the total
size of all the I/O list elements. When writing
with format control, records are written onto tape
under the control of the FORMAT statement in the
same way that format codes control the generation
of printer lines.

To avoid confusion with the logical records
of the previous section, records written with format
control are often referred to as *FORTRAN records*.
Thus, the following statement would write three
separate FORTRAN records on tape 4, since there is
no field count for the E format code.

```
        WRITE(4,23)X,Y,Z
     23 FORMAT(E20.6)
```

These records could be read by one, two,
or three separate READ statements: thus

```
        READ(4,23)A,B,C
```

or
```
        READ(4,23)A,B
        READ(4,23)C
```

or
```
        READ(4,23)A
        READ(4,23)B
        READ(4,23)C
```

Two FORTRAN records would be written if the FORMAT
statement were changed to

```
     23 FORMAT(2E20.6)
```

Note that printer lines and data cards are examples of FORTRAN records. Records written with and without FORMAT control may be written on the same file,but this is risky because of the different nature of logical and FORTRAN records and the different ways in which the information is recorded. Records written without FORMAT control should not be read with FORMAT control,and vice versa. In addition, BACKSPACE works differently since it backspaces one *FORTRAN* record.

18.7 CONCLUDING REMARKS

As the reader should be aware, much care and organization is needed when working with sequential files on tape in order to use them properly and effectively. More could be said about techniques (e.g.,buffering, blocking) which tend to increase the efficiency of programs which use sequential files. The previous sections have merely covered the details of the FORTRAN statements available to the programmer; he should now be able to try his hand at programs using these ideas.

Many details are left unmentioned since they are beyond the scope of this book. For example, the total number of units available to the programmer is an installation decision. What happens if the statement sequence WRITE,ENDFILE,WRITE,is executed? Can files be stored on discs or drums rather than on tapes? How is the actual connection made between the logical idea of a file and a particular physical I/O device? Suffice it to say that the answers to

these questions lie in mechanisms external to the
FORTRAN program, and usually need not be known by
the beginning programmer.

Anyone planning to make considerable use
of tapes and files is well advised to consult the
manuals relating to the operating system in use at
his computer installation. For example, the answers
to the questions posed above may be found in the
IBM manual "FORTRAN IV(G) Programmer's Guide".

18.8 EXERCISES

Prepare a data deck which contains 50
cards, one for each of 50 students. Each card
contains a student's name and number, together
with his marks in each of 6 particular courses.
If no mark is available for a particular course,
the corresponding field is punched with zeros.
The deck is in student-number sequence.

18.1 Write a program which reads this data
deck, writes it onto a tape, rewinds
the tape, and prints it for verification
purposes. Thus, this tape, which we will
call the Student Master File, has a record
for each student, and is in student-number
sequence.

18.2 Write a program which reads the Student
Master File created in Exercise 18.1, and
computes the number of students who have
passed each course. Assume a pass mark
to be 50 or more.

18.3 Write a program which reads the Student

Master File and computes the average for each student. A new Student Master File should be written to record the average for each student, along with the rest of the data.

18.4 Assume that additional marks become available to update a student's record (recall that some of the marks were missing). Devise a program which reads data cards, in student-number sequence, and uses the new information to update the Student Master File. Note that a new file must be written.

18.5 Suppose a new student joins the class. Write a program which will insert the new student's record into the Student Master File. Note that his student number could be such that his record is not necessarily at the end of the Student Master File. (Recall that the master file is recorded in student-number sequence.)

18.6 Suppose a similar Student Master File is available for another class, the members of which take the same six subjects. Suppose further that it is our wish to *merge* the two files to create one new Student Master File which contains the records of all the students in sequence, by student number. Write a program to accomplish this.

CHAPTER 19

ADVANCED FORMAT

Various format codes have been introduced throughout this book as they were required. This chapter introduces some specialized format codes and some techniques that simplify the writing of FORMAT statements. The final section discusses a means of constructing or modifying format codes at execution time.

Although most of the examples in this chapter are illustrated by referring to punched cards for input and printed lines for output, the concepts apply to FORTRAN records read or written on any sequential file.

19.1 G FORMAT

The G format code is a generalized code which can be used to transmit (input or output) integer, real, complex, or logical values. Example 19.1 demonstrates the use of the G code for both input and output.

```
C EXAMPLE 19.1 - DEMONSTRATE G FORMAT
      LOGICAL L
      COMPLEX C
      REAL*8 BIG
      READ10,A,L,C,BIG
   10 FORMAT(4G8.4,G15.8)
      I=321
      PRINT96,A,L,C,I,BIG
   96 FORMAT(' ',3G9.2,G9.3,G4,G12.5)
      STOP
      END
```

If the following data card were supplied,

b150.0bbbbbTbbbbbb.0256bbb150.0E0bbb-.75632946D4

G8.4	G8.4	G8.4	G8.4	G15.8
A	L	C		BIG

the line printed would be

b0.15Eb03bbbbbbbbbTb0.26E-01b150.bbbbb321b-7563.3bbbb

| G9.2 | G9.2 | G9.2 | G9.3 | G4 | G12.5 |

Note that the same result could have been obtained if the FORMAT statements used were

```
   10 FORMAT(F8.4,L8,F8.4,E8.4,D15.8)
   96 FORMAT(' ',E9.2,L9,E9.2,F5.0,4X,I4,F8.1,4X)
```

The example illustrates that the G format code can be used in place of the F, E, D, I, or L codes. The .d portion of Gw.d may be omitted for integer and logical values, and is ignored if present.

For input, the rules for the G code are the same as those for the individual codes F, E, D, I, and L; the type of the variable and the form of the number punched on the card determine which set of rules apply.

For output, integer and logical values are printed according to the rules for I and L codes, respectively. For real values, the d of Gw.d specifies the number of *significant* digits to be printed, and is also used to determine whether the value is to be printed with or without an exponent. If the magnitude of a value x is in the range $.1 \leq x < 10^d$, d significant digits are printed with a decimal point in the proper place; in such cases, the exponent is zero, and it is replaced by four blanks. If x is not in the range just specified, the rules for Ew.d or Dw.d are used, depending on the length (4 or 8 bytes) of the value. For complex values, this rule applies to the real and imaginary parts individually. It is wise to have $w \geq d + 7$ in order to have space in the field in case the exponent is to be printed.

19.2 Z FORMAT

The format code Zw is used to transmit data in hexadecimal form, as Example 19.2 shows.

```
C EXAMPLE 19.2 - Z FORMAT
      INTEGER*2 J
      J=28
      X=28.
      WRITE(6,43)J,J,X,X
   43 FORMAT(' ',I3,4X,Z4,F6.1,Z10)
```

The output of this example is the line

```
b28bbbb001Cbb28.0bb421C0000
  I3   4X  Z4   F6.1    Z10

   J        J    X       X
```

The field 001C is the hexadecimal coding of the
sixteen-bit binary integer number contained in the
half-word of memory that the variable J occupies.
Similarly, 421C0000 is the hexadecimal representation
of the contents of the word that the real variable
X occupies. Since a word, or four bytes, is the
equivalent of eight hexadecimal digits, the last
field printed has been padded on the left with two
blanks to make up the requested printer field of
width 10.

Thus the Z format code allows the programmer
to examine the actual bit configuration that the
computer uses to store a value. On input, it may be
used to set up special bit patterns in memory.

The rules for the Zw code are:

(i) On output, if the number of hexadecimal
     digits - 2, 4, 8, 16, 32, for a value of
     length 1, 2, 4, 8, 16, bytes, respectively -
     is less than the field width w, the field
     is padded on the left with blanks. If the
     number of hexadecimal digits is greater
     than w, only the w farthest-right digits are
     printed.

(ii) On input, leading, embedded, and trailing
     blanks in the input field of width w are
     treated as zeros. If w exceeds the number n
     of hexadecimal digits corresponding to the

number of bytes occupied by the variable,
the farthest-right digits of the input field
are used; if w is less than n, the input field
is padded on the left with the hexadecimal
digit 0. Only the hexadecimal digits

0, 1, 2, 3, 4, 5, 6, 7, 8, 9,
A, B, C, D, E, F, or blanks

may appear in the input field.

19.3   T FORMAT

The T format code simplifies the
construction of FORMAT statements in which the
positioning of fields in the print line is important.
The code Tw used on output does not itself print
anything, but specifies that the next field to be
printed is to start in position w of the FORTRAN
record. In this respect, its action is similar to
that of a 'tab-stop' on a typewriter.
Example 19.3 illustrates how the T format
code may be used.

```
C EXAMPLE 19.3 - T FORMAT
      X=J=10
      PRINT16,J,X
   16 FORMAT(' ',T14,'J=',I2,T38,'X=',F4.1)
```

The line printed is

```
    J=10                    X=10.0
    ↑                       ↑
    printer column 13       printer column 37
```

The code T14 specifies that the next field is to start in position 14 of the record. For printer output, this corresponds to column 13, since the first character in the record is used as the printer control character.

Since the T format code specifies where in the record the next field is to start, the codes in a FORMAT statement do not necessarily have to be given in a left-to-right order. Thus, the same printer line would have resulted from the use of the statement

```
16 FORMAT(T16,I2,T38,'X=',T1,' ',T40,F4.1,T14,'J=')
```

Although it is not normal to 'tab' backwards, as in the above example, this is sometimes done to achieve special effects. Example 19.4 shows how a high-order zero can be inserted in a field.

```
C EXAMPLE 19.4 - USE OF T FORMAT
      X=50.01
      L=K=50
      M=J=1
      WRITE(6,7)K,J,L,M,X
    7 FORMAT(' $  .00',T3,I2,T6,I2,4X,'$',I2,'.',
     *        I2,4X,'$',F5.2)
```

The values of L, M, and X are printed for comparison; the resulting line is

$50.01 $50. 1 $50.01

This effect is achieved in the following way. In composing the record, WATFOR first moves the Hollerith string specified by ' $ .00' to the first seven positions of a temporary area in memory,

315

called a *buffer*. The field for K is tabbed to
position 3, and the characters 50 overwrite, in
the buffer, the two blanks which were in positions
three and four. The field for J is tabbed to
position 6, but only the non-blank characters are
moved into the buffer. Thus the first zero
following the decimal point remains in the buffer,
but the second zero is overwritten with the value,
1, of J. The other Hollerith strings and the
fields for L, M and X are also moved into the
buffer. When the end of the FORMAT statement is
reached, the record is transmitted from the buffer
to the printer for printing.

Note that care must be taken, when T format
is used as above, to ensure that only the desired
fields are overwritten.

On input, the code Tw indicates that the
next field starts in position w of the input record.
(e.g., column w of a data card). Example 19.5 shows
how columns 61 to 80 of a data card may be read
'twice' as alphabetic data into different variables
with different format codes.

```
C EXAMPLE 19.5 - T FORMAT ON INPUT
      LOGICAL*1 COL1(20)
      INTEGER COL4(5)
      READ(5,2)COL1,COL4
    2 FORMAT(T61,20A1,T61,5A4)
```

19.4   THE SLASH (/) FORMAT CODE

The / format code is used to indicate
the end of one FORTRAN record and the start of a

316

new one. This means, for example, that more than
one printer line can be described by a single
FORMAT statement.

Example 19.6 shows how the / code may be
used to produce multi-record formats.

```
C EXAMPLE 19.6 - USE OF '/'
      A=16.
      B=25.
      I=35
      J=17
      PRINT9,A,I,J,B
    9 FORMAT(' ','NOTE'/' ',F7.0,I3/'0',I2,F6.1)
```

The output is

```
        NOTE
        bbbb16.b35

        17bb25.0
```

The / following the string NOTE indicates
that the end of the first record (print line) has
been reached, and that a new record is to be started
for any values that remain to be printed. Thus, the
values of A and I are printed on the second line,
according to the codes F7.0 and I3, respectively.
The / which follows I3 again indicates that a new
record is to be started for any values remaining to
be printed, namely, J and B. Note that a printer
control character is given at the start of each
record.

Consecutive slashes may be used, with
the result that blank records are inserted in the
output. If the FORMAT statement of Example 19.6
were changed to

```
      9 FORMAT(' ','NOTE'///' ',F7.0,I3/'0',I2,F6.1//)
```

the output would be

```
                              NOTE
           2 blank lines {
                              bbbb16.b35
           1 blank line  {
                              17bb25.0
           2 blank lines {
```

       The rule is that n consecutive slashes
at the beginning or end of a FORMAT statement cause
n blank records to be produced; n consecutive slashes
within the statement cause n-1 blank records to be
produced.

       The / code can be used on input to skip
to new records, to read some values, or to skip whole
records entirely. Example 19.7 reads A and B from
the first card, C from the second card, D from the
fourth card; furthermore, cards five and six
are skipped entirely.

```
      C EXAMPLE 19.7 - '/' ON INPUT
            READ(5,2)A,B,C,D
          2 FORMAT(2E15.7/F4.2//E9.1//)
```

       If the read statement were

```
          READ(1,2)A,B,C,D
```

values of A and B would be obtained from the first
record of the sequential file on unit 1, C from the
second record, D from the fourth record. Records
three, five, and six would be skipped entirely;

318

a subsequent read on unit 1 would input the seventh record on the file.

19.5 GROUP COUNTS

In the same way in which a field count allows a single format code to be repeated a number of times, a *group count* allows a collection of codes to be repeated. Example 19.8 illustrates the use of a group count.

```
C EXAMPLE 19.8 - GROUP COUNT
      REAL X(3)/-1.,0.,+1./
      PRINT10,(L,X(L),L=1,3)
10 FORMAT(' ',3(I3,F4.0);
```

The output is the line

$$\underbrace{bb1}_{I3}\underbrace{b-1.}_{F4.0}\underbrace{bb2}_{I3}\underbrace{bb0.}_{F4.0}\underbrace{bb3}_{I3}\underbrace{bb1.}_{F4.0}$$

The format codes to be repeated - I3, F4.0 - are enclosed in parentheses following the group count 3. Note that the same result could have been achieved with the FORMAT statement

```
10 FORMAT(' ',I3,F4.0,I3,F4.0,I3,F4.0)
```

If a group count is not specified, it is assumed to be 1. Thus the following statements are equivalent.

```
FORMAT((2I5,1X,3F4.2))
FORMAT(1(2I5,1X,3F4.2))
FORMAT(I5,I5,1X,F4.2,F4.2,F4.2)
```

The following are sample statements which
contain group counts.

```
 (i) FORMAT('0',I5,3(F6.1,'*',I3),F8.3/' ',6(2I4,I7))
 (ii) FORMAT(' ',2(I6,F4.0,3G6),4(I2//(F7.0,2Z10)),I2)
(iii) FORMAT('-',3(2G14.5,2(I1,I3)))
```

Statements (ii) and (iii) show grouped format codes
nested to the maximum allowed depth of 2.

Example 19.9 shows what happens if the
end of a FORMAT statement is reached before all
variables in the list have been processed. The
example reads an integer value N from the first
data card, followed by N real numbers punched 8 per
card. Assume N≤100.

```
      C EXAMPLE 19.9
            DIMENSION X(100)
            READ(5,3)N,(X(I),I=1,N)
          3 FORMAT(I3/(8F10.4))
```

The READ statement and FORMAT statement
work together as follows. The READ statement causes
the first card to be read. The FORMAT statement
specifies that the value of N is in columns 1 to 3
of the card. The / code indicates the end of the
current record, and the next data card is obtained.
Eight real values are taken from that card, and the
end of the FORMAT statement is reached. If N is
greater than 8, more values must be obtained, and
the next card is read. Control returns within the
FORMAT statement to the group count (here assumed
to be 1) preceding the left parenthesis which encloses
the code 8F10.4. If the end of the FORMAT statement

is reached again, and all values have still not been read, the process repeats.

Note that this effect is considerably different from what would occur for the statement

3 FORMAT(I3/8F10.4)

In fact, the latter statement would result in an error if used with the READ statement of Example 19.9 if N were greater than 8.

The rules which apply to the use of group counts follow:

(i)   Groups of format codes may be nested to a maximum depth of two. Thus, the following statement is in error.

FORMAT(3(2F4.2,2(I2,I6,4(I5,2X))))

(ii)   If the closing right parenthesis of the FORMAT statement is reached before all items in the I/O list have been processed, a new record is started and (a) control returns in the FORMAT statement to the group count associated with the left parenthesis that corresponds to the second last right parenthesis, or (b) control returns to the first code of the FORMAT statement if there are no group counts.

Some pictorial examples follow.

(i)   FORMAT(...2(...)...3(...)...)

(ii)   FORMAT(...(..2(..).)..2(...2(...)..))

(iii)   FORMAT(...)

321

19.6 SCALE FACTORS

If the reader has run many programs on the computer, he may be somewhat frustrated by the fact that discrepancies occasionally arise when calculations are done which involve real numbers with decimal fractions. For example

        PRINT,1./3.+1./3.+1./3.

produces the result 0.9999999E 00.

These problems arise because of the inaccuracy which results from the conversion of decimal fractions to hexadecimal floating-point numbers for the computer's internal use.

Although these discrepancies can usually be ignored, they can be annoying when the programmer is working on a problem that requires complete accuracy of results, for example, an accounting problem involving money and requiring accuracy to the nearest cent.

The programmer might consider doing all calculations using integer arithmetic, but this might prove inconvenient for several reasons. For example, the precision of integer values is not as great as that of double-precision values. Or it might prove bothersome to key-punch data as, for example, 345, when a notation such as 3.45 might be desired.

The use of *scale factors* in FORMAT statements can aid the programmer in the following way. A value for a real variable can be punched as, say, 3.45 on a data card, but can be read in and used in the computer as the value 345., free of any decimal

fraction. Similarly, on output, the number can be
scaled down to re-appear with a decimal fraction.
Example 19.10 is a simple illustration of this idea.

```
C EXAMPLE 19.10 - SIMPLE P-SCALING
      READ2,X
    2 FORMAT(-2PF4.2)
      PRINT3,X,X
    3 FORMAT(' ',F6.2,2X,-2PF4.2)
```

If the input card contains the value 3.45
punched in columns 1 to 4, the output line appears
as follows:

$$345.00bb3.45$$

F6.2 2X -2PF4.2

The value of X used *internally* in the computer is
345.; its value *externally* can appear as 3.45; the
scaling factor -2P, applied to the F format codes,
takes care of the conversion automatically.

The general form of the P code is sP,
where s is an unsigned or negatively signed constant;
for example,

-2P , 3P , 0P

It usually precedes a format code used for real
values; for example,

-2PD14.2 , 0PE14.7 , 1P3F6.2

The number 3 appearing between the P and F in the
last example is a field count for the F code.

The conversion effected by the scale
factor sP is described by the rule

$$\text{external number} = 10^S \times \text{internal value}$$

The result is that X is assigned the value 345.
when the data field 3.45 is read with format code
-2PF4.2; however, X re-appears printed as 3.45
when scaled by -2PF4.2.

A somewhat more complicated example shows
that P-scaling might be put to use in an accounting-
type application.

Example 19.11 reads a number of data cards,
each containing two values which represent the number
of hours worked in a week by an employee and his
hourly rate. The program calculates each employee's
weekly gross pay, and accumulates the total gross pay
for all the employees.

```
C EXAMPLE 19.11 - PAY CALCULATION
      INTEGER PAY,SUM
      PRINT18
   18 FORMAT('1',T4,'HOURS',T15,'RATE',T25,'GROSS PAY')
      SUM=0
   11 READ(5,15,END=25)HOURS,RATE
   15 FORMAT(-2PF5.2,4X,-2PF4.2)
      PAY=(IFIX(HOURS)*IFIX(RATE)+50)/100
      PRINT16,HOURS,RATE,FLOAT(PAY)
   16 FORMAT(' ',T4,-2PF5.2,T15,-2PF4.2,T25,'$*********'
     *       ,T25,-2PF10.2)
      SUM=SUM+PAY
      GO TO 11
   25 PRINT17,FLOAT(SUM)
   17 FORMAT('0TOTAL GROSS PAY',T25,'$*********',
     *        T25,-2PF10.2)
      STOP
      END
```

Some sample output follows

```
HOURS          RATE        GROSS PAY
40.00          3.50        $***140.00
25.00          1.99        $****49.75
41.00          3.00        $***123.00
45.50          2.55        $***116.03

TOTAL GROSS PAY            $***428.78
```

The data card for the first employee would be punched, starting in column 1, as

    40.00bbbb3.50

The data cards for all other employees would be punched in a similar manner.

Note that the pay is calculated as an integer value rounded to the nearest cent. The built-in function IFIX is used to give the integer values corresponding to real values HOURS and RATE, and the values of PAY and SUM are changed to real values using the built-in function FLOAT. These latter values are scaled to have two decimal places for printing.

Several examples which show the effect of P-scaling on input follow:

Format Code	External Number as Input	Internal Value
-2PF5.2	26.73	2673.
2PF5.2	26.73	.2673
3PF11.2	26532000.	26532.
0PF5.1	46.5	46.5
2PE8.2	76.58E2	7658.
2PE10.2	7658.	76.58

The last two examples show that P-scaling on input applies *only* to F-style numbers, that is, real numbers without an E or D exponent.

P-scaling on output applies to any real value, whether written in F, E, D, or G format. Examples of output follow:

Format Code	Internal Value	External Number as Output
2PE12.3	76532.	76.532E 03
-3PE12.6	76532.	0.000765E 08
3PF9.0	76532.	76532000.
-2PG9.2	76532.	0.00E 07

There is one other property of the P format code that remains to be explained. A scale factor, once encountered in a particular FORMAT statement, applies to all F, E, D, and G codes which are subsequently encountered in the same statement, unless the P-scale is replaced with another scale factor. This means that the following two statements are equivalent.

```
FORMAT(-2PF5.2,4X,-2PF4.1)
FORMAT(-2PF5.2,4X,F4.1)
```

A scale factor 0P can be used to cancel the effect of any previous scale factor. For example, in the statement

```
FORMAT(-3PF7.3,4PE17.6,0PF5.2,F3.0)
```

the codes F5.2 and F3.0 are not affected by any scale factor.

19.7 EXECUTION-TIME FORMAT

As has been seen, programs of a very general nature can be written using the FORTRAN language. For example, a program can be prepared that will calculate the over-all average mark for a class of virtually any size, and in which any student takes virtually any number of courses. The program could read in, as data, the number of students, a record of the number of courses that each student takes, and his mark in each course. An additional degree of flexibility could be obtained by using an integer variable as a unit number in certain READ statements of the program. In this way, the data to be processed could be stored either on cards or on tape; the value of the unit number to be used could be read in as a parameter to the program.

One degree of inflexibility does exist, however. Once the program has been compiled, any data to be used with the program must conform to the format specifications, present in the program, that will be used to read or print the data. This means that if the data are not punched in a compatible form, the FORMAT statements of the program have to be revised and the program has to be re-compiled.

To avoid this undesirable possibility, a facility has been included in the FORTRAN language to allow format specifications to be read into the computer, as alphabetic data, at execution time. This, in essence, allows a suitable FORMAT statement to be composed after the data have been punched; both the data and the format codes to read them can be fed into the computer at execution time, with no modification of the program.

Example 19.12 illustrates this idea of *execution-time format* or *variable format.*

```
C EXAMPLE 19.12 - VARIABLE FORMAT
      DIMENSION VEC(15),X(100)
      READ(5,2)VEC
    2 FORMAT(15A4)
      READ(5,VEC)N,(X(I),I=1,N)
      .
      .
      .
```

The first READ statement reads in all 15 elements of the array VEC, using the A format code. The second READ statement contains the name of the array VEC in place of a FORMAT statement number. The result is that, at execution time, the characters stored in the array VEC are decoded as format specifications, and these are used to read N and the first N elements of X. The character data read into the array VEC look exactly like any FORMAT statement, except that the word FORMAT does not precede the parenthesized list of codes. For example, the data card for VEC might be

$$(I3/(E14.7,2X,3F10.2/6F8.4))$$

Note that the format list could be at most 60 characters long (including the outer parentheses), since VEC has dimension 15. This number was chosen only for illustration, and could be changed to suit the programmer.

An execution-time format must be stored in an array, even if the array consists of only one element, and the array name may be used in any I/O statement in place of a FORMAT statement number. Valid statements are

```
      WRITE(I,VEC)P,Q,R
      READ(3,FMT,END=12,ERR=2)(Y(I),I=1,N)
      PRINTARRAY,A,B,C,D
```

where VEC, FMT, Y, and ARRAY are arrays.

A final example will show that execution-time formats can, in fact, be constructed and modified by the program, i.e., they need not be read in.

```
C EXAMPLE 19.13 - VARIABLE FORMAT
      REAL A(10,10)
      INTEGER DIGIT(10)/'1','2','3','4','5','6',
     *      '7','8','9','10'/
      INTEGER VF(4)/'(1H0','    ','F12.','6)' /
      READ,N
      .
      .
      .
      VF(2)=DIGIT(N)
      WRITE(6,VF)((A(I,J),J=1,N),I=1,N)
      .
      .
      .
      END
```

Example 19.13 initializes the elements of the vector DIGIT to the character strings shown. The vector VF has its four adjacent elements initialized to the character string

          (1H0bbbbF12.6)bb

A value is read in for N, and this is subsequently used in the statement

          VF(2)=DIGIT(N)

to replace the four blanks initially stored in VF(2). For example, if N equals 6, the vector VF is modified to

          (1H06bbbF12.6)bb

Recalling that blanks in a FORMAT statement are
ignored, the reader will see that the effect of
the WRITE statement is to print the elements of a
6 by 6 matrix by rows, double-spaced, with one row
per printed line.

One point must be emphasized: the variable
format consists of a sequence of *characters*. Integer
constants used in calculations are *not*, in general,
representations of character strings. Thus, for
example, if the statement

VF(2)=N

were used instead of

VF(2)=DIGIT(N)

an execution-time error would result.

A variable format may be an array of any
type that the programmer finds convenient. Usually,
however, an integer array is the easiest to work with,
particularly if the array is to be modified, as in
the last example.

19.8   <u>EXERCISES</u>

19.1 Write a program which declares four
variables I, A, C, and L to be of integer,
real, complex, and logical type, respectively.
As well, the variables I, A, C, and L should
be initialized to have the values 3225,
625.629, (32.4, 16.E5), and .FALSE.,
respectively. Then print the variables,
using the statement

PRINT17, I, A, C, L

with each of the following FORMAT
statements:

```
  (i)    17 FORMAT('0',5G16.7)
 (ii)    17 FORMAT('0',G4,3G14.6,G9)
(iii)    17 FORMAT('0',5G4.0)
 (iv)    17 FORMAT('0',G3,4G15.2)
  (v)    17 FORMAT('0',5(G16.5,4X))
 (vi)    17 FORMAT('0',5('VALUE IS',5G16.3))
(vii)    17 FORMAT('0',G15.6)
(viii)   17 FORMAT('0',8G15.6)
```

It is instructive to predict what the
results will be before actually running
the program on the computer.

19.2   Example 19.3 demonstrates how the T format
code can be used to position fields in a
print line. Write a program that calculates
a table of sines, cosines, tangents, and
square roots for x = 0, 1, 2, ..., 25.
Use the T format code to position the
headings and the columns to be printed.

19.3   The first card of a data deck contains
the size n of a square matrix A (assume
n ≤ 16). The rest of the deck consists
of n data cards, each card containing n
integer values, punched using format I5.
Write a program that reads the entire
data deck, using one READ statement.
Assume that the values are punched in row
sequence. Print the matrix and a suitable
heading, using one PRINT statement.

19.4 (a) A data deck consists of 100 real
         values, each having two decimal
         places. Write a program that reads
         the values, using a scaling factor
         to multiply each value by 100. Find
         the sum of the values, using integer
         arithmetic, and print the result,
         again using scaling to divide the
         result by 100. If the sum contains
         more than 7 digits, use an extended-
         precision variable to print the final
         result.

     (b) Repeat part (a), but this time use
         T format to read each value twice,
         once with scaling and once without
         scaling. Perform all calculations
         using real arithmetic. Compare the
         two results.

19.5 (a) Punch a set of data cards according
         to some format of your choice. The
         first data card should contain the
         necessary list of format codes to
         input your data. Write a program
         that reads the format list into an
         array, and then uses the variable-
         format feature to read the data cards
         into another array.

     (b) Modify the data deck so that the
         second data card contains a list of
         format codes that could be used to
         output the array. Write a program
         to read in the two format lists, and

then use these to read and print
your data.

19.6   Exercise 12.9 describes a figure consisting
of a set of points, some of which may be
connected by either vertical or horizontal
lines. Write a program that reads data
which describes the connections for a
particular figure of your choice, and
that prints the figure using *'s to denote
the points and .'s to denote the connections.

19.7   Write a subprogram which accepts an integer
N as input, and prints a "square" with N
asterisks on each side. The figure will
not be square, because the horizontal
spacing on the printer is different from
the vertical spacing.

19.8   Write a subprogram which accepts two
integers N and M as input, and prints a
"rectangle" with N asterisks as the width
and M asterisks as the length.

19.9   (a)   Write a subprogram which accepts the
value r as input, and outlines the
circle

$$x^2 + y^2 = r^2$$

on the printer, using the asterisk
symbol. The circle should take up
as much room as possible on the
printed page. Some indication defining
the scale should be printed.

(b)   Part (a) should suggest a technique
for "plotting" functions using the

printer. Design a subprogram which has the kind of graphic output for functions of the type

$$y = f(x).$$

19.10 Your answers for Exercise 15.2 (a), and Exercise 15.4 can be verified by reading in the constants from data cards, and printing their values, using the Z format code.

CHAPTER 20

ODDS AND ENDS

This chapter is concerned with a number of topics which seemed to have little place in any of the preceding chapters. Either their use was not required, or their introduction would have added considerable detail at an inappropriate point. Hence, it was decided to collect these ideas and present them in this final chapter.

20.1   THE DATA STATEMENT

The DATA statement is a non-executable FORTRAN statement that is used to specify the compile-time initialization of variables. In this respect, its effect is much like that of declaration statements which include initialization information. The rules for the DATA statement are similar to those of declaration statements, and a few examples should be sufficient to outline the specific differences.

The statement

```
DATA PI/3.14/,I/27/,X/2.5/,J/-3/,OK/.TRUE./
```

assigns, at compile time, the initial values 3.14, 27, 2.5, -3, and .TRUE. to the variables PI, I, X, J, and OK, respectively. The same initialization is obtained by using the statements

```
REAL PI/3.14/,X/2.5/
INTEGER I/27/,J/-3/
LOGICAL OK/.TRUE./
```

The basic difference between DATA statements and
type-declaration statements is that DATA statements
contain no type-declaration information; any variable
named in the statement has a type given by default,
or by a previous declaration statement.

Another difference is that the variable
names to be initialized may be written in a list,
followed by a list of the initializing constants.
For example, each of the statements

```
DATA PI,I,X,J,OK/3.14,27,2.5,-3,.TRUE./
DATA PI,I/3.14,27/,X/2.5/,J,OK/-3,T
```

has the same effect as the above DATA statement.

Single array elements or whole arrays may
be initialized, but array dimensions must be
declared in previous declaration statements. Consider
the statements

```
DIMENSION JP2(10),X(5)
REAL MORT(3,3),ZQ(6)
DATA JP2,MORT,X(3)/10*0,6*-1.,4*5.8/,ZQ(1)/-4.3/
```

Each of the ten elements of the integer
array JP2 is initialized to the value 0. Each of
the first six elements of the real array MORT is
initialized to the value -1.; each of the last
three elements of MORT, as well as the element X(3)
of the vector X, is initialized to the value 5.8.
The initialization of MORT is done in storage order,
that is, by columns. Furthermore, the single element
ZQ(1) of the vector ZQ is initialized to -4.3.

WATFOR allows implied DO's in DATA statements; they can be used to initialize parts of
arrays, as the following example shows.

```
DIMENSION A(3,3),X(10),Y(3)
DATA B,(X(I),I=1,7,2),Y(2),A/15*3.42E3/
```

Here, the variable B, the first, third, fifth, and
seventh elements of X, the second element of Y,
and all of the elements of the matrix A, are
initialized to the value 3.42E3. Nested implied
DO's may be used if desired. The only restriction
is that the initial value, the increment, and the
test value of any implied DO must be integer constants;
they should not be variables, as is the case in the
DO statement.

The following are several further examples
of DATA statements

```
LOGICAL L1,L2,L3
REAL*8 D1,D2
COMPLEX C1,C2
DIMENSION A(10),B(2,3),N(5),M(3),L(3)
DATA L1/.TRUE./,D1,C2,X/15.5D3,(7.2,-7.6),25.6/
DATA A,G,B(1,2),N,M(3)/10*0.,2*.04,5*1,-3/
DATA L2,C1,Q,L3/'ABCD','DEFGHI',-14.3,F/
```

Data statements may be placed almost
anywhere in a program segment. Most programmers
place them near the beginning of the segment.

20.2 HEXADECIMAL CONSTANTS

A hexadecimal constant consists of the
letter Z followed by a string of hexadecimal digits;
an example is Z1A5B. These constants may be used
as initial values in type-declaration or DATA

statements to set up special bit patterns in
memory.

Some examples are:

(i)   REAL X/Z00100000/,Y/Z7FFFFFFF/
(ii)   DATA X,Y/Z00100000,Z7FFFFFFF/
(iii) INTEGER*2 M1/ZF/,M2/Z01020304/

Examples (i) and (ii) achieve the same
result; the variables X and Y are initialized to
hexadecimal values which, incidentally, represent
the smallest and largest floating-point numbers,
respectively. Both variables are of full-word
size, and thus can contain a hexadecimal constant
of eight digits.

Example (iii) illustrates that the
constants specified can contain fewer or more
hexadecimal digits than can be stored in the
corresponding variable. If fewer digits are given
than can be stored, the constant is padded on the
left with zeros; if more are given than can
be stored, only the farthest-right are used. Both
M1 and M2 are half-word integer variables; thus,
each can store a four-digit hexadecimal constant.
Hence, Example (iii) is equivalent to the statement

INTEGER*2 M1/Z000F/,M2/Z0304/

20.3 EQUIVALENCE

Occasionally a programmer writes a very
long program, and, when finished, finds that he has
used, possibly by accident, two or more names for
the same variable. One solution is to re-write the

338

program to make the variable names consistent. A
second alternative is supplied by a feature of the
FORTRAN language.   The statement

$$\text{EQUIVALENCE(XP5,A,Q4)}$$

informs the compiler that the variables named in
the parenthesized list are to be assigned to the
same storage locations in memory. This means that
A and Q4 are synonyms for the variable XP5.

Another use for this feature is to provide
alternative ways of referencing data in a program.
For example, the statements

```
COMPLEX Z
DIMENSION X(2)
EQUIVALENCE(X,Z)
```

specify that the complex variable Z and the vector
X occupy the same two consecutive full words. Thus,
a reference to X(1) is a reference to the real part
of Z, and a reference to X(2) is a reference to the
imaginary part of Z.   Similarly, with the statements

```
LOGICAL*1 B(4)
EQUIVALENCE(I,B)
```

references to elements of B provide access to the
individual bytes of variable I.

The statements

```
DIMENSION V(5)
EQUIVALENCE(Q,V(3))
```

specify Q as a synonym for V(3).

The statements

```
DIMENSION A(10,10),B(10),C(10),D(100)
EQUIVALENCE (A,B,D),(A(1,2),C)
```

provide various ways of referencing the elements of matrix A. Vectors B and C occupy the same storage as columns one and two, respectively, of A, since two-dimensional arrays are stored by columns. Similarly the elements of the ten columns of A, in storage order, are the one hundred elements of the vector D.

Probably the most common use of the EQUIVALENCE statement is to achieve a saving of storage in programs which use large arrays. For example, suppose a program requires two large arrays specified by

DIMENSION X(100,100),Y(100,100)

It may not be possible to have this much storage available for the program. However, if the program is such that the matrix X is not needed in the part of the program that uses Y, and vice versa, X and Y can share storage if we make them equivalent; thus, the statement

EQUIVALENCE(X,Y)

could be used.

As the examples have illustrated, an array name can appear with or without subscripts in an EQUIVALENCE statement. If no subscripts are used, the first element of the array is implied. Thus, if A is an array of two dimensions, the statements

EQUIVALENCE(A,B)
EQUIVALENCE(A(1,1),B)

achieve the same result. An additional simplification is allowed; one subscript may be given to specify the position of an element of a multi-dimensional array when the array appears in an EQUIVALENCE statement. For example, given the statement

```
DIMENSION A(10,5),B(10)
```

the following two statements are acceptable, and produce the same result.

```
EQUIVALENCE(A(1,2),B)
EQUIVALENCE(A(11),B)
```

This is the only exception to the rule that an array must always be used with the same number of subscripts as it has dimensions.

Any number of variables may appear in the list, and any number of lists may appear in a single EQUIVALENCE statement. The following examples illustrate this, and, as well, illustrate that the same variable can be made equivalent to more than one other variable. The two statements, in fact, produce the same result.

```
EQUIVALENCE(A,B,C,D,E,F,G),(I,X,K,TOM),(F,T2Q)
EQUIVALENCE(A,B,C),(E,A,D),(A,T2Q,G,F),(I,X),(K,TOM,X)
```

Contradictory effects of the EQUIVALENCE statement are detected by the compiler, and are considered as errors. An example is

```
DIMENSION A(10),B(10),C(10)
EQUIVALENCE(A,B(3)),(A,C(5)),(B,C)
```

Here A(1) and B(3) are made equivalent by the first list; this implies that A(5) and B(7) are also equivalent. The second list makes A(1) equivalent to C(5), and, by implication, makes B(7) and A(5) equivalent to C(9). The third list attempts to

341

make B(1) equivalent to C(1), which is clearly a
contradiction.

One problem can arise when variables which
occupy different amounts of memory are made equivalent to one another. Consider the example

```
LOGICAL*1 I(4)
INTEGER A,B
EQUIVALENCE (I(2),B),(I,A)
```

In this case, not both of A and B can be aligned
in memory on a full-word boundary. The compiler
diagnoses this problem, and issues a warning message,
since, if left uncorrected, time-consuming execution-
time boundary alignment must take place. Ways of
avoiding invalid boundary alignment are discussed
in the next section.

Subprogram parameters may not appear in
EQUIVALENCE statements.

Finally, it should be emphasized that the
EQUIVALENCE statement is non-executable; its purpose
is to supply the compiler with information to be
used when it allocates storage for variables at
compile time.

20.4 MORE ON COMMON BLOCKS

This section adds a few details to the
information on common blocks which was given in a
previous chapter. Some of the details are connected
with valid and invalid uses of the EQUIVALENCE
statement.

The order of appearance of the variable
names in COMMON statements determines the order of

342

the storage locations for the variables in common blocks. Thus, it is illegal to attempt to make two variables equivalent in one common block, or in two different common blocks. Hence, the following EQUIVALENCE statement is invalid.

```
COMMON/BLK1/X,Y/BLK2/A,B
EQUIVALENCE(X,B)
```

However, any variable not in a common block may be made equivalent to a variable within the block, e.g.,

```
COMMON P,Q
EQUIVALENCE(Z,P)
```

If Z were an array, this could have the implicit effect of increasing the size of the common block. Thus, for the statements

```
DIMENSION Z(5)
COMMON P,Q
EQUIVALENCE(Z,P)
```

the size of the blank common block is 20 bytes, since the entire vector Z is brought into the block by the EQUIVALENCE statement; we say that the block has been extended to the right.

The first variable named in a COMMON statement is always the first element in the block in which it is stored. An attempt to extend any common block to the left by use of the EQUIVALENCE statement would violate this rule.

Thus, the statements

```
DIMENSION R(5)
COMMON S,T
EQUIVALENCE(S,R(3))
```

are invalid, since they attempt to have the elements

343

R(1) and R(2) precede S in the block.

It is not necessary that a common block be the same size in two different segments; the compiler allocates storage by using the largest size required for the block when all segments are considered. A warning is issued, however, since the condition might indicate an error in the program. For example, consider the following two statements.

```
(i)   COMMON X,Y,Z
(ii)  COMMON X,Z
```

If (i) were to be used in a main program and (ii) in a subprogram, the block size allocated would be 12 bytes. But note that the variable Y in (i) and the variable Z in (ii) are stored at the same location in the block.

To avoid problems, some programmers simply duplicate any COMMON statements, and insert the duplicates into subprograms that require them.

The lay-out of a common block can be quite different in the various segments. For example, consider the following sets of statements.

```
(i)    COMMON X,Y,Z
(ii)   COMPLEX P
       COMMON P,I
(iii)  LOGICAL*1 L(12)
       COMMON L
```

If (i) were used in one subprogram, (ii) in a second subprogram, and (iii) a third subprogram, the single blank common block established would contain 12 bytes;

these 12 bytes would have a different significance in each subprogram. This is not illegal, and is, in fact, occasionally desirable. It is the programmer's responsibility to be aware of the differences, and to make allowances, if necessary.

Normally, the compiler automatically provides the proper boundary alignment for variables used in a program. However, since COMMON and EQUIVALENCE statements specify the order in which variables are to be stored, their use can occasionally lead to assignment of storage such that proper alignment cannot be provided for some variables. For example, consider the following case.

```
LOGICAL*1 L
REAL*8 D
COMMON L,D
```

The compiler always aligns the first element of any common block on a *double-word boundary*. This means, for the example under consideration, that the double-word quantity D cannot be aligned on a double-word boundary, since the COMMON statement specifies it must be stored adjacent to the one-byte quantity L. Although this is not strictly an error, it should be avoided if possible, since it can lead to a decrease in the efficiency of the program; extra operations must be performed by the compiler at execution time to account for the improper alignment.

One way to avoid the situation is to arrange the common block so that the variables appear in decreasing order according to length, i.e., all double-word variables are placed first, all full word variables second, all half-word variables third, and all byte variables last. Proper alignments will result, since the block starts on a double-word boundary. An alternative is to pad the block with dummy names. For the example above, the statements

```
LOGICAL*1 L,UNUSED(7)
REAL*8 D
COMMON L,UNUSED,D
```

result in proper alignment for all variables.

Similar methods can be used to correct improper alignment caused by the use of the EQUIVALENCE statement.

20.5   BLOCK DATA SUBPROGRAMS

A block data subprogram is a special subprogram which is specifically used to assign initial values to variables in common blocks. The following example illustrates a number of points.

```
BLOCK DATA
IMPLICIT COMPLEX*8(C),LOGICAL(U-W)
DIMENSION P(6)
COMMON/BLK1/X(3),YZ/BLK2/U,V,W
COMMON P/BLK3/C1,C2
DATA X,V,C2/3*0.,.TRUE.,(1.,2.)/
INTEGER*2 YZ/-35/,P*4
EQUIVALENCE(P,IQ)
DATA IQ/2/
END
```

The first statement of such subprograms is always BLOCK DATA, and, as with every subprogram, the last statement is always END. If an IMPLICIT

346

statement is used, it must be the second statement in the subprogram. A block data subprogram is never called; note that it does not have a name. Moreover, there are never any executable statements in the subprogram.

There must be at least one COMMON statement, since the purpose of the subprogram is to provide initializing data for variables in common blocks. The example illustrates that initial values may be entered into more than one common block by a single block data subprogram. Note that not all variables in a block need be initialized. However, all variables in a particular block must be specified in COMMON statements; this is required so that the compiler is made aware of the complete structure of the block in order to perform the proper initialization.

Block data subprograms are not required for programs written to be compiled by WATFOR, since WATFOR allows variables in common blocks to be initialized by statements in any program segment. However, if used as described above, much of the information about the various common blocks in a job is localized in one program segment. This serves a valuable documentary purpose, and also simplifies the changing of any initial values in blocks, if changes are required.

Most FORTRAN compilers require that variables in common blocks be initialized only by means of block data subprograms. Thus, such subprograms should be used if a program is likely to be compiled by a compiler other than WATFOR.

20.6 <u>SUBPROGRAM ARGUMENTS</u>

This section contains a number of details about subprogram arguments. These details will likely be of interest only to experienced programmers, or to those who plan to make extensive use of subprogram capabilities.

*   *   *

Hollerith strings may be used as subprogram parameters, as shown by the following example.

```
CALL OUTMES('THIS IS AN EXAMPLE.',5,18,Y)
```

WATFOR treats a Hollerith string used in this way as if the characters forming the string, taken in groups of four, are the values of elements of a real vector; blanks are supplied on the right of the last element if the length of the string is not a multiple of four. The implication is that WATFOR requires that the corresponding dummy parameter of the called subprogram be a real vector of the appropriate dimension.

In the above example, the Hollerith string is considered as a real vector of dimension five. The subprogram OUTMES could contain a statement supplying this dimension for a real array used as the corresponding dummy parameter. Alternatively, an execution-time dimension could be used. For example, the PRINT statement in the following sequence

```
      SUBROUTINE OUTMES(X,N,M,P)
      DIMENSION X(N)
      .
      .
      PRINT22,X
   22 FORMAT(' ',5A4)
      .
      .
      END
```

would produce the printed line

THIS IS AN EXAMPLE.

*   *   *

A subprogram should not change the value
of any parameter for which the calling argument is a
constant, an expression, or a DO-parameter. Unexpected
results can occur if this rule is violated. Consider
a subprogram which contains the following statements:

```
      SUBROUTINE SQVAR(N,X,M)
      .
      .
      .
      N=N+1
      M=N
      .
      .
      .
      X=X**2
      .
      .
      .
      END
```

A calling program segment containing the following
statements violates the above rule for each argument.

```
      DO 1 I=1,20
      .
      .
      CALL SQVAR(2,3.*SIN(A),I)
      .
      .
    1 CONTINUE
```

An equivalent call to SQVAR, which obeys
the rule, could be accomplished as follows:

```
      DO 1 I=1,20
      .
      .
      L=2
      K=I
      Z=3.*SIN(A)
      CALL SQVAR(L,Z,K)
      .
      .
    1 CONTINUE
```

*   *   *

The following details relate to the means
by which argument values are transmitted to a subprogram when it is called.

Consider the subprogram which contains
the following statements

```
      SUBROUTINE THING4(X,N,P)
      .
      .
      X=X+2
      .
      .
      N=P*X
      .
      .
      RETURN
      .
      .
      END
```

The variables X, N, and P are considered to be
dummy variables, that is, they have no values until
the subprogram is called, at which time each is
assigned the value of the corresponding argument.
The compiler does, however, reserve space in memory
to be occupied by the values of X, N, and P; a

350

full word is reserved for each of them.

When the subprogram is called by a statement such as

CALL THING4(Z,K,28.7)

part of the effect of the call is to copy the values
of the arguments Z, K, and 28.7 into the storage
locations reserved for X, N, and P. Thus, when
the subprogram operates on X, N, and P, it is, in
effect, operating on copies of the values of the
calling arguments. When a RETURN is executed in
the subprogram, the values in the storage locations
reserved for the parameters X, N, and P are copied
back into the storage locations reserved for the
values of the arguments in the calling program.
This copying action is performed automatically by
the compiler, and the technique is referred to as
call by value.

Call by value is the method most frequently
used to pass arguments back and forth between calling
and called segments. There is another technique,
referred to as *call by location*, available to the
programmer. To illustrate how this is used, suppose
the above SUBROUTINE statement is replaced by the
statement

SUBROUTINE THING4(/X/,/N/,P)

The slashes around the parameter names X and N
specify that they are to be treated by the compiler
as call-by-location parameters. This means that
the compiler reserves no storage - in the subprogram -
for the values of X and N. Parameter P has storage

reserved for it, since it is a call-by-value parameter.

When the subprogram is called by a statement such as

CALL THING4(Z,K,28.7)

the value 28.7 is copied into the space reserved
for P in the subprogram. However, the values of
Z and K are not copied. Instead, the addresses
of the memory locations occupied by Z and K are
supplied to the subprogram. Any references that
the subprogram makes to its parameters X and N
are, in fact, references (by means of these
addresses) to the actual values of Z and K, not
to copies of Z and K, as is the case for call-by-
value parameters. When a RETURN is executed, only
the call-by-value parameters are copied back into
the calling program; in the above case, only the
value of P is copied back.

Although call by location is treated
here as if it were a new concept, in actual fact,
the technique has been used earlier in this book.
Array names used as dummy parameters are treated
automatically by the compiler as call-by-location
parameters. This is done in order to avoid the
wasteful duplication of memory space for arrays.
As well, no time-consuming copying of the arrays
needs to take place at the time of a call. Subprogram names used as dummy parameters are also
treated automatically as call-by-location parameters.

*   *   *

A few additional rules must be added,
concerning parameters in ENTRY statements. Call-
by-location parameters may be used in ENTRY statements within a subprogram. However, a parameter
must be used consistently, by location or by value,
if it appears in more than one entry point of a
subprogram. Thus the statements

```
SUBROUTINE MAX(/N/)
.
.
ENTRY MIN(N)
.
.
END
```

are in error.

A subprogram parameter must not be used
in any executable statement of the subprogram prior
to its appearance in a parameter list. The statements

```
FUNCTION F(X,A,N)
.
.
X=3.*Q
.
.
ENTRY G(X,Q)
.
.
END
```

violate this rule, since Q is used before it appears
in the parameter list of entry point G. This rule
is required, since the compiler must give special
treatment to names used as parameters.

A common use of multiple entry points is
to supply initial values to a subprogram by a call
to a particular entry point, with subsequent calls
being made to other entry points. Consider the

following example of this idea.

```
          SUBROUTINE FIRST(X,A,Y,K,Q,Z,L,T,M,S)
          RETURN
          ENTRY OTHER(P)
          .
          .
          .
          END
```

A call to FIRST will cause the values of the
corresponding arguments to be copied into the
storage locations reserved for the parameters.
These values will then be available for computations
if subsequent calls are made to entry point OTHER;
on such calls, only a value for P will be copied
into the subprogram.

      Contrast this with the effect obtained
if the first statement is replaced by

```
     SUBROUTINE FIRST(/X/,/A/,/Y/,K,Q,Z,L,T,M,S)
```

In this case, for a call to FIRST, the subprogram
is supplied with the addresses of the arguments
corresponding to X, A, and Y, and with copies of
argument values for the other parameters. For
subsequent calls to OTHER, the *current* values of
the arguments which correspond to X, A, and Y,
are used wherever the subprogram references X, A,
and Y; on the other hand, the *copies* obtained for
the other parameters will be used for references
to them in the subprogram.

20.7 ADDITIONAL RULES FOR FORMAT-FREE INPUT

The following rules are given to complete the list of features of format-free input.

(i) Any field containing a T or an F may be used as input for a logical variable. The field is scanned from left to right, and the first T or F encountered determines the logical value as .TRUE. or .FALSE., respectively.

For example:

```
LOGICAL L1,L2,L3
READ, L1,L2,L3
```

with the data card

CAT, ALFA, BATTLE

results in the assignment T, F, T, for L1, L2, L3, respectively.

(ii) Data items may be separated by one comma and/or blanks.

For example:

READ, A,B

with data fields punched as 4.2bb,bbbb3.8 yields the same result as 4.2,3.8 or 4.2b3.8

(iii) Hexadecimal constants may be used as input. Thus,

READ,X,Y

with the data card

Z41100000,ZC1200000

assigns the indicated hexadecimal numbers
to X and Y (these numbers are the floating-
point representations of 1. and -2.,
respectively).

(iv) If successive elements of the read list
are to be assigned the same value, a
replication factor may be used. For
example,

    DIMENSION A(100)
    READ,A

could have the data card

    50*1.,50*-1.

20.8 ORDERING OF CERTAIN STATEMENTS IN A PROGRAM

WATFOR is a *one-pass* compiler. This means
that each statement of a program is processed only
once by the compiler; any translation to machine-
language instructions is done on this single pass
over the program. This is in contrast to some
compilers which may process the statements of a
program segment two or more times; the program is
stored, possibly in a modified form, in the main
memory or on peripheral devices such as tapes or
discs, so that the compiler can process the program
additional times, until the translation is complete.

To simplify the construction of a one-pass
compiler, certain restrictions are made on the
ordering of statements within a program. The
restrictions are:

(i) If a variable name appears in an EQUIVALENCE

356

statement and has not appeared previously
in an explicit declaration statement,
the variable is assumed to have the
standard length and type given by default.
If the variable then appears in an explicit
declaration statement following the
EQUIVALENCE statement, the length of the
variable must not be changed.

Thus,

```
EQUIVALENCE(I,X),(Z,P)
REAL*8 X
COMPLEX Z
INTEGER P
```

is considered invalid by WATFOR. However,

```
COMPLEX Z
REAL*8 X
EQUIVALENCE(I,X),(Z,P)
INTEGER P
```

is acceptable.

(ii)   If a variable is initialized, the statement
in which it is initialized must follow any
COMMON or EQUIVALENCE statements which
mention the variable. Thus,

```
INTEGER*2 J/3/,K/4/
COMMON J
EQUIVALENCE(K,L)
```

is considered invalid by WATFOR, but the
sequence

```
INTEGER*2 J,K
COMMON J
EQUIVALENCE(K,L)
DATA J,K/2,4/
```

is acceptable.

357

20.9 <u>EXERCISES</u>

20.1 Consider any program you have written
which involves FORMAT statements. Remove
the FORMAT statements, and modify the I/O
statements to reference arrays, which
contain execution-time format specifications.
Initialize these arrays, using DATA statements, so that they have the same list of
format codes as in the original FORMAT
statements. Remember to include the
parentheses at each end of the list of
codes. Verify that you have done the job
correctly by running the program on the
computer.

20.2 Exercise 15.2 (b) involves the conversion
of binary integers to their corresponding
decimal equivalents. Your work can easily
be verified by the computer in the following
way.

(i) Convert the binary integers, by hand,
to hexadecimal integers.

(ii) Write a program which initializes
integer variables to each of these
hexadecimal values. Then have the
program print the values.

20.3 Exercise 15.3 involves converting a number
of hexadecimal floating-point constants
into their corresponding decimal equivalents.
Your work can be verified as in Exercise
20.2. However, this time the hexadecimal
values must be assigned to real variables.

20.4   Repeat Exercises 20.2 and 20.3, but instead of *initializing* the variables with hexadecimal values, read these values into the computer from data cards.

20.5   Verify your answers to Exercise 15.5 by reading the hexadecimal values from data cards, performing the required calculations, and printing the results.

20.6   Consider any FORTRAN program you have written which involves integer variables. Declare an integer array M which has as many elements as there are integer variables in your program. Then use an EQUIVALENCE statement to make each integer variable equivalent to one element of the array M. Now it is possible to print the current values of all the integer variables by using the statement

```
PRINT,M
```

This can be useful when debugging programs; try it.

20.7   Write a subprogram which accepts a Hollerith string of length twelve as input. The subprogram is to count the number of occurrences of the character E, and to return this value to the calling program. HINT: Since the string must be stored in four-character substrings in a real array, you could consider using an EQUIVALENCE statement in the subprogram which

associates the array with a logical array
of twelve elements. However, the real
array must be copied first, since subprogram parameters cannot be used in
EQUIVALENCE statements.

20.8 (a) Predict the output of the following
program and verify your prediction
by running the program on the computer.

```
M=N=1
CALL ONE(M)
CALL TWO(N)
PRINT,M,N
STOP
END
SUBROUTINE ONE(I)
RETURN
ENTRY TWO(J)
I=I+2
J=J+2
RETURN
END
```

(b) Repeat part (a) but replace the
SUBROUTINE statement by

```
SUBROUTINE ONE(/I/)
```

CHAPTER 21

CHARACTER MANIPULATION IN WATFIV

When writing programs that store and
reference character data in the manner described
in Chapter 17, the programmer has to pay special
attention to the type and length of the variables
used to contain the character strings. If the
character strings can be stored in integer, real,
logical, or complex variables or arrays, they are
fairly easy to manipulate. Those which do not
fit become awkward to handle, and usually extra
programming is required. WATFIV contains a type-
declaration statement which helps solve this problem
by allowing character strings to be recognized as
a data form. This chapter describes this additional
character-handling ability.

21.1   CHARACTER VARIABLES

Recall that a set of characters enclosed
in quotes is referred to as a character string.
Examples of character strings are:

(i)   'JOKE'
(ii)   'X=(A+B)*C+39'
(iii) 'TO BE OR NOT TO BE'

Variables capable of being assigned
values which are character strings are said to be
character variables. A character variable can be
any valid FORTRAN symbolic name which is declared

in a CHARACTER declaration statement. For example,
the statement

CHARACTER*4 A/'JOKE'/

declares A to be a character variable. Furthermore,
A is initialized so that it contains the character
string JOKE. In the statement

CHARACTER*7 B/'CHARLES'/,C/'JAMES'/

B and C are declared to be character variables
which can contain seven characters. B is initialized
to contain the string CHARLES. C has assigned to
it the string JAMES, which consists of fewer than
seven characters. In this case, the compiler
automatically inserts blanks on the right.

The *length* of a character variable is the
number of bytes that are reserved for the variable.
The default or standard length is one, and the
maximum length is 255. Recall that each byte of
the IBM 360 memory is capable of storing one
character. Occasionally we use the terms 'byte'
and 'character' interchangeably.

The following examples further demonstrate
how character strings can be formed.

(i)   CHARACTER*4 A/'LIFE'/,B*9/'ALBATROSS'/
(ii)   CHARACTER*8 C/8HABCDEFGH/
(iii) CHARACTER Z(5)/'A','B','C','D','E'/
(iv)   CHARACTER H*11/'HORSE'/,W*8/'ABCDEFGHIJK'/
(v)   CHARACTER TAB*5(3,2)/3*'XXXXX',3*'YYYYY'/

Example (i) assigns the character strings
LIFE and ALBATROSS to the character variables A and
B, respectively.

Example (ii) illustrates the use of the H-type Hollerith to define a character string.

Example (iii) declares Z to be a character array with five elements, each occupying one byte. The five elements contain the letters A, B, C, D, and E.

In Example (iv), we have the situation where there are only five characters in the string, whereas the variable is capable of storing eleven characters. As previously stated, blanks are inserted on the right. In the case of W in Example (iv), the letters IJK are truncated, since the character string has eleven characters, and the variable can store only eight.

Example (v) uses a replication factor, and sets the first column of TAB to XXXXX's and the second column to YYYYY's.

21.2 INPUT/OUTPUT OF CHARACTER STRINGS

If we wish to print character data, we may use either format-free I/O or the A format code. Consider Example 21.1.

```
C EXAMPLE 21.1
      CHARACTER C*7/'CHARLIE'/
      CHARACTER A*4/'CHAR'/,B*3/'LIE'/
      PRINT 7,A,B
    7 FORMAT(1X,A4,A3)
      PRINT,C,A,B
      STOP
      END
```

The following two lines would be printed

```
CHARLIE
CHARLIE  CHAR  LIE
```

The strings CHAR and LIE are printed using the format codes A4 and A3, respectively, to form the first line. The format-free PRINT statement causes the three values on the second line to be printed, separated from one another by a blank character.

As we have seen previously, constants may appear in output lists; they are printed literally. This holds for character strings; thus, if the statements

```
NUM=4
LEVEL=29
PRINT,'NUM=',NUM,'LEVEL=',LEVEL
```

were executed, the output would be

```
NUM=      4 LEVEL=       29
```

The A format code may be used to input values for character variables, as described in Section 17.4. Alternatively, the format-free I/O facility may be used; in this case, character strings read as data must be enclosed in quotes. If the following statements were executed

```
CHARACTER A*4, B*3, C*4
READ,A,B,C
```

with the data card

```
'ABC', 'DOGS', 'IT''S'
```

then A would be assigned the value ABC, padded on the right with one blank, B would be assigned the

value DOG, and C would be assigned the value IT'S.
Note that, if a quote is required as input, two
successive quotes must be punched. The commas
separating the three character strings on the data
card could be replaced by blanks.

21.3   OPERATIONS WITH CHARACTER VARIABLES

If the statements

```
INTEGER C,A/123/,B/456/
C=A+B
```

were executed, C would be assigned the integer
result 579. However, if the statements

```
CHARACTER*3 C,A/'123'/,B/'456'/
C=A+B
```

were written, a *compile-time* error message would
be issued following the assignment statement, since
arithmetic operations are not defined for character
strings.

However, character assignment statements
can be used to assign values to character variables;
all variables or constants or array elements,
including the variable on the left-hand side of the
equal sign, must be of type character. Examples of
valid assignment statements using character variables
are:

```
CHARACTER A*6/'ABCDEF'/,B*6,D*8,E*5,F*7(3)
B=A
F(2)=A
E='54321'
D=A
```

The value of the A in the statement D=A will be

padded on the right with blanks, since it is shorter
than D.   If the right-hand element is too long, it
will be truncated from the right during replacement.
However, the compiler will warn that this will
occur.

21.4   COMPARISON OF CHARACTER VARIABLES

Character variables and character constants
can be used as operands with the relational operators
in order to perform comparisons.   For example, the
statements

```
CHARACTER A*5
   •
   •
   •
IF(A.EQ.'ENTRY')GO TO 20
```

compare the value of the character variable A with
the character string ENTRY, and transfer control to
the statement numbered 20 if they are the same.
Both operands must be of character type.   If operands
of unequal length are used, the shorter operand is
considered as if it were padded on the right with
blanks to the length of the longer operand.
The other relational operators can be
used as well.   For example, in the statements

```
CHARACTER X*10,Y*10
   •
   •
   •
IF(X.LT.Y)PRINT,X
```

if the character string X is "less" than the
character string Y, this implies that the value of
X precedes the value of Y in alphabetical order.

Again, if X and Y were of different lengths, the shorter string would be padded with blanks to the length of the longer string.   Exercise 21.6 will introduce the concept of order when characters other than letters are used.

Example 17.5 arranges, in alphabetical order, one hundred four-letter words read from data cards.   If, in the example, the array WORD were declared as

CHARACTER WORD*80(100)

and two FORMAT statements were written as

2 FORMAT (A80)

and

7 FORMAT(' ',A80)

then the program would input one hundred cards, and arrange character strings of length 80 in alphabetical order.

21.5   ADDITIONAL RULES FOR CHARACTER VARIABLES

This section contains a number of details concerning the use of character variables in programs.

(i)   The IMPLICIT statement can be used to set up a "first-letter rule" for character variables of a specified length.   For example, the statement

IMPLICIT CHARACTER*9(A),CHARACTER(B-E)

specifies that variables beginning with

367

the letter A are of character type and of
length 9. Variables starting with letters
B through E are character variables of
length 1.

(ii) Character variables may appear in DIMENSION
statements or in DATA statements. The
statement

```
CHARACTER A*3(10),B*10/'1234567890'/
```

is equivalent to the statements

```
CHARACTER A*3,B*10
DIMENSION A(10)
DATA B/'1234567890'/
```

(iii) Character strings or variables may be used
as subprogram arguments, as shown in the
following statements.

```
CHARACTER A*3(10),B,C(20)
CALL SUB(B,'A9B3',A,C(3))
```

Parameters in a SUBROUTINE or FUNCTION
statement may be character variable names
or array names, as demonstrated below.

```
FUNCTION CALC(A,B)
CHARACTER A*10,B*5(40)
```

Wherever a parameter is a character
variable, the corresponding argument must
also be a character variable of the same
length. If the parameter is an array,
then the corresponding argument must also
be an array.

(iv) Character variables may appear in COMMON
statements, and be thus accessible to

other program segments.

(v) Function subprograms of type character
are **not** allowed.

21.6 EXERCISES

21.1 Exercises 17.1 through 17.5 are problems
dealing with character manipulation.
Repeat these exercises using CHARACTER
variables where appropriate.

21.2 A data card contains a sequence of the
four characters - plus, minus, asterisk,
and slash.

(i) Write a program that reads the data
card, then determines and prints the
number of occurrences of each type
of character.

(ii) If two asterisks occur adjacently,
they are to be counted as only one
character. Include this feature in
your program.

21.3 (a) Write a program that reads 25 data
cards, each containing a "word" which
consists of up to 16 letters, stores
them in a character array WORD, and
then arranges the words in alphabetical
order.

(b) Repeat (a), storing the words in an
integer array.

(c) Write a program that reads 25 data
cards and stores them in an array
as in (a). Your program should then

read in another word called KEY, and
determine whether KEY is in the array.
Print an appropriate message to
indicate whether KEY is in the array.

(d) The number of comparisons can be
reduced if the 25 words are arranged
in alphabetical order before
determining if KEY is in the array.
Write a program that reads the 25
words, sorts them, reads KEY, and
determines if KEY is in the array.
The number of comparisons should be
output, as well as an appropriate
message.

21.4 Write a program that accepts two integers
I and J as input, and then prints a
rectangle of width I and length J, using
the asterisk as the character to outline
the rectangle.

21.5 Write a function subprogram

FUNCTION INDEX(STRING,LS,THING,LT)

where STRING and THING are two character
strings with length LS and LT, respectively.
The function INDEX should return to the
calling program a value indicating the
numerical position of the first occurrence
of THING in STRING. If LT is greater than
LS, or THING is not found in STRING, the
function should return a zero value to the
calling program.

21.6   The letters of the alphabet can be
       arranged in what we call "alphabetical
       order". The internal representation of
       the letters has been chosen to make this
       ordering easy. The other characters,
       such as numbers and special characters,
       also have their own internal representation.
       Write a program that sorts all the
       characters available on the keypunch. Your
       output should be the ordered characters,
       printed in both A and Z format.

CHAPTER 22

ADDITIONAL I/O FEATURES IN WATFIV

In this Chapter, we describe a number of
other I/O features, in particular, FORTRAN direct-
access capabilities and NAMELIST capabilities. Also,
the core-to-core I/O facilities, as implemented in
WATFIV, are described.

The programmer should be aware that
direct-access I/O is a very specialized method.
In general, before writing programs which use this
feature, he should check with his installation for
any local rules concerning the use of direct-access
I/O.

22.1 DIRECT-ACCESS FILES

In Chapter 18, we discussed the use of
magnetic tapes for the storage and processing of
data files. Vast quantities of data can be recorded
rapidly and economically using tape. However, this
procedure possesses a disadvantage: because of the
sequential nature of tape, half of a file must be
processed in order to read a record in the centre
of the file. This can mean a retrieval time in the
order of several minutes for that particular part
of the file. This retrieval time is, of course, a
function of the tape unit being used and of the
actual length of the file; thus, the average retrieval
time can vary from fractions of a second to minutes,
depending on the circumstances.

This timing problem is the reason that magnetic tapes are seldom used to store records which have to be retrieved at random. Fortunately, many file processing applications are of a sequential nature, and magnetic tapes are ideal in such cases; however, when random retrieval of information is required, we use *direct-access devices* such as magnetic drums, disks, or data cells.

It is beyond the scope of this book to describe the physical details of the various direct-access storage devices. However, these devices use a variety of hardware techniques to achieve a common goal; that goal is to read a record from any part of the file into computer memory within a fraction of a second. These hardware techniques include multiple read/write heads, moving read/write heads, and different physical arrangements of the storage media.

22.2 DIRECT-ACCESS FILES IN FORTRAN

The user can consider that his file consists of a number of records, each of which has an *index* which indicates the relative position of the record in the file. The first record has index 1, the second has index 2, etc., with the indices increasing by unity for each record up to the end of the file. Thus, the index is a way of referring *directly* to a record within the file. Any one of these records can be located and read into memory in less than one second. FORTRAN files which are set up in this way are known as *direct-access files*, and are created and processed using *direct-access I/O* statements.

Suppose we wish to set up a direct-access file with one record for each of the 1869 students in a school. Furthermore, assume that the students have been assigned student identification numbers from 1 to 1869. In order to begin our file of information, we punch a card containing student number and name, for each of the 1869 students. Example 22.1 illustrates a simple program for creating the file and storing this information.

```
C EXAMPLE 22.1 - CREATING A DIRECT-ACCESS FILE
      INTEGER STUDNO,NAME(5)
      DEFINE FILE 12(2000,150,E,INT)
      DO 22 I=1, 1869
      READ 3, STUDNO, NAME
   22 WRITE(12'STUDNO,4)NAME
    3 FORMAT(I4,5A4)
    4 FORMAT(5A4)
      STOP
      END
```

The DEFINE FILE statement causes a portion of available random-access memory to be allocated to unit number 12 (also referred to as data set reference number 12, or, informally, as file 12). This file is to have 2000 records, each of 150 bytes in length. The E indicates that each record will be read or written using format control. INT is an integer variable, and is known as the *associated variable*; its purpose will be described later.

The statement numbered 22 causes the records to be written into the file. It is an example of the general WRITE statement discussed on page 292, i.e.,

WRITE(unit,fmt)list

In this case, the 'unit' parameter is replaced by 12'STUDNO[†], which means "file 12, that specific record whose index is the current integer value of STUDNO". The 'fmt' and 'list' are 4 and NAME, respectively.

The program reads a student number and name from each card, and stores only the name in the record indexed according to the student number. This procedure is repeated in the DO-loop for each of the 1869 cards. Note that the cards are not required to be in any particular sequence. The direct-access WRITE statement will seek out the proper record prior to transferring the name from memory to random-access storage.

Note that we reserved 2000 records, although there were only 1869 students. This is to allow for an increase in student population. Also, note that we used only 20 bytes of the 150 bytes reserved for each record. This permits us, at some future time, to store additional information about a student, such as examination marks. In the meantime, the 130 unused positions contain blanks. These blanks were stored to fill out the record when the name was written into the first 20 bytes.

[†] On a Model 026 keypunch, use @ for '.

Example 22.2 shows how the file can be expanded to record marks for a particular examination. A card is prepared containing student number and mark for each examination, and this is the data deck for the program.

```
C EXAMPLE 22.2
      INTEGER STUDNO,NAME(5),ASSOC
      DEFINE FILE 12(2000,150,E,ASSOC)
    4 READ (5,1,END=5)STUDNO,MARK
      READ(12'STUDNO,2)NAME
      WRITE(12'STUDNO,3)NAME,MARK
      GO TO 4
    1 FORMAT(I4,I3)
    2 FORMAT(5A4)
    3 FORMAT(5A4,I3)
    5 STOP
      END
```

The program reads a card, and subsequently reads the corresponding student record from file 12. The FORTRAN statement

```
      READ(12'STUDNO,2)NAME
```

causes the specific record indexed by the value of STUDNO to be read from file 12, using FORMAT statement 2. The values read are stored in the five elements of the subscripted variable NAME. Then the record is re-written into the same physical location in file 12; this time, the name and mark are recorded.

Note that, once again, the cards in the input-data deck can be in random sequence, and only those students who have received a mark on the examination have their records *updated*. Note also that, in order to add a mark to a record, we have to *read* it first, then write it. This is because

it is not possible to write onto a *part* of a record.
Each WRITE causes the entire record to be altered.
Thus, if there is any information in a record which
must be retained, the record must be read first, and
then written, with all the information to be recorded
placed in the output list of the WRITE statement.

A DEFINE FILE statement is included
in Example 22.2; it specifies the same
characteristics with which the file was originally
created.

The program in Example 22.3 prepares a
list giving student number, name, and examination
mark for each of a selected group of students.
This selected group is identified by punching the
student number of each onto separate cards; these
cards form the data deck for the program.

```
C EXAMPLE 22.3
      INTEGER STUDNO,NAME(5)
      DEFINE FILE 12(2000,150,E,INT)
    4 READ(5,1,END=5)STUDNO
      READ(12'STUDNO,2)NAME,MARK
      PRINT 3,STUDNO,NAME,MARK
      GO TO 4
    5 STOP
    1 FORMAT(I4)
    2 FORMAT(5A4,I3)
    3 FORMAT('0',I8,3X,5A4,I6)
      END
```

The program reads a data card, reads the
appropriate record in the direct-access file, and
prints one line. This procedure is repeated for
each of the data cards. If the data cards are in
a random sequence by student number, the output

listing will be in the same sequence.

The example illustrates a weakness in our planning in the previous examples. A problem arises when *no* mark has been previously recorded for a particular student. Execution of the statement

READ(12'STUDNO,2)NAME,MARK

then results in assigning a value of zero to the integer variable MARK, since the record contains blanks rather than a three-digit integer. There is no indication that this is not a legitimate mark of zero. Exercise 22.5 suggests one method for over-coming this difficulty. Of course, there are other ways of applying controls in a situation like this. The matter is raised here only to bring the general problem to the attention of the reader.

22.3   DIRECT ACCESS WITH FORMAT CONTROL

The previous examples have been concerned with a direct-access file with which FORMAT statements were used to control input/output. This section is meant to consolidate some of the ideas, and to summarize the various rules.

(i)   The file is always set up using a DEFINE FILE statement of the following type:

DEFINE FILE unit(number,size,E,associated variable)

This statement must be executed prior to reading or writing into the file. It may appear more than once in a program and/or its associated subprograms, but second and subsequent definitions of a file are ignored.

378

The 'unit' could be any integer from
1 to 99 inclusive, depending on the
conventions used in any particular
installation. The reader must be aware
of these local conventions before using
direct-access features of FORTRAN.

The 'number' is an integer constant
which indicates the number of records in
the file.

The 'size' is an integer constant
which indicates the number of bytes in
each record.

The letter E indicates that I/O will
be done under format control.

The 'associated variable' is an integer
variable. When a read or write operation
has been executed involving the record
with index n, the associated variable is
assigned the integer value n+1. Thus,
this variable has a value which is the
index of the next sequential record in the
file following a read or write operation.
This can be useful to read a direct-access
file sequentially, as in Example 22.4.

```
C EXAMPLE 22.4
      DEFINE FILE 12(2000,150,E,INT)
      INTEGER NAME(5)
      INT=123
      DO 5 J=1,10
      READ(12'INT,4)NAME
    5 PRINT 6,NAME
      STOP
    4 FORMAT(5A4)
    6 FORMAT('0',5A4)
      END
```

In Example 22.4, the DO-loop is executed ten times. The first READ causes record 123 to be read. Then INT is set to 124, as it is the associated variable. The second READ thus causes record 124 to be retrieved. Ultimately, each of the records 123 to 132 (inclusive) is read and printed.

The associated variable has all of the usual properties of an integer variable, but has some restrictions. It can not appear as part of the 'list' of a READ or a WRITE statement involving direct-access I/O on the associated file. Also, it can not appear as a subprogram parameter. However, the COMMON mechanism may be used to pass it to a subprogram.

(ii) Records are written using statements of the form

```
WRITE(unit'index,fmt)list
```

The 'unit' is an integer variable or integer constant of length four which has a value between 1 and 99, and which corresponds to the file which will be written. This file has been previously defined using a DEFINE FILE statement.

The 'index' is an integer expression whose value indicates the index of the record to be written, for example,

```
WRITE(4'2*I+1,6)X,Y
```

'Fmt' is a statement number which refers to the FORMAT statement to be used. If execution-time format is being used, 'fmt' is the name of the array containing a string of characters which specifies the format.

'List' defines the data to be written, and has properties similar to those of 'lists' for other output statements defined in this book. For example, a 'list' will usually contain one or more FORTRAN variable names, separated by commas, as list elements. However, a list can be empty, or it can contain FORTRAN expressions as list elements. In the latter case, these expressions are evaluated, and the results are the data to be written.

Example 22.5 gives an illustration of the use of the empty list.

This program causes twenty blank characters to be written in the first twenty byte-positions of each of the 2000 records in file 12. In fact, the remaining 130 byte-positions in each record are also automatically filled with blanks.

```
C EXAMPLE 22.5
      DEFINE FILE 12(2000,150,E,INT)
      DO 22 I=1,2000
   22 WRITE(12'I,4)
    4 FORMAT('                    ')
      STOP
      END
```

(iii)   Records are read using statements of the
        form

        READ(unit'index,fmt,ERR=d)list

The parameters 'unit', 'index', 'fmt', and 'list'
have already been defined in our discussion
of WRITE. The 'ERR=d' is optional, and
is used to cause a transfer of control to
the statement numbered d, if an error
should occur in reading.

(iv)   The record being written can be thought
        of as a line on the printer. This line
        has a width equal to the number of bytes
        in the record. If we write with a FORMAT
        statement which uses only part of a line,
        the remainder is filled with blanks. On
        the other hand, if the FORMAT statement
        requires more positions than the record
        allows, an error message occurs. For
        example, it is not possible to use the
        following sequence of statements for
        file 12, which was defined in earlier
        examples.

        WRITE(12'125,4)Z
      4 FORMAT(140X,F18.3)

The FORMAT statement implies a record of
158 bytes, and the record size for file
12 is defined as having only 150 bytes.
However, the following sequence of statements would work:

```
      WRITE(12'125,4)Z,T
    4 FORMAT(120X,E20.3)
```

Here *two* records are written. First, Z is
written in record 125. Then, since the
end of the FORMAT statement is reached, a
new record is begun (this is comparable to
a new print line); consequently, T is
written in record 126. Each of these
records has 120 blanks, followed by Z or
T recorded in E20.3 format, followed by
10 blanks.

Format for the READ statement can
be considered as being analogous to that
used for reading punched cards. However,
each 'card' is logically extended to have
a number of columns equal to the number
of bytes in the record. The statement

```
      READ(12'235,5)(NAME(I),I=1,5)
    5 FORMAT(//5A4)
```

would cause records 235 and 236 to be
skipped. Then the contents of the first
20 bytes of record 237 would be read into
the array NAME using format 5A4. The
associated variable would have the value
238 after the READ was completed.

(v)   Several direct-access files can be defined
in one DEFINE FILE statement. As an
example, consider

```
   DEFINE FILE 8(100,25,E,IV),3(6908,120,E,LGV)
```

(vi)   REWIND, ENDFILE, and BACKSPACE statements
       which reference direct-access files are
       ignored.

22.4   DIRECT ACCESS WITHOUT FORMAT CONTROL

Data can be recorded more efficiently, both
from the point of view of file space and machine time,
if they are read and written without format control.
This means that the information written is an exact
image of its representation in memory. For example,
consider the following sequence of statements.

```
DEFINE FILE 3(1200,30,U,INT)
X=3.468
WRITE(3'172)X
```

Here file 3 is defined to have 1200 records. Each
of those records is 30 *words* (120 bytes), since the
file will be written or read without format control
(indicated by the letter U). The WRITE statement
causes the four bytes containing the value of the
real variable X to be written into the first full
word (four bytes) of record 172. The remainder of
the record is padded with zeros. Under no condition
could the list of elements associated with the
WRITE statement create a record which requires more
than 30 full words. For example, the statements

```
DEFINE FILE 3(1200,30,U,INT)
REAL X(40)/40*1.3/
WRITE(3'172)X
```

would cause an error to occur. This is because the
array X requires 40 words, and the record size
is only 30 words.

If the DEFINE FILE statement has the letter U as its fourth parameter, the file must always be read or written without format control. Furthermore, the third parameter (record size) must be given as the number of full words. Subsequent READ and WRITE statements associated with this file must omit the format parameter. In other respects, the READ/WRITE statements are the same as those described in the previous section.

22.5   DIRECT ACCESS WITH OR WITHOUT FORMAT CONTROL

It may be convenient to define a direct-access file so that it can be read or written with *or* without format control. This is done by using the letter L as the fourth parameter in the DEFINE FILE statement. The third parameter (record size) must then be indicated in bytes. The statement

DEFINE FILE 27(1800,200,L,INT)

defines file 27 with 1800 records, each of 200 bytes, and the records can be read or written with or without format control, as required.

22.6   THE FIND STATEMENT

The direct-access READ statement must perform two functions.

(i)   It must find the record on the direct-access storage medium (a process which usually requires the physical movement of the storage medium or read-write heads). This could take up to one second.

385

(ii) It must transfer the data from the record in the direct-access storage device to computer memory.

The FIND statement permits the programmer to perform the first of these functions in advance, thus reducing the time required to process the READ statement. For example, when the FIND statement is encountered, the sequence

```
FIND(17'127)
   .
   .
   .
READ(17'127)X,Y,Z
   .
   .
   .
```

will cause the direct-access control mechanism to begin to locate record 127 in file 17. Then the processing of statements by the computer will continue while the record is being located. By the time the READ instruction is encountered, the record may be located, in which case the READ can be executed more quickly, as only a data transfer is necessary. If the record has not yet been found, processing will pause temporarily, and the READ statement will subsequently be executed.

The FIND statement is always of the form

```
FIND(unit'index)
```

where 'unit' and 'index' are defined as they are for the READ or WRITE statement. After the record has been 'found', the associated variable has a value equal to the value of index in the FIND statement.

22.7 NAMELIST I/O

The NAMELIST feature of FORTRAN provides
a method of doing I/O without reference to a FORMAT
statement. In this sense, it is similar to WATFOR's
special format-free I/O features. Consider the
following example, which illustrates basically how
NAMELIST can be used to output variables.

```
C EXAMPLE 22.6 - OUTPUT USING NAMELIST
      DIMENSION IGD(3)
      COMPLEX XRAY
      REAL*8 A1/-13.7D0/
      NAMELIST/ALPHA/XRAY,LAMBDA,IGD,A1
      LAMBDA=5
      IGD(1)=6
      IGD(2)=-16
      IGD(3)=0
      XRAY=(25.38,-0.05)
    3 WRITE(6,ALPHA)
      STOP
      END
```

The non-executable NAMELIST statement declares the
FORTRAN symbolic name ALPHA to be the name of the
list of variables XRAY,LAMBDA,IGD,A1. The NAMELIST
name ALPHA can then be used in a subsequent WRITE
statement to print the values of all the variables
which appear in the list. This is done in the
WRITE statement numbered 3; there, ALPHA is used
where one might normally expect a format specification
to appear.

If this simple program were executed, the
output resulting from statement 3 would appear as
follows:

387

```
&ALPHA
XRAY=(25.38,0.05),LAMBDA=5,IGD=6,-16,0,A1=-13.7D0,&END
```

Note that the compiler supplies formatting automatically, and explicitly identifies each variable
printed. In the case of an array, for example, IGD,
the elements of the array are printed in storage
order, separated by commas. The significance of the
additional fields &ALPHA and &END will become more
apparent when we discuss NAMELIST input.

The next example illustrates that more
than one NAMELIST name can be declared in a program,
and that variables can appear in more than one list.

```
C EXAMPLE 22.7 - MORE NAMELISTS
      NAMELIST/X/A,B,C/Z/P,A,Q,S
      NAMELIST/Y/C,P
      .
      .
      .
      WRITE(6,Y)
      .
      .
      .
      IF(A.NE.B)WRITE(6,X)
      .
      .
      .
      WRITE(6,Z)
      STOP
      END
```

The first statement declares two NAMELIST
names, X and Z, and the second declares one NAMELIST
name, Y. If the program were to assign values of
-1.25, 3.89, 6.2, 16.2, -13., 7500., respectively,
to the variables A,B,C,P,Q,S, and, if all three
WRITE statements were executed in the order shown,
the output would appear as follows:

```
      &Y
      C=6.2,P=16.2,&END
      &X
      A=-1.25,B=3.89,C=6.2,&END
      &Z
      P=16.2,A=-1.25,Q=-13.,S=7500.,&END
```

The NAMELIST feature is often used as a simple and
convenient means of producing output for debugging
a program. It can be used to input values to a
program, but the rules are somewhat more detailed,
as the following example will show.

```
      C EXAMPLE 22.8 - NAMELIST INPUT
            COMPLEX Z
            DIMENSION X(3),B(2)
            NAMELIST/INLST/I,X,B,P,J,C,Z/VVB/A,B,X
      16 READ(5,INLST)
             .
             .
             .
            READ(5,VVB)
             .
             .
             .
            STOP
            END
```

A data card to be read by the READ statement
numbered 16 could be punched as

```
    &INLST B(2)=-5.3,J=11,Z=(0.,-2.5),X=1.,-7.,6.,&END
    ↑
    column 2
```

   Column one of the card must be blank.
The field &INLST[†], punched in columns two to seven,
indicates that a *NAMELIST data group* follows. At

[†] On a Model 026 keypunch, a '+' is used instead
of '&'.

least one blank column separates this field from
any data items which follow. A data item, for
example, B(2)=-5.3, specifically identifies the
variable or array element and the value it is to
receive as a result of the READ operation. Each
data item is followed immediately by a comma, and
the special field &END marks the end of the data
group.

   This particular card assigns values to
the variables J and Z, to the array element B(2),
and to all three elements of array X. Note that
the names J,Z,B,X, appear in the list declared for
NAMELIST name INLST in the program. Names not
appearing in the list INLST may not appear in the
data group. If an array name without subscripts
appears, followed by a list of constants, the
constants are assigned to the elements of the array
in storage order. It is not necessary to specify
values in the data group for all variables appearing
in the NAMELIST list; the current value of any
omitted variable (I,C,B(1),P, in Example 22.8)
is left unchanged by the READ statement.

   Data items may not contain embedded blanks.
For example,

    AbBCb=7.3b,XbY=b6b5bb,

are not valid data items, whereas

    ABC=7.3,bbXY=65.,

are valid.

   The usual rules of agreement between the
type of variable and type of constant apply for

NAMELIST input. Logical constants are punched as
T or F or .TRUE. or .FALSE., as in the DATA statement.
Furthermore, a replication factor can be used, as
in the DATA statement, if a particular constant is
to be assigned to a succession of elements of an
array. For example,

$$X=2*0.,1.,$$

could have been used to read values for all three
elements of the array X of Example 22.8.

Data items for one NAMELIST data group
may be punched on more than one card, but each
card must begin with a complete variable or array
name or a constant. Column one of each card must
be blank. The following illustration shows how the
data group for Example 22.8 could have been punched
on four cards.

```
column 2
↓
&INLST
     B(2)=-5.3,  Z=(0.,-2.5),
                       X=1.,-7.,6.,
     J=11,  &END
```

Now we explain the significance of the
header field &INLST. When a READ statement using
a NAMELIST name INLST is executed, the next
card in the card reader is read and examined. If
this card does not contain &INLST in columns 2 to
7, the next card is read, and the process is
repeated until a card containing &INLST is found.
Then, the items in that data group are used to
satisfy the READ request.

There are several other rules that must be followed when using NAMELIST. These are as follows.

(i)   A NAMELIST name may appear in a program only in a NAMELIST statement or a READ or WRITE statement.

(ii)   NAMELIST statements must be placed after any other declaration statements that name variables appearing in the NAMELIST lists.

(iii) A subprogram parameter may not be used in a NAMELIST list.

(iv)   As with the general form of the READ and WRITE statements described in Chapter 18, the unit number may be other than 5 or 6, and may be an integer variable. For example, the statements

```
NAMELIST/XYZ/A,B,C
     .
     .
     .
WRITE(7,XYZ)
     .
     .
     .
```

may be used in one program to punch a NAMELIST data group to be read by another program.

(v)   END and ERR returns may be specified in READ statements. An example is

```
READ(I,INLST,END=107)
```

22.8 DUMPLIST STATEMENT

The DUMPLIST statement of WATFIV was
designed especially as a program debugging aid.
Here is how it works:

(i)   A DUMPLIST statement is essentially a
NAMELIST statement, except that the word
DUMPLIST replaces the word NAMELIST.
Sample statements are

```
DUMPLIST/ABC/X,PVZ,LOGY/LIST1/A,ROVER
DUMPLIST/HERE/IFOR,ONE,M,KEEN
```

(ii) A DUMPLIST list name need never appear in
a READ or WRITE statement.

(iii) A DUMPLIST statement has *no* effect if the
program in which it appears executes
normally.

(iv) However, if execution of the program is
terminated because of an error condition,
WATFIV will automatically generate
NAMELIST-like output of all DUMPLIST
lists appearing in program segments which
have been entered. The values printed
are those which the variables had when the
program was terminated.

To avoid producing too much output, try to select
only a few key variables when constructing your
DUMPLIST statements. Usually a bug in a program can
be spotted by examining the final values of a few
carefully chosen variables.

22.9   CORE-TO-CORE INPUT/OUTPUT

In previous sections, we have discussed the general input/output statements

```
READ(unit,fmt,END=n,ERR=m)list
WRITE(unit,fmt)list
```

and their particular forms and applications in terms of I/O with card readers, printers, punches, tapes, and direct-access devices. In each of these cases, 'unit' referred to a specific physical device (or part of a physical device) which was external to the main memory. For example, if 'unit' were 5, a READ would cause a card or cards to be read sequentially from the card reader.

WATFIV allows another form of the 'unit' parameter in these generalized statements. When 'unit' is a variable of type character, the character string thus referenced is treated as an I/O device similar to the card reader or printer. The interesting thing is that no actual I/O device is involved; the effect is to create a memory-to-memory transfer of data, under format control. This format control gives the programmer the facility to trans-form data from one form to another within the computer. This feature is called *core-to-core I/O*, and has many useful and interesting applications.

Let us consider a number of simple examples to illustrate the mechanics of the process. Then we will introduce more comprehensive examples, and will conclude with a summary of the rules.

```
C EXAMPLE 22.9
      CHARACTER*11 A/'1.234-86.45'/
      READ(A,2)X,Y
    2 FORMAT(F5.3,F6.2)
      Z=X+Y
      PRINT,Z
      STOP
      END
```

In Example 22.9, the character variable
A may be considered as a card of 11 columns. The
READ statement references 'unit' A; since 'unit A'
has been declared a character variable, the contents
of variable A are 'read' in the same way as we
would read information from an eleven-column card.
The reading is under control of FORMAT statement 2.
Thus, the real variables X and Y are assigned the
values 1.234 and -86.45, respectively.

If the FORMAT statement were incorrect
in any way, an error message would occur.

Let us consider a few modifications of
the FORMAT statement, together with their effects.

(i)   2 FORMAT(F4.2,F7.2)
      The variable X is assigned the value 1.23,
      but an error occurs for Y, since the field
      4-86.45 can not be interpreted by the
      format code F7.2.

(ii) 2 FORMAT(F4.2,2X,F4.1)
      The variables X and Y are assigned the
      values 1.23 and 86.4, respectively. The
      2X causes the 4- to be skipped, and 5,
      the eleventh character, is ignored.

(iii)   2 FORMAT(F5.2,F8.2)

An error occurs because the FORMAT statement attempts to reference 13 characters,
whereas A has a capacity of only 11
characters.

(iv)   2 FORMAT(F5.3/F6.2)

Here, X is assigned the value 1.234
according to the format code F5.3.   The
'/' indicates that a new record is to be
used for the value of Y.   An error message
results, indicating that we have run out
of data, since the character variable A
consists of only one string or record.

To allow for the possibility of reading
more than one record in core-to-core I/O, the 'unit'
may be a character array.   For example, if we define
A by

    CHARACTER A*11(2)/'1.234','-86.45'/

then the statements

        READ(A,2)X,Y
        2 FORMAT(F5.3/F6.2)

result in values of 1.234 and -86.45 for X and Y,
respectively.   In effect, the elements of array A
can be considered as a collection of sequential
records.   Example 22.10 provides another illustration
of this idea.

```
C EXAMPLE 22.10
      INTEGER X/2579/
      CHARACTER*20 B(5)/5*' '/,Y/'ZZZ'/
      WRITE(B,2)X,Y
    2 FORMAT(I10,3X,'ABC'/A20)
      PRINT,B
      STOP
      END
```

In Example 22.10, the WRITE statement
references the character array B. The 5 elements
of the array B can be considered as 5 lines on the
printer, each one having 20 print positions. Thus,
after the WRITE is executed, elements B(1) and
B(2) would contain

bbbbbb2579bbbABCbbbb

and

ZZZbbbbbbbbbbbbbbbbb

respectively; the values of B(3), B(4), and B(5)
are not affected. No carriage-control character
need be used in the FORMAT statement, since no
actual printing takes place.

Consider the following FORMAT statements
and their corresponding effects.

(i)   2 FORMAT('A'/'B'/'C'/I4/A18)
      After the WRITE statement of Example 22.10
      is executed, the contents of array B are
      as follows:

B(1)   Abbbbbbbbbbbbbbbbbbb
B(2)   Bbbbbbbbbbbbbbbbbbbb
B(3)   Cbbbbbbbbbbbbbbbbbbb

397

```
          B(4)   2579bbbbbbbbbbbbbbbb
          B(5)   ZZZbbbbbbbbbbbbbbbbb
```

(ii)   2 FORMAT(I10,A20)

Here an error message results because the length of the first element of B is only 20, and the FORMAT statement is attempting to store 30 characters in it.

(iii)   2 FORMAT(//I10/A20/)

Here twenty blanks are stored in each of B(1), B(2), and B(5); B(3) and B(4) are as follows:

```
          B(3)   bbbbbb2579bbbbbbbbbb
          B(4)   ZZZbbbbbbbbbbbbbbbbb
```

(iv)   2 FORMAT(////I10/A20)

This results in an error message, since we are trying to write six records, and the character array contains only five elements.

The core-to-core 'unit' may also be specified as a character-array element. An example is

          READ(B(I),2)list

This has the effect of starting the READ at the Ith element or record of B.

22.10   RE-READS WITH CORE-TO-CORE I/O

One of the important applications of core-to-core I/O is the provision of a method of reading a record several times using different FORMAT statements. For example, an input deck can consist of cards with several different data formats in any order. Thus, before we read a card, we have no idea which of several FORMAT statements to use. Example 22.11 assumes that the input cards are of three types, and each type is identified by a code of 1, 2, or 3 in column 80. Core-to-core I/O can be used to overcome the problem, as indicated in the following example.

```
C EXAMPLE 22.11
      CHARACTER*79 STRING
      INTEGER TYPE
      READ 2,STRING,TYPE
    2 FORMAT(A79,I1)
      GO TO (4,5,6),TYPE
      PRINT,'ERROR IN CARD-',STRING,TYPE
      STOP
    4 READ(STRING,7)list
    7 FORMAT(...)
        .
        .
        .
    5 READ(STRING,8)list
    8 FORMAT(...)
        .
        .
        .
    6 READ(STRING,9)list
    9 FORMAT(...)
        .
        .
        .
      END
```

Here the first 79 columns of the card are read into a character variable STRING, and column 80 is read into TYPE. Then the type of card is determined, using the computed GO TO statement.

Subsequently, the first 79 columns are re-read from STRING, using core-to-core I/O and the appropriate FORMAT statement.

22.11 MODIFYING EXECUTION-TIME FORMATS

Another important application of core-to-core I/O is the convenient ability which it gives to the programmer to modify execution-time formats. For example, in the statement

```
        CHARACTER*13 F(1)/'(1H0,10X,1H*)'/
            •
            •
            •
        WRITE(6,F)
```

the format parameter in the WRITE statement is given as the character variable F. F is initialized to the character string

```
        (1H0,10X,1H*)
```

and this is a list of format codes. Thus, the WRITE statement results in an asterisk's being printed in the eleventh print position. A character array, or a character array element, can be used to store the string of format codes. An array of a different type could also be used.

```
        C EXAMPLE 22.12
              CHARACTER*13 F(1)
              DO 3 I=1,20
              WRITE(F,2)I
            2 FORMAT('(1H0,',I2,'X,1H*)')
            3 WRITE(6,F)
              STOP
              END
```

400

In this example, we have two WRITE statements within the range of the DO-loop. The first WRITE sets up a format list in the character variable F using core-to-core I/O. It is used as an execution-time format for the second WRITE. Note that, each time through the loop, the contents of F are changed according to the current value of I. The effect is that twenty lines are printed, each containing one asterisk, where the asterisk is in print position 2 of line 1, print position 3 of line 2, etc.

22.12 CORE-TO-CORE I/O SUMMARY

Core-to-core I/O uses the two generalized statements

```
READ(unit,fmt)list
WRITE(unit,fmt)list
```

'Unit' is either a character variable, a subscripted character variable, or a character array name. If 'unit' is an array, each element of that array is considered as a sequential record whose length is indicated by the number of bytes in each element of the character array.

The 'fmt' parameter is either a statement number of a FORMAT statement or the name of an execution-time format list.

The 'list' is similar to the list used in other I/O operations in FORTRAN.

22.13 <u>EXERCISES</u>

22.1 Prepare a data deck for the program in
      Example 22.1, and use the program and
      data deck to create a direct-access student
      record file. It is unlikely that you will
      want to prepare 1869 data cards so be sure
      to change the DO statement to suit your
      special requirements.

      Choose your student numbers so that they
      begin at 1 and use consecutive integers.
      Assign the student numbers to the student
      names at random.

22.2 (a) Write programs which read the student
          record file and list student
          number and name for each record in
          the file
          (i)   in increasing sequence by student
                number.
          (ii) in decreasing sequence by student
                number.

22.3 Suppose we are required to print the
      student record file in alphabetic order
      by name. Since the original student
      numbers were assigned at random, the
      solution to the problem is not trivial.
      There are many ways to solve the problem
      and the following is one solution.
      (a) Prepare a data deck which contains
          one card for each student in the
          file. Each card should contain only
          the student number. Sort this

deck manually so that the sequence of student numbers will represent the students in alphabetic order by name. Write a program which reads this data deck and prints the file in alphabetic sequence.

(b)   The data deck prepared for (a) is really a 'list' of pointers to the records. This list could be permanently stored in a direct-access file and used whenever an alphabetic listing is required. Write a program to create this special file; subsequently, use the file to produce an alphabetic listing.

(c)   Instead of creating a special file to store the list, as suggested in (b), we could place a 'pointer' in each record; this indicates the next record in alphabetic sequence. Thus, if we know the position of the first record in alphabetic order, we could print the entire file in alphabetic sequence. Write a program which reads the data deck prepared for (a) and modifies the entire file to add the appropriate pointers to each record. Note that the last record (alphabetically) must have a special pointer (zero for example) to indicate the end of the 'chain'.

22.4 Keeping a file up-to-date always presents
      special problems. For example, suppose that
      we wish to add two new students to the
      student record file, and that we also wish
      to delete one particular student who has
      withdrawn. First we must assign student
      numbers to the two new students. Then we
      must prepare a data deck which contains
      three cards, one for each of the new
      students, and one for the student who is
      to be removed from the file. These data
      cards contain not only student number and
      name, but also a special code which indicates
      the action to be taken. For example, the
      new students could be indicated by code 1,
      and the student to be deleted could be
      indicated by code 2.

      (a) Write a program which updates the file
           as created in Exercise 22.1.
      (b) Write a program which updates the file
           or files as modified in Exercise 22.3
           (b) and Exercise 22.3 (c).

22.5 In Example 22.3, we encountered a problem:
      it was impossible to tell whether or not
      a mark of zero was legitimate. One way of
      overcoming the problem is to read the
      record twice. The first time we use A
      format, and test for blank characters in
      the MARK field of the record. Subsequently,
      when we read the record using the second
      format, we are aware of the status of
      this field.

(a)   Modify the program to use this
      technique, and have it print 'NO MARK'
      whenever there is a blank MARK field.

(b)   When you have studied core-to-core
      I/O, modify the program to make use
      of this feature.

22.6   A card contains one or more integer
       constants, separated from one another by
       semicolons. Write a generalized program
       which reads cards of this type and which
       calculates and prints the sum of the
       integers on each card. Test your program
       using the following data cards.

column 1
↓
123;-86;12678;+35
-8;+3;-0;+0;896;34286

22.7   (a)   Key-punch the program of Example 22.12
             and verify that it works by testing
             it on the computer.

       (b)   Modify the program by replacing the
             DO statement with the following four
             statements

```
J=5
DO 3 K=1,11
I=J**2
J=J-1
```

             Run the program, and note the pattern
             of asterisks. What function are you
             plotting, and for what values of the
             variables?

APPENDIX A

FORTRAN BUILT-IN FUNCTIONS

The following table summarizes the
built-in functions that are available with FORTRAN
processors for the IBM 360. Several notational
conveniences are used to simplify the table.

The following symbols are used to denote
the type of arguments:

    i2 any half-word integer expression

    i4 any full-word integer expression

    r4 any single-precision real expression

    r8 any double-precision real expression

    c8 any complex expression

    c16 any extended-precision complex
        expression

These symbols are also used to denote the type of
result of the functions.

The symbols a, a1, a2, represent arguments
in general; a1 and a2 are used specifically to
represent first and second arguments. Some functions
may be used with an unspecified number of arguments;
this is shown by the use of dots (...) with the
function name.

MATHEMATICAL SIGNIFICANCE	FUNCTION NAME WITH ARGUMENTS	DEFINITION	
Square Root	SQRT(r4)	$\sqrt{a}$	
	DSQRT(r8)		r8
	CSQRT(c8)		c8
	CDSQRT(c16)		c16
Sine	SIN(r4)	sin a	r4
	DSIN(r8)		r8
	CSIN(c8)		c8
	CDSIN(c16)	a in radians	c16
Cosine	COS(r4)	cos a	r4
	DCOS(r8)		r8
	CCOS(c8)		c8
	CDCOS(c16)	a in radians	c16
Tangent	TAN(r4)	tan a	r4
	DTAN(r8)	a in radians	r8
Cotangent	COTAN(r4)	cot a	r4
	DCOTAN(r8)	a in radians	r8
Arcsine	ARSIN(r4)	x=arcsin a	r4
	DARSIN(r8)	$-\frac{\pi}{2} \leq x \leq \frac{\pi}{2}$	r8
Arccosine	ARCOS(r4)	x=arccos a	r4
	DARCOS(r8)	$0 \leq x \leq \pi$	r8
Arctangent	ATAN(r4)	x=arctan a	r4
	DATAN(r8)	$-\frac{\pi}{2} \leq x \leq \frac{\pi}{2}$	r8
	ATAN2(r4,r4)	x=arctan(a1/a2)	r4
	DATAN2(r8,r8)	$-\pi \leq x \leq \pi$	r8

MATHEMATICAL SIGNIFICANCE	FUNCTION NAME WITH ARGUMENTS	DEFINITION	TYPE OF RESULT
Exponential	EXP(r4) DEXP(r8) CEXP(c8) CDEXP(c16)	e^a	r4 r8 c8 c16
Natural Logarithm	ALOG(r4) DLOG(r8) CLOG(c8) CDLOG(c16)	$\log_e a$	r4 r8 c8 c16
Common Logarithm	ALOG10(r4) DLOG10(r8)	$\log_{10} a$	r4 r8
Hyperbolic Sine	SINH(r4) DSINH(r8)	$\sinh a$	r4 r8
Hyperbolic Cosine	COSH(r4) DCOSH(r8)	$\cosh a$	r4 r8
Hyperbolic Tangent	TANH(r4) DTANH(r8)	$\tanh a$	r4 r8
Error Function	ERF(r4) DERF(r8)	$\mathrm{erf}(a) = \dfrac{2}{\sqrt{\pi}} \int_0^a e^{-t^2} dt$	r4 r8
	ERFC(r4) DERFC(r8)	$1 - \mathrm{erf}(a)$	r4 r8
Gamma Function	GAMMA(r4) DGAMMA(r8)	$\Gamma(a) = \int_0^\infty t^{a-1} e^{-t} dt$	r4 r8
	ALGAMA(r4) DLGAMA(r8)	$\mathrm{loggamma}(a) = \log_e \Gamma(a)$	r4 r8

MATHEMATICAL SIGNIFICANCE	FUNCTION NAME WITH ARGUMENTS	DEFINITION	TYPE OF RESULT
Absolute Value	IABS(i4) ABS(r4) DABS(r8)	$\lvert a \rvert$	i4 r4 r8
	CABS(c8) CDABS(c16)	$\sqrt{x^2+y^2}$ for x+iy	r4 r8
Type Conversion	FLOAT(i4) DFLOAT(i4)	Convert from integer to real	r4 r8
	IFIX(r4) HFIX(r4)	Convert from real to integer	i4 i2
	SNGL(r8)	Most significant part of double-precision value	r4
	DBLE(r4)	Convert single- to double-precision	r8
	CMPLX(r4,r4) DCMPLX(r8,r8)	Convert two real values to complex	c8 c16
	REAL(c8)	Obtain real part of complex value	r4
	AIMAG(c8)	Obtain imaginary part to complex value	r4
Complex Conjugate	CONJG(c8) DCONJG(c16)	$\bar{a}=x-iy$ for a=x+iy	c8 c16

409

MATHEMATICAL SIGNIFICANCE	FUNCTION NAME WITH ARGUMENTS	DEFINITION	TYPE OF RESULT
Transfer of Sign	SIGN(r4,r4) ISIGN(i4,i4) DSIGN(r8,r8)	$\lvert a1\rvert \, sgn(a2)$, where $sgn(a)=\begin{cases} 1 & a>0 \\ 1 & a=0 \\ -1 & a<0 \end{cases}$	r4 i4 r8
Truncation	INT(r4) AINT(r4) IDINT(r8)	$sgn(a)\left[\lvert a\rvert\right]$, where $\left[x\right]$ is the largest integer $\leq x$	i4 r4 i4
Modular Arithmetic	MOD(i4,i4) AMOD(r4,r4) DMOD(r8,r8)	$a1-sgn(x)\left[\lvert x\rvert\right]a2$ where $x=a1/a2$	i4 r4 r8
Positive Difference	DIM(r4,r4) IDIM(i4,i4)	$a1-min(a1,a2)$	r4 i4
Largest Value	AMAX0(i4,i4,..) AMAX1(r4,r4,..) MAX0(i4,i4,..) MAX1(r4,r4,..) DMAX1(r8,r8,..)	$max(a1,a2,..)$	r4 r4 i4 i4 r8
Smallest Value	AMIN0(i4,i4,..) AMIN1(r4,r4,..) MIN0(i4,i4,..) MIN1(r4,r4,..) DMIN1(r8,r8,..)	$min(a1,a2,..)$	r4 r4 i4 i4 r8

410

APPENDIX B

WATFOR DIAGNOSTIC MESSAGES

The WATFOR FORTRAN compiler has been
designed to aid the programmer in the debugging
process that is inherent in most programming tasks.
To do this, the compiler provides checking of the
source program, at compile time, for violations of
the rules of the language. An error is indicated
by printing a coded message on the printer listing
of the source program, usually following the statement in which the violation occurred. If no serious
errors occur, the resulting machine-language program
may be executed.

Although WATFOR cannot detect errors in
the logic of a program, it can continue to check,
at execution time, for conditions which indicate
an oversight on the part of the programmer. Again,
the error is noted by a coded message on the
printed output, and execution of the program is
terminated.

At compile time, there are three levels
of error message that may appear - *Extension,
Warning, Error.*

An Extension message is meant to indicate
that the programmer has used an extension, allowed
by WATFOR[†], of the FORTRAN language; the purpose

---

† Uses of format-free I/O are not flagged.

411

is to warn the programmer that his program will
not likely be accepted by any other FORTRAN
compiler. For example, the statement

PRINT25,X**2+Y**2

would receive an IO-C extension message.

A Warning message indicates that the
compiler has made some assumption about the program.
For example, the statement

GZORGUMPLATZ=4.5

would be flagged with a VA-2 warning message to
indicate that WATFOR had recognized a variable name
longer than six characters, but had proceeded by
truncating the name to use only the six farthest-
left characters, and had ignored the rest.

An Error message indicates a language
violation severe enough to prevent execution.

A complete list of codes that WATFOR can
produce while diagnosing a program follows in this
appendix. A few words should be said about how to
interpret these codes. In most cases, the message
printed supplies some information in addition to
the actual code; this information relates to the
condition encountered, and may include, for example,
the number of the line[†] or the name of the subprogram in which the condition occurred. Execution-
time messages include a feature which lists all the

[†] The line number appears to the left of each
statement on the printer listing.

412

subprograms involved when an error is found in a subprogram. The list names the calling segment, the segment which calls the calling segment, etc., all the way back to the main program, which is referenced as M/PROG. Some printouts include a descriptive phrase which should be read in the context of the message found in the code table. For example, the statement

$$DO \ 1 \ X=1,10 \qquad (assume \ X \ is \ real)$$

will be flagged with the message DO-5 NAMELY X. The text for DO-5 is 'INVALID DO PARAMETER'. The message should be construed as: An invalid DO-parameter, namely, X, has been detected at compile time.

WATFOR will allow 'undefined variables' to be output, but these are easily detected by the programmer, as the printed values are quite striking. For example, an undefined full-word integer value appears as −2139062144; an undefined real value appears as −0.4335017E−77.

'ASSIGN STATEMENTS AND VARIABLES'
AS-2   'ATTEMPT TO REDEFINE AN ASSIGNED VARIABLE IN AN ARITHMETIC STATEMENT'
AS-3   'ASSIGNED VARIABLE USED IN AN ARITHMETIC EXPRESSION'
AS-4   'ASSIGNED VARIABLE CANNOT BE HALF WORD INTEGER'
AS-5   'ATTEMPT TO REDEFINE AN ASSIGN VARIABLE IN AN INPUT LIST'

'BLOCK DATA STATEMENTS'
BD-0   'EXECUTABLE STATEMENT IN BLOCK DATA SUBPROGRAMME'
BD-1   'IMPROPER BLOCK DATA STATEMENT'

'CARD FORMAT AND CONTENTS'
CC-0   'COLUMNS 1-5 OF CONTINUATION CARD NOT BLANK'
             PROBABLE CAUSE - STATEMENT PUNCHED TO LEFT OF COLUMN 7
CC-1   'TOO MANY CONTINUATION CARDS (MAXIMUM OF 7)'
CC-2   'INVALID CHARACTER IN FORTRAN STATEMENT '$' INSERTED IN SOURCE LISTING'
CC-3   'FIRST CARD OF A PROGRAMME IS A CONTINUATION CARD'
             PROBABLE CAUSE - STATEMENT PUNCHED TO LEFT OF COLUMN 7
CC-4   'STATEMENT TOO LONG TO COMPILE (SCAN-STACK OVERFLOW)'
CC-5   'BLANK CARD ENCOUNTERED'
CC-6   'KEYPUNCH USED DIFFERS FROM KEYPUNCH SPECIFIED ON JOB CARD'
CC-7   'FIRST CHARACTER OF STATEMENT NOT ALPHABETIC'
CC-8   'INVALID CHARACTER(S) CONCATENTATED WITH FORTRAN KEYWORD'
CC-9   'INVALID CHARACTERS IN COL 1-5. STATEMENT NUMBER IGNORED'
             PROBABLE CAUSE - STATEMENT PUNCHED TO LEFT OF COLUMN 7

'COMMON'
CM-0   'VARIABLE PREVIOUSLY PLACED IN COMMON'
CM-1   'NAME IN COMMON LIST PREVIOUSLY USED AS OTHER THAN VARIABLE'
CM-2   'SUBPROGRAMME PARAMETER APPEARS IN COMMON STATEMENT'
CM-3   'INITIALIZING OF COMMON SHOULD BE DONE IN A BLOCK DATA SUBPROGRAMME'
CM-4   'ILLEGAL USE OF BLOCK NAME'

'FORTRAN TYPE CONSTANTS'
CN-0   'MIXED REAL*4,REAL*8 IN COMPLEX CONSTANT'
CN-1   'INTEGER CONSTANT GREATER THAN 2,147,483,647 (2**31-1)'
CN-2   'EXPONENT OVERFLOW OR UNDERFLOW CONVERTING CONSTANT IN SOURCE STATEMENT'
CN-3   'EXPONENT ON REAL CONSTANT GREATER THAN 99'
CN-4   'REAL CONSTANT HAS MORE THAN 16 DIGITS, TRUNCATED TO 16'
CN-5   'INVALID HEXADECIMAL CONSTANT'
CN-6   'ILLEGAL USE OF DECIMAL POINT'
CN-8   'CONSTANT WITH E-TYPE EXPONENT HAS MORE THAN 7 DIGITS, ASSUME D-TYPE'
CN-9   'CONSTANT OR STATEMENT NUMBER GREATER THAN 99999'

'COMPILER ERRORS'
CP-0   'DETECTED IN PHASE RELOC'
CP-1   'DETECTED IN PHASE LINKR'
CP-2   'DUPLICATE PSEUDO STATEMENT NUMBERS'
CP-4   'DETECTED IN PHASE ARITH'
CP-5   'COMPILER INTERRUPT'

'DATA STATEMENT'
DA-0   'REPLICATION FACTOR GREATER THAN 32767, ASSUME 32767'
DA-1   'NON-CONSTANT IN DATA STATEMENT'
DA-2   'MORE VARIABLES THAN CONSTANTS IN DATA STATEMENT'
DA-3   'ATTEMPT TO INITIALIZE A SUBPROGRAMME PARAMETER IN A DATA STATEMENT'
DA-4   'NON-CONSTANT SUBSCRIPTS IN A DATA STATEMENT INVALID IN /360 FORTRAN'
DA-5   '/360 FORTRAN DOES NOT HAVE IMPLIED DO IN DATA STATEMENT'
DA-6   'NON-AGREEMENT BETWEEN TYPE OF VARIABLE AND CONSTANT IN DATA STATEMENT'
DA-7   'MORE CONSTANTS THAN VARIABLES IN DATA STATEMENT'
DA-8   'VARIABLE PREVIOUSLY INITIALIZED. LATEST VALUE USED'
             CHECK COMMON/EQUIVALENCED VARIABLES
DA-9   'INITIALIZING BLANK COMMON NOT ALLOWED IN /360 FORTRAN'
DA-A   'INVALID DELIMITER IN CONSTANT LIST PORTION OF DATA STATEMENT'
DA-B   'TRUNCATION OF LITERAL CONSTANT HAS OCCURRED'

'DIMENSION STATEMENTS'
DM-0   'NO DIMENSIONS SPECIFIED FOR A VARIABLE IN A DIMENSION STATEMENT'
DM-1   'OPTIONAL LENGTH SPECIFICATION IN DIMENSION STATEMENT IS ILLEGAL'
DM-2   'INITIALIZATION IN DIMENSION STATEMENT IS ILLEGAL'
DM-3   'ATTEMPT TO RE-DIMENSION A VARIABLE'
DM-4   'ATTEMPT TO DIMENSION AN INITIALIZED VARIABLE'

'DO LOOPS'
DO-0   'ILLEGAL STATEMENT USED AS OBJECT OF DO'
DO-1   'ILLEGAL TRANSFER INTO THE RANGE OF A DO-LOOP'
DO-2   'OBJECT OF A DO STATEMENT HAS ALREADY APPEARED'
DO-3   'IMPROPERLY NESTED DO-LOOPS'
DO-4   'ATTEMPT TO REDEFINE A DO-LOOP PARAMETER WITHIN RANGE OF LOOP'
DO-5   'INVALID DO-LOOP PARAMETER'
DO-6   'TOO MANY NESTED DO'S (MAXIMUM OF 20)'
DO-7   'DO-PARAMETER IS UNDEFINED OR OUTSIDE RANGE'
DO-8   'THIS DO LOOP WILL TERMINATE AFTER FIRST TIME THROUGH'
DO-9   'ATTEMPT TO REDEFINE A DO-LOOP PARAMETER IN AN INPUT LIST'

'EQUIVALENCE AND/OR COMMON'
EC-0   'TWO EQUIVALENCED VARIABLES APPEAR IN COMMON'
EC-1   'COMMON BLOCK HAS DIFFERENT LENGTH THAN IN A PREVIOUS SUBPROGRAMME'
EC-2   'COMMON AND/OR EQUIVALENCE CAUSES INVALID ALIGNMENT. EXECUTION SLOWED'
        REMEDY - ORDER VARIABLES IN DESCENDING ORDER BY LENGTH
EC-3   'EQUIVALENCE EXTENDS COMMON DOWNWARDS'
EC-7   'COMMON/EQUIVALENCE STATEMENT DOES NOT PRECEDE PREVIOUS USE OF VARIABLE'
EC-8   'VARIABLE USED WITH NON-CONSTANT SUBSCRIPT IN COMMON/EQUIVALENCE LIST'
EC-9   'A NAME SUBSCRIPTED IN AN EQUIVALENCE STATEMENT WAS NOT DIMENSIONED'

'END STATEMENTS'
EN-0   'NO END STATEMENT IN PROGRAMME -- END STATEMENT GENERATED'
EN-1   'END STATEMENT USED AS STOP STATEMENT AT EXECUTION'
EN-2   'IMPROPER END STATEMENT'
EN-3   'FIRST STATEMENT OF SUBPROGRAMME IS END STATEMENT'

'EQUAL SIGNS'
EQ-6   'ILLEGAL QUANTITY ON LEFT OF EQUALS SIGN'
EQ-8   'ILLEGAL USE OF EQUAL SIGN'
EQ-A   'MULTIPLE ASSIGNMENT STATEMENTS NOT IN /360 FORTRAN'

'EQUIVALENCE STATEMENTS'
EV-0   'ATTEMPT TO EQUIVALENCE A VARIABLE TO ITSELF'
EV-1   'ATTEMPT TO EQUIVALENCE A SUBPROGRAMME PARAMETER'
EV-2   'LESS THAN 2 MEMBERS IN AN EQUIVALENCE LIST'
EV-3   'TOO MANY EQUIVALENCE LISTS (MAX = 255)'
EV-4   'PREVIOUSLY EQUIVALENCED VARIABLE RE-EQUIVALENCED INCORRECTLY'

'POWERS AND EXPONENTIATION'
EX-0   'ILLEGAL COMPLEX EXPONENTIATION'
EX-2   'I**J WHERE I=J=0'
EX-3   'I**J WHERE I=0, J.LT.0'
EX-6   '0.0**Y WHERE Y.LE.0.0'
EX-7   '0.0**J WHERE J=0'
EX-8   '0.0**J WHERE J.LT.0'
EX-9   'X**Y WHERE X.LT.0.0, Y.NE.0.0'

'ENTRY STATEMENT'
EY-0   'SUBPROGRAMME NAME IN ENTRY STATEMENT PREVIOUSLY DEFINED'
EY-1   'PREVIOUS DEFINITION OF FUNCTION NAME IN AN ENTRY IS INCORRECT'
EY-2   'USE OF SUBPROGRAMME PARAMETER INCONSISTENT WITH PREVIOUS ENTRY POINT'
EY-3   'ARGUMENT NAME HAS APPEARED IN AN EXECUTABLE STATEMENT'
        BUT WAS NOT A SUBPROGRAMME PARAMETER
EY-4   'ENTRY STATEMENT NOT PERMITTED IN MAIN PROGRAMME'
EY-5   'ENTRY POINT INVALID INSIDE A DO-LOOP'
EY-6   'VARIABLE WAS NOT PREVIOUSLY USED AS A PARAMETER - PARAMETER ASSUMED'

'FORMAT'
    SOME FORMAT ERROR MESSAGES GIVE CHARACTERS IN WHICH ERROR WAS DETECTED
FM-0   'INVALID CHARACTER IN INPUT DATA'
FM-2   'NO STATEMENT NUMBER ON A FORMAT STATEMENT'
FM-5   'FORMAT SPECIFICATION AND DATA TYPE DO NOT MATCH'
FM-6   'INCORRECT SEQUENCE OF CHARACTERS IN INPUT DATA'
FM-7   'NON-TERMINATING FORMAT'

FT-0   'FIRST CHARACTER OF VARIABLE FORMAT NOT A LEFT PARENTHESIS'
FT-1   'INVALID CHARACTER ENCOUNTERED IN FORMAT'
FT-2   'INVALID FORM FOLLOWING A SPECIFICATION'
FT-3   'INVALID FIELD OR GROUP COUNT'
FT-4   'A FIELD OR GROUP COUNT GREATER THAN 255'
FT-5   'NO CLOSING PARENTHESIS ON VARIABLE FORMAT'
FT-6   'NO CLOSING QUOTE IN A HOLLERITH FIELD'
FT-7   'INVALID USE OF COMMA'
FT-8   'INSUFFICIENT SPACE TO COMPILE A FORMAT STATEMENT (SCAN-STACK OVERFLOW)'
FT-9   'INVALID USE OF P SPECIFICATION'
FT-A   'CHARACTER FOLLOWS CLOSING RIGHT PARENTHESIS'
FT-B   'INVALID USE OF PERIOD(.)'
FT-C   'MORE THAN THREE LEVELS OF PARENTHESES'
FT-D   'INVALID CHARACTER BEFORE A RIGHT PARENTHESIS'
FT-E   'MISSING OR ZERO LENGTH HOLLERITH ENCOUNTERED'
FT-F   'NO CLOSING RIGHT PARENTHESIS'

'FUNCTIONS AND SUBROUTINES'
FN-0   'NO ARGUMENTS IN A FUNCTION STATEMENT'
FN-3   'REPEATED ARGUMENT IN SUBPROGRAMME OR STATEMENT FUNCTION DEFINITION'
FN-4   'SUBSCRIPTS ON RIGHT HAND SIDE OF STATEMENT FUNCTION'
                PROBABLE CAUSE - VARIABLE TO LEFT OF = NOT DIMENSIONED
FN-5   'MULTIPLE RETURNS ARE INVALID IN FUNCTION SUBPROGRAMMES'
FN-6   'ILLEGAL LENGTH MODIFIER IN TYPE FUNCTION STATEMENT'
FN-7   'INVALID ARGUMENT IN ARITHMETIC OR LOGICAL STATEMENT FUNCTION'
FN-8   'ARGUMENT OF SUBPROGRAMME IS SAME AS SUBPROGRAMME NAME'

'GO TO STATEMENTS'
GO-0   'STATEMENT TRANSFERS TO ITSELF OR A NON-EXECUTABLE STATEMENT'
GO-1   'INVALID TRANSFER TO THIS STATEMENT'
GO-2   'INDEXED OF COMPUTED 'GOTO' IS NEGATIVE,ZERO OR UNDEFINED'
GO-3   'ERROR IN VARIABLE OF 'GO TO' STATEMENT'
GO-4   'INDEX OF ASSIGNED 'GO TO' IS UNDEFINED OR NOT IN RANGE'

'HOLLERITH CONSTANTS'
HO-0   'ZERO LENGTH SPECIFIED FOR H-TYPE HOLLERITH'
HO-1   'ZERO LENGTH QUOTE-TYPE HOLLERITH'
HO-2   'NO CLOSING QUOTE OR NEXT CARD NOT CONTINUATION CARD'
HO-3   'HOLLERITH CONSTANT SHOULD APPEAR ONLY IN CALL STATEMENT'
HO-4   'UNEXPECTED HOLLERITH OR STATEMENT NUMBER CONSTANT'

'IF STATEMENTS (ARITHMETIC AND LOGICAL)'
IF-0   'STATEMENT INVALID AFTER A LOGICAL IF'
IF-3   'ARITHMETIC OR INVALID EXPRESSION IN LOGICAL IF'
IF-4   'LOGICAL, COMPLEX, OR INVALID EXPRESSION IN ARITHMETIC IF'

'IMPLICIT STATEMENT'
IM-0   'INVALID MODE SPECIFIED IN AN IMPLICIT STATEMENT'
IM-1   'INVALID LENGTH SPECIFIED IN AN IMPLICIT OR TYPE STATEMENT'
IM-2   'ILLEGAL APPEARANCE OF $ IN A CHARACTER RANGE'
IM-3   'IMPROPER ALPHABETIC SEQUENCE IN CHARACTER RANGE'
IM-4   'SPECIFICATION MUST BE SINGLE ALPHABETIC CHARACTER, 1ST CHARACTER USED'
IM-5   'IMPLICIT STATEMENT DOES NOT PRECEDE OTHER SPECIFICATION STATEMENTS'
IM-6   'ATTEMPT TO ESTABLISH THE TYPE OF A CHARACTER MORE THAN ONCE'
IM-7   '/360 FORTRAN ALLOWS ONE IMPLICIT STATEMENT PER PROGRAMME'
IM-8   'INVALID ELEMENT IN IMPLICIT STATEMENT'
IM-9   'INVALID DELIMITER IN IMPLICIT STATEMENT'

'INPUT/OUTPUT'
IO-0   'MISSING COMMA IN I/O LIST OF I/O OR DATA STATEMENT'
IO-2   'STATEMENT NUMBER IN I/O STATEMENT NOT A FORMAT STATEMENT NUMBER'
IO-3   'FORMATTED LINE TOO LONG FOR I/O DEVICE (RECORD LENGTH EXCEEDED)'
IO-6   'VARIABLE FORMAT NOT AN ARRAY NAME'
IO-8   'INVALID ELEMENT IN INPUT LIST OR DATA LIST'
IO-9   'TYPE OF VARIABLE UNIT NOT INTEGER IN I/O STATEMENTS'
IO-A   'HALF-WORD INTEGER VARIABLE USED AS UNIT IN I/O STATEMENTS'
IO-B   'ASSIGNED INTEGER VARIABLE USED AS UNIT IN I/O STATEMENTS'
IO-C   'INVALID ELEMENT IN AN OUTPUT LIST'
IO-D   'MISSING OR INVALID UNIT IN I/O STATEMENT'
IO-E   'MISSING OR INVALID FORMAT IN READ/WRITE STATEMENT'
IO-F   'INVALID DELIMITER IN SPECIFICATION PART OF I/O STATEMENT'
IO-G   'MISSING STATEMENT NUMBER AFTER END= OR ERR='
IO-H   '/360 FORTRAN DOESN'T ALLOW END/ERR RETURNS IN WRITE STATEMENTS'
IO-J   'INVALID DELIMITER IN I/O LIST'
IO-K   'INVALID DELIMITER IN STOP, PAUSE, DATA, OR TAPE CONTROL STATEMENT'

'JOB CONTROL CARDS'
JB-1   'JOB CARD ENCOUNTERED DURING COMPILATION'
JB-2   'INVALID OPTION(S) SPECIFIED ON JOB CARD'
JB-3   'UNEXPECTED CONTROL CARD ENCOUNTERED DURING COMPILATION'

'JOB TERMINATION'
KO-0   'JOB TERMINATED IN EXECUTION BECAUSE OF COMPILE TIME ERROR'
KO-1   'FIXED-POINT DIVISION BY ZERO'
KO-2   'FLOATING-POINT DIVISION BY ZERO'
KO-3   'TOO MANY EXPONENT OVERFLOWS'
KO-4   'TOO MANY EXPONENT UNDERFLOWS'
KO-5   'TOO MANY FIXED-POINT OVERFLOWS'
KO-6   'JOB TIME EXCEEDED'
KO-7   'COMPILER ERROR - INTERRUPTION AT EXECUTION TIME,RETURN TO SYSTEM'
KO-8   'INTEGER IN INPUT DATA IS TOO LARGE (MAXIMUM IS 2147483647)'

'LOGICAL OPERATIONS'
LG-2   '.NOT. USED AS A BINARY OPERATOR'

'LIBRARY ROUTINES'
LI-0   'ARGUMENT OUT OF RANGE DGAMMA OR GAMMA. (1.382E-76 .LT. X .LT. 57.57)'
LI-1   'ABSOLUTE VALUE OF ARGUMENT .GT. 174.673, SINH,COSH,DSINH,DCOSH'
LI-2   'SENSE LIGHT OTHER THAN 0,1,2,3,4 FOR SLITE OR 1,2,3,4 FOR SLITET'
LI-3   'REAL PORTION OF ARGUMENT .GT. 174.673, CEXP OR CDEXP'
LI-4   'ABS(AIMAG(Z)) .GT. 174.673 FOR CSIN, CCOS, CDSIN OR CDCOS OF Z'
LI-5   'ABS(REAL(Z)) .GE. 3.537E15 FOR CSIN, CCOS, CDSIN OR CDCOS OF Z'
LI-6   'ABS(AIMAG(Z)) .GE. 3.537E15 FOR CEXP OR CDEXP OF Z'
LI-7   'ARGUMENT .GT. 174.673, EXP OR DEXP'
LI-8   'ARGUMENT IS ZERO, CLOG, CLOG10, CDLOG OR CDLG10'
LI-9   'ARGUMENT IS NEGATIVE OR ZERO, ALOG, ALOG10, DLOG OR DLOG10'
LI-A   'ABS(X) .GE. 3.537E15 FOR SIN, COS, DSIN OR DCOS OF X'
LI-B   'ABSOLUTE VALUE OF ARGUMENT .GT. 1, FOR ARSIN, ARCOS, DARSIN OR DARCOS'
LI-C   'ARGUMENT IS NEGATIVE, SQRT OR DSQRT'
LI-D   'BOTH ARGUMENTS OF DATAN2 OR ATAN2 ARE ZERO'
LI-E   'ARGUMENT TOO CLOSE TO A SINGULARITY, TAN, COTAN, DTAN OR DCOTAN'
LI-F   'ARGUMENT OUT OF RANGE DLGAMA OR ALGAMA. (0.0 .LT. X .LT. 4.29E73)'
LI-G   'ABSOLUTE VALUE OF ARGUMENT .GE. 3.537E15, TAN, COTAN, DTAN, DCOTAN'
LI-H   'FEWER THAN TWO ARGUMENTS FOR ONE OF MINO, MIN1, AMINO, ETC.'

'MIXED MODE'
MD-2   'RELATIONAL OPERATOR HAS A LOGICAL OPERAND'
MD-3   'RELATIONAL OPERATOR HAS A COMPLEX OPERAND'
MD-4   'MIXED MODE - LOGICAL WITH ARITHMETIC'
MD-6   'WARNING - SUBSCRIPT IS COMPLEX. REAL PART USED'

417

'MEMORY OVERFLOW'
MO-0   'SYMBOL TABLE OVERFLOWS OBJECT CODE. SOURCE ERROR CHECKING CONTINUES'
MO-1   'INSUFFICIENT MEMORY TO ASSIGN ARRAY STORAGE. JOB ABANDONED'
MO-2   'SYMBOL TABLE OVERFLOWS COMPILER, JOB ABANDONED'
MO-3   'DATA AREA OF SUBPROGRAMME TOO LARGE -- SEGMENT SUBPROGRAMME'
MO-4   'GETMAIN CANNOT PROVIDE BUFFER FOR WATLIB'

'NAMELIST'
NA-0   'MULTIPLY DEFINED NAMELIST NAME'
NA-1   'NAMELIST NOT IMPLEMENTED'

'PARENTHESES'
PC-0   'UNMATCHED PARENTHESES'
PC-1   'INVALID PARENTHESIS COUNT'

'PAUSE, STOP STATEMENTS'
PS-0   'STOP WITH OPERATOR MESSAGE NOT ALLOWED. SIMPLE STOP ASSUMED'
PS-1   'PAUSE WITH OPERATOR MESSAGE NOT ALLOWED. TREATED AS CONTINUE'

'RETURN STATEMENT'
RE-0   'FIRST CARD OF SUBPROGRAMME IS A RETURN STATEMENT'
RE-1   'RETURN I, WHERE I IS ZERO,NEGATIVE OR TOO LARGE'
RE-2   'MULTIPLE RETURN NOT VALID IN FUNCTION SUBPROGRAMME'
RE-3   'VARIABLE IN MULTIPLE RETURN IS NOT A SIMPLE INTEGER VARIABLE'
RE-4   'MULTIPLE RETURN NOT VALID IN MAIN PROGRAMME'

'ARITHMETIC AND LOGICAL STATEMENT FUNCTIONS'
    PROBABLE CAUSE OF SF ERRORS - VARIABLE ON LEFT OF = WAS NOT DIMENSIONED
SF-1   'PREVIOUSLY REFERENCED STATEMENT NUMBER ON STATEMENT FUNCTION'
SF-2   'STATEMENT FUNCTION IS THE OBJECT OF A LOGICAL IF STATEMENT'
SF-3   'RECURSIVE STATEMENT FUNCTION, NAME APPEARS ON BOTH SIDES OF ='
SF-5   'ILLEGAL USE OF A STATEMENT FUNCTION'

'SUBPROGRAMMES'
SR-0   'MISSING SUBPROGRAMME'
SR-2   'SUBPROGRAMME ASSIGNED DIFFERENT MODES IN DIFFERENT PROGRAMME SEGMENTS'
SR-4   'INVALID TYPE OF ARGUMENT IN SUBPROGRAMME REFERENCE'
SR-5   'SUBPROGRAMME ATTEMPTS TO REDEFINE A CONSTANT,TEMPORARY OR DO PARAMETER'
SR-6   'ATTEMPT TO USE SUBPROGRAMME RECURSIVELY'
SR-7   'WRONG NUMBER OF ARGUMENTS IN SUBPROGRAMME REFERENCE'
SR-8   'SUBPROGRAMME NAME PREVIOUSLY DEFINED -- FIRST REFERENCE USED'
SR-9   'NO MAIN PROGRAMME'
SR-A   'ILLEGAL OR BLANK SUBPROGRAMME NAME'

'SUBSCRIPTS'
SS-0   'ZERO SUBSCRIPT OR DIMENSION NOT ALLOWED'
SS-1   'SUBSCRIPT OUT OF RANGE'
SS-2   'INVALID VARIABLE OR NAME USED FOR DIMENSION'

'STATEMENTS AND STATEMENT NUMBERS'
ST-0   'MISSING STATEMENT NUMBER'
ST-1   'STATEMENT NUMBER GREATER THAN 99999'
ST-3   'MULTIPLY-DEFINED STATEMENT NUMBER'
ST-4   'NO STATEMENT NUMBER ON STATEMENT FOLLOWING TRANSFER STATEMENT'
ST-5   'UNDECODEABLE STATEMENT'
ST-7   'STATEMENT NUMBER SPECIFIED IN A TRANSFER IS A NON-EXECUTABLE STATEMENT'
ST-8   'STATEMENT NUMBER CONSTANT MUST BE IN A CALL STATEMENT'
ST-9   'STATEMENT SPECIFIED IN A TRANSFER STATEMENT IS A FORMAT STATEMENT'
ST-A   'MISSING FORMAT STATEMENT'

'SUBSCRIPTED VARIABLES'
SV-0   'WRONG NUMBER OF SUBSCRIPTS'
SV-1   'ARRAY NAME OR SUBPROGRAMME NAME USED INCORRECTLY WITHOUT LIST'
SV-2   'MORE THAN 7 DIMENSIONS NOT ALLOWED'
SV-3   'DIMENSION TOO LARGE'
SV-4   'VARIABLE WITH VARIABLE DIMENSIONS IS NOT A SUBPROGRAMME PARAMETER'
SV-5   'VARIABLE DIMENSION NEITHER SIMPLE INTEGER VARIABLE NOR S/P PARAMETER'

'SYNTAX ERRORS'
SX-0   'MISSING OPERATOR'
SX-1   'SYNTAX ERROR-SEARCHING FOR SYMBOL,NONE FOUND'
SX-2   'SYNTAX ERROR-SEARCHING FOR CONSTANT,NONE FOUND'
SX-3   'SYNTAX ERROR-SEARCHING FOR SYMBOL OR CONSTANT,NONE FOUND'
SX-4   'SYNTAX ERROR-SEARCHING FOR STATEMENT NUMBER,NONE FOUND'
SX-5   'SYNTAX ERROR-SEARCHING FOR SIMPLE INTEGER VARIABLE,NONE FOUND'
SX-C   'ILLEGAL SEQUENCE OF OPERATORS IN EXPRESSION'
SX-D   'MISSING OPERAND OR OPERATOR'

'I/O OPERATIONS'
UN-0   'CONTROL CARD ENCOUNTERED ON UNIT 5 DURING EXECUTION'
                PROBABLE CAUSE - MISSING DATA OR IMPROPER FORMAT STATEMENTS
UN-1   'END OF FILE ENCOUNTERED'
UN-2   'I/O ERROR'
UN-3   'DATA SET REFERENCED FOR WHICH NO DD CARD SUPPLIED'
UN-4   'REWIND, ENDFILE, BACKSPACE REFERENCES UNIT 5, 6, 7'
UN-5   'ATTEMPT TO READ ON UNIT 5 AFTER IT HAS HAD END-OF-FILE'
UN-6   'UNIT NUMBER IS NEGATIVE,ZERO,GREATER THAN 7 OR UNDEFINED'
UN-7   'TOO MANY PAGES'
UN-8   'ATTEMPT TO DO SEQUENTIAL I/O ON A DIRECT ACCESS FILE'
UN-9   'WRITE REFERENCES 5 OR READ REFERENCES 6, 7'
UN-A   'ATTEMPT TO READ MORE DATA THAN CONTAINED IN LOGICAL RECORD'
UN-B   'TOO MANY PHYSICAL RECORDS IN A LOGICAL RECORD.INCREASE RECORD LENGTH.'

'UNDEFINED VARIABLES'
UV-0   'UNDEFINED VARIABLE - SIMPLE VARIABLE'
UV-1   'UNDEFINED VARIABLE - EQUIVALENCED, COMMONED, OR DUMMY PARAMETER'
UV-2   'UNDEFINED VARIABLE - ARRAY MEMBER'
UV-3   'UNDEFINED VARIABLE - ARRAY NAME WHICH WAS USED AS A DUMMY PARAMETER'
UV-4   'UNDEFINED VARIABLE - SUBPROGRAMME NAME USED AS DUMMY PARAMETER'
UV-5   'UNDEFINED VARIABLE - ARGUMENT OF THE LIBRARY SUBPROGRAMME NAMED'
UV-6   'VARIABLE FORMAT CONTAINS UNDEFINED CHARACTER(S)'

'VARIABLE NAMES'
VA-0   'ATTEMPT TO REDEFINE TYPE OF A VARIABLE NAME'
VA-1   'SUBROUTINE NAME OR COMMON BLOCK NAME USED INCORRECTLY'
VA-2   'VARIABLE NAME LONGER THAN SIX CHARACTERS. TRUNCATED TO SIX'
VA-3   'ATTEMPT TO REDEFINE THE MODE OF A VARIABLE NAME'
VA-4   'ATTEMPT TO REDEFINE THE TYPE OF A VARIABLE NAME'
VA-6   'ILLEGAL USE OF A SUBROUTINE NAME'
VA-8   'ATTEMPT TO USE A PREVIOUSLY DEFINED NAME AS FUNCTION OR ARRAY'
VA-9   'ATTEMPT TO USE A PREVIOUSLY DEFINED NAME AS A STATEMENT FUNCTION'
VA-A   'ATTEMPT TO USE A PREVIOUSLY DEFINED NAME AS A SUBPROGRAMME NAME'
VA-B   'NAME USED AS A COMMON BLOCK PREVIOUSLY USED AS A SUBPROGRAMME NAME'
VA-C   'NAME USED AS SUBPROGRAMME PREVIOUSLY USED AS A COMMON BLOCK NAME'
VA-D   'ILLEGAL DO-PARAMETER,ASSIGNED OR INITIALIZED VARIABLE IN SPECIFICATION'
VA-E   'ATTEMPT TO DIMENSION A CALL-BY-NAME PARAMETER'

'EXTERNAL STATEMENT'
XT-0   'INVALID ELEMENT IN EXTERNAL LIST'
XT-1   'INVALID DELIMITER IN EXTERNAL STATEMENT'
XT-2   'SUBPROGRAMME PREVIOUSLY EXTERNALLED'

419

APPENDIX C

WATFIV DIAGNOSTIC MESSAGES

Since the comments of Appendix B generally
apply to WATFIV, only differences are noted here.

(i) WATFIV uses a slightly different coding
scheme from WATFOR for identifying error
messages; for example, the error code IO-2
has a significance under WATFIV different
from its significance under WATFOR. The
user should be careful to consult the
appropriate list of error messages. A
complete list of WATFIV codes and messages
is given below.

(ii) WATFIV prints the value of an undefined
variable as a string of U's. For example,
if J is undefined when the statements

```
I=3
K=2
PRINT,I,J,K
```

are executed, the output appears as

3 UUUUUUUUUUUU 2

(iii) WATFIV considers character variables to be
part of the FORTRAN language. Consequently,
uses of character variable features are
generally not flagged with Extension
messages. Only those features over-and-
above the original specifications of the
SHARE FORTRAN Committee are flagged.

'ASSEMBLER LANGUAGE SUBPROGRAMS'
AL-0   'MISSING END CARD ON ASSEMBLY LANGUAGE OBJECT DECK'
AL-1   'ENTRY-POINT OR CSECT NAME IN AN OBJECT DECK WAS PREVIOUSLY
         DEFINED.FIRST DEFINITION USED'

'BLOCK DATA STATEMENTS'
BD-0   'EXECUTABLE STATEMENTS ARE ILLEGAL IN BLOCK DATA SUBPROGRAMS'
BD-1   'IMPROPER BLOCK DATA STATEMENT'

'CARD FORMAT AND CONTENTS'
CC-0   'COLUMNS 1-5 OF CONTINUATION CARD ARE NOT BLANK.
         PROBABLE CAUSE:STATEMENT PUNCHED TO LEFT OF COLUMN 7'
CC-1   'LIMIT OF 5 CONTINUATION CARDS EXCEEDED'
CC-2   'INVALID CHARACTER IN FORTRAN STATEMENT.
         A '$' WAS INSERTED IN THE SOURCE LISTING'
CC-3   'FIRST CARD OF A PROGRAM IS A CONTINUATION CARD.
         PROBABLE CAUSE:STATEMENT PUNCHED TO LEFT OF COLUMN 7'
CC-4   'STATEMENT TOO LONG TO COMPILE (SCAN-STACK OVERFLOW)'
CC-5   'A BLANK CARD WAS ENCOUNTERED'
CC-6   'KEYPUNCH USED DIFFERS FROM KEYPUNCH SPECIFIED ON JOB CARD'
CC-7   'THE FIRST CHARACTER OF THE STATEMENT WAS NOT ALPHABETIC'
CC-8   'INVALID CHARACTER(S) ARE CONCATENATED WITH THE FORTRAN KEYWORD'
CC-9   'INVALID CHARACTERS IN COLUMNS 1-5.STATEMENT NUMBER IGNORED.
         PROBABLE CAUSE:STATEMENT PUNCHED TO LEFT OF COLUMN 7'

'COMMON'
CM-0   'THE VARIABLE IS ALREADY IN COMMON'
CM-1   'OTHER COMPILERS MAY NOT ALLOW COMMONED VARIABLES TO BE INITIALIZED IN
        OTHER THAN A BLOCK DATA SUBPROGRAM'
CM-2   'ILLEGAL USE OF A COMMON BLOCK OR NAMELIST NAME'

'FORTRAN TYPE CONSTANTS'
CN-0   'MIXED REAL*4,REAL*8 IN COMPLEX CONSTANT;REAL*8 ASSUMED FOR BOTH'
CN-1   'AN INTEGER CONSTANT MAY NOT BE GREATER THAN 2,147,483,647 (2**31-1)'
CN-2   'THE EXPONENT OF A REAL CONSTANT IS GREATER THAN 99,THE MAXIMUM'
CN-3   'A REAL CONSTANT HAS MORE THAN 16 DIGITS.IT WAS TRUNCATED TO 16'
CN-4   'INVALID HEXADECIMAL CONSTANT'
CN-5   'ILLEGAL USE OF A DECIMAL POINT'
CN-6   'CONSTANT WITH MORE THAN 7 DIGITS BUT E-TYPE EXPONENT, ASSUMED TO BE
        REAL*4'
CN-7   'CONSTANT OR STATEMENT NUMBER GREATER THAN 99999'
CN-8   'AN EXPONENT OVERFLOW OR UNDERFLOW OCCURRED WHILE CONVERTING A CONSTANT
        IN A SOURCE STATEMENT'

'COMPILER ERRORS'
CP-0   'COMPILER ERROR - LANDR/ARITH'
CP-1   'COMPILER ERROR.LIKELY CAUSE:MORE THAN 255 DO STATEMENTS'
CP-4   'COMPILER ERROR - INTERRUPT AT COMPILE TIME,RETURN TO SYSTEM'

'CHARACTER VARIABLE'
CV-0   'A CHARACTER VARIABLE IS USED WITH A RELATIONAL OPERATOR'
CV-1   'LENGTH OF A CHARACTER VALUE ON RIGHT OF EQUAL SIGN EXCEEDS THAT ON
        LEFT. TRUNCATION WILL OCCUR'
CV-2   'UNFORMATTED CORE-TO-CORE I/O NOT IMPLEMENTED'

422

'DATA STATEMENT'
DA-0 'REPLICATION FACTOR IS ZERO OR GREATER THAN 32767.
       IT IS ASSUMED TO BE 32767'
DA-1 'MORE VARIABLES THAN CONSTANTS'
DA-2 'ATTEMPT TO INITIALIZE A SUBPROGRAM PARAMETER IN A DATA STATEMENT'
DA-3 'OTHER COMPILERS MAY NOT ALLOW NON-CONSTANT SUBSCRIPTS IN DATA
       STATEMENTS'
DA-4 'TYPE OF VARIABLE AND CONSTANT DO NOT AGREE (MESSAGE ISSUED ONCE FOR AN
       ARRAY)'
DA-5 'MORE CONSTANTS THAN VARIABLES'
DA-6 'A VARIABLE WAS PREVIOUSLY INITIALIZED.THE LATEST VALUE IS USED.
       CHECK COMMONED AND EQUIVALENCED VARIABLES'
DA-7 'OTHER COMPILERS MAY NOT ALLOW INITIALIZATION OF BLANK COMMON'
DA-8 'A HOLLERITH CONSTANT HAS BEEN TRUNCATED'
DA-9 'OTHER COMPILERS MAY NOT ALLOW IMPLIED DO-LOOPS IN DATA STATEMENTS'

'DEFINE FILE STATEMENTS'
DF-0 'THE UNIT NUMBER IS MISSING'
DF-1 'INVALID FORMAT TYPE'
DF-2 'THE ASSOCIATED VARIABLE IS NOT A SIMPLE INTEGER VARIABLE'
DF-3 'NUMBER OF RECORDS OR RECORD SIZE IS ZERO OR GREATER THAN 32767'

'DIMENSION STATEMENTS'
DM-0 'NO DIMENSIONS ARE SPECIFIED FOR A VARIABLE IN A DIMENSION STATEMENT'
DM-1 'THE VARIABLE HAS ALREADY BEEN DIMENSIONED'
DM-2 'CALL-BY-LOCATION PARAMETERS MAY NOT BE DIMENSIONED'
DM-3 'THE DECLARED SIZE OF ARRAY EXCEEDS SPACE PROVIDED BY CALLING ARGUMENT'

423

'DO LOOPS'

DO-0 'THIS STATEMENT CANNOT BE THE OBJECT OF A DO-LOOP'
DO-1 'ILLEGAL TRANSFER INTO THE RANGE OF A DO-LOOP'
DO-2 'THE OBJECT OF THIS DO-LOOP HAS ALREADY APPEARED'
DO-3 'IMPROPERLY NESTED DO-LOOPS'
DO-4 'ATTEMPT TO REDEFINE A DO-LOOP PARAMETER WITHIN THE RANGE OF THE LOOP'
DO-5 'INVALID DO-LOOP PARAMETER'
DO-6 'ILLEGAL TRANSFER TO A STATEMENT WHICH IS INSIDE THE RANGE OF A DO-LOOP'
DO-7 'A DO-LOOP PARAMETER IS UNDEFINED OR OUT OF RANGE'
DO-8 'BECAUSE OF ONE OF THE PARAMETERS,THIS DO-LOOP WILL TERMINATE AFTER THE FIRST TIME THROUGH'
DO-9 'A DO-LOOP PARAMETER MAY NOT BE REDEFINED IN AN INPUT LIST'
DO-A 'OTHER COMPILERS MAY NOT ALLOW THIS STATEMENT TO END A DO-LOOP'

'EQUIVALENCE AND/OR COMMON'

EC-0 'EQUIVALENCED VARIABLE APPEARS IN A COMMON STATEMENT'
EC-1 'A COMMON BLOCK HAS A DIFFERENT LENGTH THAN IN A PREVIOUS SUBPROGRAM:GREATER LENGTH USED'
EC-2 'COMMON AND/OR EQUIVALENCE CAUSES INVALID ALIGNMENT. EXECUTION SLOWED.REMEDY:ORDER VARIABLES BY DECREASING LENGTH'
EC-3 'EQUIVALENCE EXTENDS COMMON DOWNWARDS'
EC-4 'A SUBPROGRAM PARAMETER APPEARS IN A COMMON OR EQUIVALENCE STATEMENT'
EC-5 'A VARIABLE WAS USED WITH SUBSCRIPTS IN AN EQUIVALENCE STATEMENT BUT HAS NOT BEEN PROPERLY DIMENSIONED'

'END STATEMENTS'
EN-0   'MISSING END STATEMENT:END STATEMENT GENERATED'
EN-1   'AN END STATEMENT WAS USED TO TERMINATE EXECUTION'
EN-2   'AN END STATEMENT CANNOT HAVE A STATEMENT NUMBER. STATEMENT NUMBER
        IGNORED'
EN-3   'END STATEMENT NOT PRECEDED BY A TRANSFER'

'EQUAL SIGNS'
EQ-0   'ILLEGAL QUANTITY ON LEFT OF EQUALS SIGN'
EQ-1   'ILLEGAL USE OF EQUAL SIGN'
EQ-2   'OTHER COMPILERS MAY NOT ALLOW MULTIPLE ASSIGNMENT STATEMENTS'
EQ-3   'MULTIPLE ASSIGNMENT IS NOT IMPLEMENTED FOR CHARACTER VARIABLES'

'EQUIVALENCE STATEMENTS'
EV-0   'ATTEMPT TO EQUIVALENCE A VARIABLE TO ITSELF'
EV-2   'A MULTI-SUBSCRIPTED EQUIVALENCED VARIABLE HAS BEEN INCORRECTLY
        RE-EQUIVALENCED.REMEDY:DIMENSION THE VARIABLE FIRST'

'POWERS AND EXPONENTIATION'
EX-0   'ILLEGAL COMPLEX EXPONENTIATION'
EX-1   'I**J WHERE I=J=0'
EX-2   'I**J WHERE I=0, J.LT.0'
EX-3   '0.0**Y WHERE Y.LE.0.0'
EX-4   '0.0**J WHERE J=0'
EX-5   '0.0**J WHERE J.LT.0'
EX-6   'X**Y WHERE X.LT.0.0, Y.NE.0.0'

425

'ENTRY STATEMENT'
EY-0 'ENTRY-POINT NAME WAS PREVIOUSLY DEFINED'
EY-1 'PREVIOUS DEFINITION OF FUNCTION NAME IN AN ENTRY IS INCORRECT'
EY-2 'THE USAGE OF A SUBPROGRAM PARAMETER IS INCONSISTENT WITH A PREVIOUS ENTRY-POINT'
EY-3 'A PARAMETER HAS APPEARED IN A EXECUTABLE STATEMENT BUT IS NOT A SUBPROGRAM PARAMETER'
EY-4 'ENTRY STATEMENTS ARE INVALID IN THE MAIN PROGRAM'
EY-5 'ENTRY STATEMENT INVALID INSIDE A DO-LOOP'

'FORMAT'
SOME FORMAT ERROR MESSAGES GIVE CHARACTERS IN WHICH ERROR WAS DETECTED
FM-0 'IMPROPER CHARACTER SEQUENCE OR INVALID CHARACTER IN INPUT DATA'
FM-1 'NO STATEMENT NUMBER ON A FORMAT STATEMENT'
FM-2 'FORMAT CODE AND DATA TYPE DO NOT MATCH'
FM-4 'FORMAT PROVIDES NO CONVERSION SPECIFICATION FOR A VALUE IN I/O LIST'
FM-5 'AN INTEGER IN THE INPUT DATA IS TOO LARGE.
     (MAXIMUM=2,147,483,647=2**31-1)'
FM-6 'A REAL NUMBER IN THE INPUT DATA IS OUT OF MACHINE RANGE (1.E-78,1.E+75)'
FM-7 'UNREFERENCED FORMAT STATEMENT'
FT-0 'FIRST CHARACTER OF VARIABLE FORMAT IS NOT A LEFT PARENTHESIS'
FT-1 'INVALID CHARACTER ENCOUNTERED IN FORMAT'
FT-2 'INVALID FORM FOLLOWING A FORMAT CODE'
FT-3 'INVALID FIELD OR GROUP COUNT'
FT-4 'A FIELD OR GROUP COUNT GREATER THAN 255'
FT-5 'NO CLOSING PARENTHESIS ON VARIABLE FORMAT'
FT-6 'NO CLOSING QUOTE IN A HOLLERITH FIELD'
FT-7 'INVALID USE OF COMMA'
FT-8 'FORMAT STATEMENT TOO LONG TO COMPILE (SCAN-STACK OVERFLOW)'
FT-9 'INVALID USE OF P FORMAT CODE'

426

```
FT-A  'INVALID USE OF PERIOD(.)'
FT-B  'MORE THAN THREE LEVELS OF PARENTHESES'
FT-C  'INVALID CHARACTER BEFORE A RIGHT PARENTHESIS'
FT-D  'MISSING OR ZERO LENGTH HOLLERITH ENCOUNTERED'
FT-E  'NO CLOSING RIGHT PARENTHESIS'
FT-F  'CHARACTERS FOLLOW CLOSING RIGHT PARENTHESIS'
FT-G  'WRONG QUOTE USED FOR KEY-PUNCH SPECIFIED'
FT-H  'LENGTH OF HOLLERITH EXCEEDS 255'

'FUNCTIONS AND SUBROUTINES'
FN-1  'A PARAMETER APPEARS MORE THAN ONCE IN A SUBPROGRAM OR STATEMENT
       FUNCTION DEFINITION'
FN-2  'SUBSCRIPTS ON RIGHT-HAND SIDE OF STATEMENT FUNCTION.
       PROBABLE CAUSE:VARIABLE TO LEFT OF EQUAL SIGN NOT DIMENSIONED'
FN-3  'MULTIPLE RETURNS ARE INVALID IN FUNCTION SUBPROGRAMS'
FN-4  'ILLEGAL LENGTH MODIFIER'
FN-5  'INVALID PARAMETER'
FN-6  'A PARAMETER HAS THE SAME NAME AS THE SUBPROGRAM'

'GO TO STATEMENTS'
GO-0  'THIS STATEMENT COULD TRANSFER TO ITSELF'
GO-1  'THIS STATEMENT TRANSFERS TO A NON-EXECUTABLE STATEMENT'
GO-2  'ATTEMPT TO DEFINE ASSIGNED GOTO INDEX IN AN ARITHMFTIC STATEMENT'
GO-3  'ASSIGNED GOTO INDEX MAY BE USED ONLY IN ASSIGNED GOTO AND ASSIGN
       STATEMENTS'
GO-4  'THE INDEX OF AN ASSIGNED GOTO IS UNDEFINED OR OUT OF RANGE,OR INDEX OF
       COMPUTED GOTO IS UNDEFINED'
GO-5  'ASSIGNED GOTO INDEX MAY NOT BE AN INTEGER*2 VARIABLE'
```

427

```
'HOLLERITH CONSTANTS'
HO-0  'ZERO LENGTH SPECIFIED FOR H-TYPE HOLLERITH'
HO-1  'ZERO LENGTH QUOTE-TYPE HOLLERITH'
HO-2  'NO CLOSING QUOTE OR NEXT CARD NOT A CONTINUATION CARD'
HO-3  'UNEXPECTED HOLLERITH OR STATEMENT NUMBER CONSTANT'

'IF STATEMENTS (ARITHMETIC AND LOGICAL)'
IF-0  'AN INVALID STATEMENT FOLLOWS THE LOGICAL IF'
IF-1  'ARITHMETIC OR INVALID EXPRESSION IN LOGICAL IF'
IF-2  'LOGICAL,COMPLEX OR INVALID EXPRESSION IN ARITHMETIC IF'

'IMPLICIT STATEMENT'
IM-0  'INVALID DATA TYPE'
IM-1  'INVALID OPTIONAL LENGTH'
IM-3  'IMPROPER ALPHABETIC SEQUENCE IN CHARACTER RANGE'
IM-4  'A SPECIFICATION IS NOT A SINGLE CHARACTER.THE FIRST CHARACTER IS USED'
IM-5  'IMPLICIT STATEMENT DOES NOT PRECEDE OTHER SPECIFICATION STATEMENTS'
IM-6  'ATTEMPT TO DECLARE THE TYPE OF A CHARACTER MORE THAN ONCE'
IM-7  'ONLY ONE IMPLICIT STATEMENT PER PROGRAM SEGMENT ALLOWED. THIS ONE
       IGNORED'
```

'INPUT/OUTPUT'
IO-0   'I/O STATEMENT REFERENCES A STATEMENT WHICH IS NOT A FORMAT STATEMENT'
IO-1   'A VARIABLE FORMAT MUST BE AN ARRAY NAME'
IO-2   'INVALID ELEMENT IN INPUT LIST OR DATA LIST'
IO-3   'OTHER COMPILERS MAY NOT ALLOW EXPRESSIONS IN OUTPUT LISTS'
IO-4   'ILLEGAL USE OF END= OR ERR= PARAMETERS'
IO-5   'INVALID UNIT NUMBER'
IO-6   'INVALID FORMAT'
IO-7   'ONLY CONSTANTS,SIMPLE INTEGER*4 VARIABLES,AND CHARACTER VARIABLES ARE
        ALLOWED AS UNIT'
IO-8   'ATTEMPT TO PERFORM I/O IN A FUNCTION WHICH IS CALLED IN AN OUTPUT
        STATEMENT'
IO-9   'UNFORMATTED WRITE STATEMENT MUST HAVE A LIST'

'JOB CONTROL CARDS'
JB-0   'CONTROL CARD ENCOUNTERED DURING COMPILATION;
        PROBABLE CAUSE:MISSING $ENTRY CARD'
JB-1   'MIS-PUNCHED JOB OPTION'

'JOB TERMINATION'
KO-0   'SOURCE ERROR ENCOUNTERED WHILE EXECUTING WITH RUN=FREE'
KO-1   'LIMIT EXCEEDED FOR FIXED-POINT DIVISION BY ZERO'
KO-2   'LIMIT EXCEEDED FOR FLOATING-POINT DIVISION BY ZERO'
KO-3   'EXPONENT OVERFLOW LIMIT EXCEEDED'
KO-4   'EXPONENT UNDERFLOW LIMIT EXCEEDED'
KO-5   'FIXED-POINT OVERFLOW LIMIT EXCEEDED'
KO-6   'JOB-TIME EXCEEDED'
KO-7   'COMPILER ERROR - EXECUTION TIME:RETURN TO SYSTEM'
KO-8   'TRACEBACK ERROR. TRACEBACK TERMINATED'

'LOGICAL OPERATIONS'
LG-0 '.NOT. WAS USED AS A BINARY OPERATOR'

'LIBRARY ROUTINES'
LI-0 'ARGUMENT OUT OF RANGE DGAMMA OR GAMMA. (1.382E-76 .LT. X .LT. 57.57)'
LI-1 'ABSOLUTE VALUE OF ARGUMENT .GT. 174.673, SINH,COSH,DSINH,DCOSH'
LI-2 'SENSE LIGHT OTHER THAN 0,1,2,3,4 FOR SLITE OR 1,2,3,4 FOR SLITET'
LI-3 'REAL PORTION OF ARGUMENT .GT. 174.673, CEXP OR CDEXP'
LI-4 'ABS(AIMAG(Z)) .GT. 174.673 FOR CSIN, CCOS, CDSIN OR CDCOS OF Z'
LI-5 'ABS(REAL(Z)) .GE. 3.537E15 FOR CSIN, CCOS, CDSIN OR CDCOS OF Z'
LI-6 'ABS(AIMAG(Z)) .GE. 3.537E15 FOR CEXP OR CDEXP OF Z'
LI-7 'ARGUMENT .GT. 174.673, EXP OR DEXP'
LI-8 'ARGUMENT IS ZERO, CLOG, CLOG10, CDLOG, CDLOG OR CDLG10'
LI-9 'ARGUMENT IS NEGATIVE OR ZERO, ALOG, ALOG10, DLOG OR DLOG10'
LI-A 'ABS(X) .GE. 3.537E15 FOR SIN, COS, DSIN OR DCOS OF X'
LI-B 'ABSOLUTE VALUE OF ARGUMENT .GT. 1. FOR ARSIN, ARCOS, DARSIN OR DARCOS'
LI-C 'ARGUMENT IS NEGATIVE, SQRT OR DSQRT'
LI-D 'BOTH ARGUMENTS OF DATAN2 OR ATAN2 ARE ZERO'
LI-E 'ARGUMENT TOO CLOSE TO A SINGULARITY, TAN, COTAN, DTAN OR DCOTAN'
LI-F 'ARGUMENT OUT OF RANGE,DLGAMA OR ALGAMA. (0.0 .LT. X .LT. 4.29E73)'
LI-G 'ABSOLUTE VALUE OF ARGUMENT .GE. 3.537E15, TAN, COTAN, DTAN, DCOTAN'
LI-H 'LESS THAN TWO ARGUMENTS FOR ONE OF MIN0,MIN1,AMIN0,ETC.'

'MIXED MODE'
MD-0 'RELATIONAL OPERATOR HAS LOGICAL OPERAND'
MD-1 'RELATIONAL OPERATOR HAS COMPLEX OPERAND'
MD-2 'MIXED MODE - LOGICAL OR CHARACTER WITH ARITHMETIC'
MD-3 'OTHER COMPILERS MAY NOT ALLOW SUBSCRIPTS OF TYPE COMPLEX,LOGICAL OR
       CHARACTER'

430

'MEMORY OVERFLOW'
MO-0 'INSUFFICIENT MEMORY TO COMPILE THIS PROGRAM.REMAINDER WILL BE ERROR
       CHECKED ONLY'
MO-1 'INSUFFICIENT MEMORY TO ASSIGN ARRAY STORAGE. JOB ABANDONED'
MO-2 'SYMBOL TABLE EXCEEDS AVAILABLE SPACE,JOB ABANDONED'
MO-3 'DATA AREA OF SUBPROGRAM EXCEEDS 24K -- SEGMENT SUBPROGRAM'
MO-4 'INSUFFICIENT MEMORY TO ALLOCATE COMPILER WORK AREA OR WATLIB BUFFER'

'NAMELIST STATEMENTS'
NL-0 'NAMELIST ENTRY MUST BE A VARIABLE,NOT A SUBPROGRAM PARAMETER'
NL-1 'NAMELIST NAME PREVIOUSLY DEFINED'
NL-2 'VARIABLE NAME TOO LONG'
NL-3 'VARIABLE NAME NOT FOUND IN NAMELIST'
NL-4 'INVALID SYNTAX IN NAMELIST INPUT'
NL-6 'VARIABLE INCORRECTLY SUBSCRIPTED'
NL-7 'SUBSCRIPT OUT OF RANGE'

'PARENTHESES'
PC-0 'UNMATCHED PARENTHESIS'
PC-1 'INVALID PARENTHESIS NESTING IN I/O LIST'

'PAUSE, STOP STATEMENTS'
PS-0 'OPERATOR MESSAGES NOT ALLOWED:SIMPLE STOP ASSUMED FOR STOP,
       CONTINUE ASSUMED FOR PAUSE'

'RETURN STATEMENT'
RE-1 'RETURN I, WHERE I IS OUT OF RANGE OR UNDEFINED'
RE-2 'MULTIPLE RETURN NOT VALID IN FUNCTION SUBPROGRAM'
RE-3 'VARIABLE IS NOT A SIMPLE INTEGER'
RE-4 'A MULTIPLE RETURN IS NOT VALID IN THE MAIN PROGRAM'

431

'ARITHMETIC AND LOGICAL STATEMENT FUNCTIONS'
      PROBABLE CAUSE OF SF ERRORS - VARIABLE ON LEFT OF = WAS NOT DIMENSIONED
SF-1   'A PREVIOUSLY REFERENCED STATEMENT NUMBER APPEARS ON A STATEMENT
         FUNCTION DEFINITION'
SF-2   'STATEMENT FUNCTION IS THE OBJECT OF A LOGICAL IF STATEMENT'
SF-3   'RECURSIVE STATEMENT FUNCTION DEFINITION:NAME APPEARS ON BOTH SIDES OF
         EQUAL SIGN.LIKELY CAUSE:VARIABLE NOT DIMENSIONED'
SF-4   'A STATEMENT FUNCTION DEFINITION APPEARS AFTER THE FIRST EXECUTABLE
         STATEMENT'
SF-5   'ILLEGAL USE OF A STATEMENT FUNCTION NAME'

'SUBPROGRAMS'
SR-0   'MISSING SUBPROGRAM'
SR-1   'SUBPROGRAM REDEFINES A CONSTANT,EXPRESSION,DO-PARAMETER OR ASSIGNED
         GOTO INDEX'
SR-2   'THE SUBPROGRAM WAS ASSIGNED DIFFERENT TYPES IN DIFFERENT PROGRAM
         SEGMENTS'
SR-3   'ATTEMPT TO USE A SUBPROGRAM RECURSIVELY'
SR-4   'INVALID TYPE OF ARGUMENT IN REFERENCE TO A SUBPROGRAM'
SR-5   'WRONG NUMBER OF ARGUMENTS IN A REFERENCE TO A SUBPROGRAM'
SR-6   'A SUBPROGRAM WAS PREVIOUSLY DEFINED. THE FIRST DEFINITION IS USED'
SR-7   'NO MAIN PROGRAM'
SR-8   'ILLEGAL OR MISSING SUBPROGRAM NAME'
SR-9   'LIBRARY PROGRAM WAS NOT ASSIGNED THE CORRECT TYPE'
SR-A   'METHOD FOR ENTERING SUBPROGRAM PRODUCES UNDEFINED VALUE FOR
         CALL-BY-LOCATION PARAMETER'

432

'SUBSCRIPTS'
SS-0   'ZERO SUBSCRIPT OR DIMENSION NOT ALLOWED'
SS-1   'ARRAY SUBSCRIPT EXCEEDS DIMENSION'
SS-2   'INVALID SUBSCRIPT FORM'
SS-3   'SUBSCRIPT IS OUT OF RANGE'

'STATEMENTS AND STATEMENT NUMBERS'
ST-0   'MISSING STATEMENT NUMBER'
ST-1   'STATEMENT NUMBER GREATER THAN 99999'
ST-2   'STATEMENT NUMBER HAS ALREADY BEEN DEFINED'
ST-3   'UNDECODEABLE STATEMENT'
ST-4   'UNNUMBERED EXECUTABLE STATEMENT FOLLOWS A TRANSFER'
ST-5   'STATEMENT NUMBER IN A TRANSFER IS A NON-EXECUTABLE STATEMENT'
ST-6   'ONLY CALL STATEMENTS MAY CONTAIN STATEMENT NUMBER ARGUMENTS'
ST-7   'STATEMENT SPECIFIED IN A TRANSFER STATEMENT IS A FORMAT STATEMENT'
ST-8   'MISSING FORMAT STATEMENT'
ST-9   'SPECIFICATION STATEMENT DOES NOT PRECEDE STATEMENT FUNCTION DEFINITIONS
         OR EXECUTABLE STATEMENTS'
ST-A   'UNREFERENCED STATEMENT FOLLOWS A TRANSFER'

'SUBSCRIPTED VARIABLES'
SV-0   'THE WRONG NUMBER OF SUBSCRIPTS WERE SPECIFIED FOR A VARIABLE'
SV-1   'AN ARRAY OR SUBPROGRAM NAME IS USED INCORRECTLY WITHOUT A LIST'
SV-2   'MORE THAN 7 DIMENSIONS ARE NOT ALLOWED'
SV-3   'DIMENSION OR SUBSCRIPT TOO LARGE (MAXIMUM 10**8-1)'
SV-4   'A VARIABLE USED WITH VARIABLE DIMENSIONS IS NOT A SUBPROGRAM PARAMETER'
SV-5   'A VARIABLE DIMENSION IS NOT ONE OF SIMPLE INTEGER VARIABLE,SUBPROGRAM
         PARAMETER,IN COMMON'

'SYNTAX ERRORS'
SX-0   'MISSING OPERATOR'
SX-1   'EXPECTING OPERATOR'
SX-2   'EXPECTING SYMBOL'
SX-3   'EXPECTING SYMBOL OR OPERATOR'
SX-4   'EXPECTING CONSTANT'
SX-5   'EXPECTING SYMBOL OR CONSTANT'
SX-6   'EXPECTING STATEMENT NUMBER'
SX-7   'EXPECTING SIMPLE INTEGER VARIABLE'
SX-8   'EXPECTING SIMPLE INTEGER VARIABLE OR CONSTANT'
SX-9   'ILLEGAL SEQUENCE OF OPERATORS IN EXPRESSION'
SX-A   'EXPECTING END-OF-STATEMENT'

'TYPE STATEMENTS'
TY-0   'THE VARIABLE HAS ALREADY BEEN EXPLICITLY TYPED'
TY-1   'THE LENGTH OF THE EQUIVALENCED VARIABLE MAY NOT BE CHANGED.
        REMEDY: INTERCHANGE TYPE AND EQUIVALENCE STATEMENTS'

'I/O OPERATIONS'
UN-0   'CONTROL CARD ENCOUNTERED ON UNIT 5 AT EXECUTION.
        PROBABLE CAUSE:MISSING DATA OR INCORRECT FORMAT'
UN-1   'END OF FILE ENCOUNTERED (IBM CODE IHC217)'
UN-2   'I/O ERROR (IBM CODE IHC218)'
UN-3   'NO DD STATEMENT WAS SUPPLIED (IBM CODE IHC219)'
UN-4   'REWIND,ENDFILE,BACKSPACE REFERENCES UNIT 5, 6 OR 7'
UN-5   'ATTEMPT TO READ ON UNIT 5 AFTER IT HAS HAD END-OF-FILE'
UN-6   'AN INVALID VARIABLE UNIT NUMBER WAS DETECTED (IBM CODE IHC220)'
UN-7   'PAGE-LIMIT EXCEEDED'
UN-8   'ATTEMPT TO DO DIRECT ACCESS I/O ON A SEQUENTIAL FILE OR VICE VERSA.
        POSSIBLE MISSING DEFINE FILE STATEMENT (IBM CODE IHC231)'

UN-9 'WRITE REFERENCES 5 OR READ REFERENCES 6 OR 7'
UN-A 'DEFINE FILE REFERENCES A UNIT PREVIOUSLY USED FOR SEQUENTIAL I/O (IBM CODE IHC235)'
UN-B 'RECORD SIZE FOR UNIT EXCEEDS 32767,OR DIFFERS FROM DD STATEMENT SPECIFICATION (IBM CODES IHC233,IHC237)'
UN-C 'FOR DIRECT ACCESS I/O THE RELATIVE RECORD POSITION IS NEGATIVE,ZERO,OR TOO LARGE (IBM CODE IHC232)'
UN-D 'AN ATTEMPT WAS MADE TO READ MORE INFORMATION THAN LOGICAL RECORD CONTAINS (IBM CODE IHC236)'
UN-E 'FORMATTED LINE EXCEEDS BUFFER LENGTH (IBM CODE IHC212)'
UN-F 'I/O ERROR - SEARCHING LIBRARY DIRECTORY'
UN-G 'I/O ERROR - READING LIBRARY'
UN-H 'ATTEMPT TO DEFINE THE OBJECT ERROR FILE AS A DIRECT ACCESS FILE (IBM CODE IHC234)'
UN-I 'RECFM OTHER THAN V(B) IS SPECIFIED FOR I/O WITHOUT FORMAT CONTROL (IBM CODE IHC214)'
UN-J 'MISSING DD CARD FOR WATLIB.NO LIBRARY ASSUMED'
UN-K 'ATTEMPT TO READ OR WRITE PAST THE END OF CHARACTER VARIABLE BUFFER'
UN-L 'ATTEMPT TO READ ON AN UNCREATED DIRECT ACCESS FILE (IHC236)'

'UNDEFINED VARIABLES'
UV-0 'VARIABLE IS UNDEFINED'
UV-3 'SUBSCRIPT IS UNDEFINED'
UV-4 'SUBPROGRAM IS UNDEFINED'
UV-5 'ARGUMENT IS UNDEFINED'
UV-6 'UNDECODABLE CHARACTERS IN VARIABLE FORMAT'

'VARIABLE NAMES'
VA-0 'A NAME IS TOO LONG.IT HAS BEEN TRUNCATED TO SIX CHARACTERS'
VA-1 'ATTEMPT TO USE AN ASSIGNED OR INITIALIZED VARIABLE OR DO-PARAMETER IN A
       SPECIFICATION STATEMENT'
VA-2 'ILLEGAL USE OF A SUBROUTINE NAME'
VA-3 'ILLEGAL USE OF A VARIABLE NAME'
VA-4 'ATTEMPT TO USE A PREVIOUSLY DEFINED NAME AS A FUNCTION OR AN ARRAY'
VA-5 'ATTEMPT TO USE A PREVIOUSLY DEFINED NAME AS A SUBROUTINE'
VA-6 'ATTEMPT TO USE A PREVIOUSLY DEFINED NAME AS A SUBPROGRAM'
VA-7 'ATTEMPT TO USE A PREVIOUSLY DEFINED NAME AS A COMMON BLOCK'
VA-8 'ATTEMPT TO USE A FUNCTION NAME AS A VARIABLE'
VA-9 'ATTEMPT TO USE A PREVIOUSLY DEFINED NAME AS A VARIABLE'
VA-A 'ILLEGAL USE OF A PREVIOUSLY DEFINED NAME'

'EXTERNAL STATEMENT'
XT-0 'A VARIABLE HAS ALREADY APPEARED IN AN EXTERNAL STATEMENT'

APPENDIX D

SOME DIFFERENCES BETWEEN WATFOR AND WATFIV

This appendix summarizes the principal areas in which the FORTRAN language implemented by WATFIV differs from that implemented by WATFOR. The differences are minor, and are not likely to affect the inexperienced or student programmer. For the most part, these differences have arisen since an attempt was made, with WATFIV, to eliminate some incompatibilities between WATFOR and IBM's compilers.

1. WATFOR does not support the direct-access I/O, NAMELIST, and CHARACTER variable features described in Chapters 21 and 22.

2. WATFIV allows format-free I/O statements of the form

    ```
    READ(unit,*,END=m,ERR=n)list
    WRITE(unit,*)list
    ```

    For example, READ(5,*)list is equivalent to READ,list.

3. With WATFIV, a complex number printed by a format-free output statement has enclosing parentheses.

4. An integer variable of length 2 may not be used as the unit number in I/O statements in WATFIV.

5. With WATFIV, source programs punched on a Model 026 keypunch are not allowed to use $ as an alphabetic character in symbolic

names. This character is used to indicate statement number arguments, for example, CALL RTN(X,$1), since the Model 026 has no & character.

6. Real or double precision constants with exponents need not have an explicit decimal point when used in source programs compiled by WATFIV. For example, in the constant 38E+2, the decimal point is assumed to be immediately to the left of the exponent.

7. With WATFIV, the index of a computed GO TO may be zero or negative, in which case control passes to the statement following the GO TO. With WATFOR, the program is terminated with an error message.

8. If a function subprogram has multiple entry points, WATFIV allocates storage for the variables which are the function and entry point names as if they were equivalent. WATFOR allocates separate storage for each name.

9. With WATFOR, a Hollerith constant used as a subprogram argument must correspond to a parameter which is an array of type real. With WATFIV, the Hollerith may correspond to an array of any type.

10. WATFIV will allow an array element used as an argument to correspond to a parameter which is an array name. The array element is considered to be the first element of the dummy array in the called subprogram; the rest of the dummy array

is taken to be the storage immediately
following the argument element. This can
be useful, for example, to pass the
individual columns of a matrix to a subprogram which operates on a vector. As
an illustration consider:

```
      DIMENSION A(5,10)
         ⋮
      DO 1 I=1,10
    1 CALL RTN(A(1,I))
         ⋮
      END
      SUBROUTINE RTN(X)
      DIMENSION X(10)
         ⋮
```

Note that the following rule must be
obeyed: the size of the dummy array (in
bytes) must not exceed the storage provided
by the calling argument. The latter
storage is measured from the specified
element to the last element of the array
(inclusive).

11.   WATFIV uses the dimensions (including the
values of object-time dimensions) declared
for arrays which are subprogram parameters
when subscript calculations are performed.
WATFOR implicitly assumes that a dummy
array has the dimensions of any actual
array passed to it. For example, consider
the following statements:

```
      DIMENSION A(10,10)
      I=5
      J=7
    3 CALL SUBR(A,I,J)
      .
      .
      .
      END
      SUBROUTINE SUBR(X,M,N)
      DIMENSION X(M,N)
      .
      .
      .
```

Under WATFIV, when SUBR is called from statement 3, X is treated as if it had dimensions 5 and 7. Under WATFOR, X is treated as if it had dimensions 10 and 10.

The note of point 10 applies here as well.

INDEX

Page numbers in italics indicate the principal reference